AF326626

Self-Discipline and Mental Toughness 5-in-1

The Complete Guide to Beat Procrastination, Build Good Habits, Grow Willpower & Self-Control, Stay Focused, and Reach Your Goals

TABLE OF CONTENTS

OVERALL INTRODUCTION
THE SCIENCE OF LASTING CHANGE

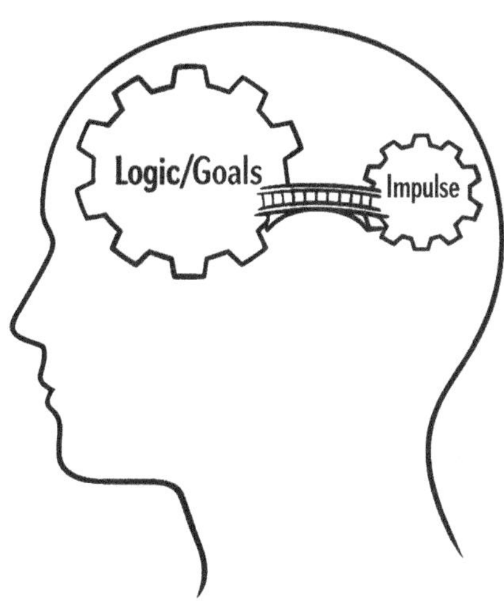

Success does not happen by accident. It is the result of specific choices you make every hour of the day. Many people believe that self-discipline is a rare gift. They think some individuals are simply born with the ability to wake up early, work hard, and avoid temptation. Science shows a different reality. Discipline is a skill you can learn and improve through practice. You are not stuck with the level of willpower you have today. You can expand it.

This book provides a roadmap to help you take control of your mind and your actions. We will look at how your brain works and why it often tries to take the easy path. By using proven methods, you can train yourself to act even when you do not feel motivated. You will learn how to stop waiting for the "right time" and start building the life you want right now. The difference between those who achieve their goals and those who do not is often found in their ability to manage their internal resistance.

The Biology of Your Choices

Your brain is a complex organ with competing interests. It has two main systems that fight for control over your behavior. The first is the prefrontal cortex. Located right behind your forehead, this part of the brain handles logic, planning, and long-term goals. It is the "adult" in the room. It understands that skipping a workout today will hurt your health a year from now.

The second system is the limbic system, which is much older in evolutionary terms. It seeks immediate pleasure and wants to avoid pain or stress at all costs. This part of the brain is responsible for your "fight or flight" response, but it also controls your desire for sugar, social media, and rest. When you procrastinate, your limbic system is winning. It wants the quick hit of dopamine from scrolling on your phone instead of the long-term reward of finishing a project.

To build mental toughness, you must strengthen the prefrontal cortex. Dr. Robert Sapolsky, a neurobiologist at Stanford University, notes that the prefrontal cortex is the part of the brain that "makes you do the harder thing when it is the right thing to do." This book gives you the tools to help that logical part of your brain win more often. We do this through neuroplasticity. This is the brain's ability to reorganize itself by forming new neural connections. When you repeat a disciplined action, the physical pathway for that action becomes stronger and more efficient.

The Myth of Motivation

Relying on motivation is a mistake. Motivation is a feeling, and feelings change constantly. You might feel excited to start a new diet on Monday but lose that feeling by Wednesday afternoon when you are tired. If you only work when you feel like it, your progress will be inconsistent. This is the primary trap that keeps people from reaching their full potential. They wait for a "spark" that may never come.

Self-discipline is the ability to follow through on a plan after the initial excitement has worn off. It is about creating systems that work regardless of your mood. Think of discipline as a battery. It can run low if you use it too much on small, unimportant choices. We call this "decision fatigue." This is why successful people like Steve Jobs or

Barack Obama often wore the same style of clothing every day. They saved their mental energy for the tasks that actually move the needle. By automating small parts of your life, you save your willpower for the moments that truly matter.

Building Mental Toughness and Grit

Mental toughness is not about being a robot without emotions. It is about your response to pressure, boredom, and failure. People with high levels of mental toughness can stay focused on a task even when it becomes repetitive or difficult. They do not quit at the first sign of discomfort. In fact, they view discomfort as a sign of growth.

Research by psychologist Angela Duckworth shows that "grit"—a combination of passion and perseverance—is a better predictor of success than IQ or talent. In her studies of West Point cadets and National Spelling Bee finalists, she found that those who survived the toughest challenges were not necessarily the most naturally gifted. They were the ones who refused to quit. You can build this grit by intentionally putting yourself in challenging situations. Each time you finish a difficult task or say no to a distraction, you are "leveling up" your mental strength.

The Five Pillars of Self-Mastery

To provide a complete transformation, this guide is divided into five specific sections. Each one targets a different part of the self-discipline puzzle.

1. Beat Procrastination Now Procrastination is rarely about laziness. It is usually about emotional regulation. You avoid a task because it makes you feel anxious, bored, or overwhelmed. We will explore the "Action-First" model, which suggests that you do not need to feel like doing something to start it. Once you start, the motivation often follows the action. You will learn how to break the cycle of "I'll do it tomorrow" by using the five-second rule and other cognitive shifts.

2. Build Good Habits That Stick Habits are the compound interest of self-improvement. If you improve by just 1% every day, you will be 37 times better by the end of a year. We will look at the "Habit Loop"—the cue, the craving, the response, and the reward. You will learn how to "stack" habits so that your current routines trigger your new, better behaviors. This section is about making success automatic so you don't have to think about it.

3. Grow Willpower and Self-Control Willpower is a finite resource, but it can be expanded. We will discuss the famous "Marshmallow Test" by Dr. Walter Mischel and what it teaches us about delayed gratification. You will learn how to manage your blood sugar, sleep, and stress levels to keep your willpower at its peak. We will also cover implementation intentions—"if-then" plans that help you decide how to handle temptation before it even arrives.

4. Stay Focused in a World of Distraction We live in an economy that profits from your lack of focus. Every app and notification is designed to steal your attention. Deep work, a term coined by Cal Newport, is the ability to focus without distraction on a cognitively demanding task. This section teaches you how to create a "monk mode" environment and how to retrain your brain to handle boredom without reaching for your phone.

5. Reach Your Goals with Precision A goal without a plan is just a wish. Many people fail because their goals are too vague. "I want to be fit" is not a plan. "I will walk for 30 minutes at 6:00 AM every morning" is a plan. We will use the SMART criteria—Specific, Measurable, Achievable, Relevant, and Time-bound—to build your roadmap. You will learn how to track your progress and pivot when life gets in the way.

The Role of Environment

Most people try to change their behavior through sheer force of will. This is the hardest way to change. If you want to stop eating junk food but keep cookies on your kitchen counter, you are forcing your brain to fight a battle every time you walk into the room. Eventually, your willpower will fail.

A more effective strategy is to change your environment. If you want to read more, put a book on your pillow. If you want to exercise, lay out your gym clothes the night before. By making the good habit easy and the bad habit difficult, you reduce the amount of discipline required to succeed. We will spend a significant amount of time in this book discussing how to "prime" your surroundings for the person you want to become.

The Psychological Cost of Inaction

We must also talk about the cost of not changing. Every time you break a promise to yourself, your self-esteem drops. You begin to view yourself as someone who does not follow through. This creates a negative feedback loop. Conversely, every time you keep a promise to yourself—no matter how small—you build "self-efficacy." This is the belief in your own ability to succeed.

When you complete the chapters in this book, you are not just gaining information. You are building a new identity. You are becoming a person who is in control. You are becoming a person who can be trusted by the most important person in your life: yourself.

How to Use This Book

This is not a book to be read once and put on a shelf. It is a manual for living. You should approach it with a pen in hand. Highlight the sections that speak to your specific struggles. Complete the reflection questions at the end of each book.

The content is organized to be cumulative. While you can jump to the section on focus, it will be more effective if you have already learned how to build habits and manage your willpower. The goal is to create a "Unified Discipline System" where each part of your life supports the others.

We have included a checklist and a resource list at the end of the collection to keep you on track. Use these tools to measure your growth. The goal is not perfection. Perfection is a trap that leads to procrastination. The goal is being better today than you were yesterday. If you stumble, you simply start again with the next choice. Discipline is a lifelong pursuit, not a destination.

BOOK ONE
BEAT PROCRASTINATION NOW

INTRODUCTION

WHY YOUR BRAIN CHOOSES DELAY OVER ACTION

Procrastination is not a time-management problem. It is an emotion-management problem. If you have ever sat at your desk with a clear to-do list and a looming deadline, yet found yourself cleaning your kitchen or scrolling through social media, you have experienced this internal conflict. You know what you should be doing. You likely even want to do it to avoid the stress of a last-minute rush. Yet, you remain paralyzed. To defeat this habit, you must first understand that you are not lazy. You are experiencing a breakdown in how your brain processes discomfort.

The Internal Tug-of-War

Inside your head, a constant battle rages between two specific areas: the limbic system and the prefrontal cortex. The limbic system is one of the oldest and most dominant parts of the human brain. Its primary job is survival. It focuses on the present moment and seeks immediate rewards while avoiding immediate pain. In the past, this system kept humans alive by encouraging them to eat when food was available and flee when a predator appeared. Today, that same system views a difficult work project or a hard conversation as a "predator" to be avoided.

On the other side is the prefrontal cortex. This is the newer, more "human" part of your brain. It allows you to think about the future, plan your career, and understand the consequences of your actions. It is the part of you that knows that if you do not finish your report today, you will be stressed on Friday. The problem is that the prefrontal cortex is like a muscle that tires easily. The limbic system, however, is like an automatic reflex. It never gets tired. When you are stressed, hungry, or exhausted, your prefrontal cortex loses its grip, and the limbic system takes over. This is why you procrastinate most when you are already feeling overwhelmed.

The Evolution of the Procrastinating Mind

To understand why your brain functions this way, we must look at our evolutionary history. For 99% of human history, the world was an "immediate-return environment." If you hunted an animal, you ate. If you found a berry bush, you consumed the fruit. There was no concept of a "quarterly report" or "saving for retirement." Our brains evolved to prioritize the "now" because the "later" was never guaranteed.

In our modern "delayed-return environment," most of our actions today do not yield rewards for weeks, months, or years. You study today for a degree in four years. You save money today for a retirement decades away. Your ancient brain struggles with this logic. It views the effort spent on a long-term goal as a waste of energy because the reward is not immediate. Procrastination is essentially your caveman brain trying to save you from wasting energy on a future that it does not believe in.

The Dopamine Loop and Modern Distraction

When you choose to delay a task, your brain receives a small, immediate reward. By clicking away from a difficult spreadsheet and onto a video or a news site, you feel a brief sense of relief. This relief is fueled by dopamine, a chemical in the brain linked to pleasure and motivation. Your brain learns very quickly that "avoidance equals relief."

This creates a dangerous cycle. The more you procrastinate, the more your brain reinforces the idea that avoiding hard work is a good strategy for feeling better in the short term. Over time, this becomes a deep-seated habit. You aren't just "putting things off"; you are literally rewiring your brain to seek the path of least resistance. Breaking this cycle requires more than just a better calendar. It requires a fundamental shift in how you respond to the feeling of resistance.

The Fear of Failure and Perfectionism

Many people procrastinate because they are perfectionists. This sounds like a contradiction. If you want things to be perfect, why would you wait until the last minute? The answer lies in your ego. If you start a project early and give it your full effort but still fail, you have no excuse. It means you weren't good enough. However, if you wait until the very last night to start, you have a built-in excuse. If the work is subpar, you can tell yourself, "I just didn't have enough time. I could have done better if I had started sooner."

This is a self-protection mechanism. By procrastinating, you protect your sense of identity. You avoid the "danger" of finding out your true limits. This is what psychologists call "self-handicapping." To beat procrastination, you must give yourself permission to be average, at least in the first draft. You must learn to separate your work from your worth.

The Zeigarnik Effect and Mental Clutter

There is a psychological phenomenon known as the Zeigarnik Effect, named after Soviet psychologist Bluma Zeigarnik. While sitting in a busy restaurant, she noticed that waiters could remember complex, unpaid orders perfectly. However, the moment the bill was paid, the information vanished from their minds. She concluded that our brains remember uncompleted or interrupted tasks much better than completed ones.

When you have a long list of things you are avoiding, those tasks don't just sit there. They take up "mental RAM." They sit in the back of your mind, causing a low level of constant anxiety. This cognitive load makes you feel tired, even if you haven't done any physical work. This is why a day spent procrastinating often feels more exhausting than a day spent working. You are carrying the weight of all those unfinished tasks.

By starting—even for just five minutes—you begin to close those open loops in your brain. Once a task is started, the Zeigarnik Effect actually works in your favor. Your brain will want to finish what it has begun so it can clear that mental space. The tension of the "unfinished" becomes a fuel that pulls you toward the finish line.

The "Present Self" vs. The "Future Self"

Research in social psychology suggests that we view our "Future Self" as a complete stranger. Using fMRI scans, researchers found that when people think about themselves ten years in the future, the brain activity in the ventromedial prefrontal cortex looks nearly identical to when they think about a complete stranger.

Because you don't feel a strong emotional connection to your future self, you are happy to "borrow" time and energy from them. You tell yourself, "Future Me will have more willpower" or "Future Me will be in the mood to do this." In reality, your future self will have the same level of energy and the same distractions as you do now. Procrastination is essentially pushing the pain of a task onto a person you don't really know.

The Six Pillars of Resistance

To beat procrastination, you must identify the specific "flavor" of resistance you are feeling. Resistance is rarely a vague cloud; it usually stems from one of six distinct areas.

1. Lack of Clarity

If a task is vague, your brain will interpret it as a threat. When you write "Start business" on your to-do list, your prefrontal cortex has no idea what the first physical movement should be. Because it cannot visualize the path, it shuts down. You must move from the abstract to the concrete.

2. Low Self-Efficacy

If you do not believe you are capable of doing the task well, you will avoid it to protect your ego. This is the "Imposter Syndrome" trap. You delay because as long as you haven't started, you haven't "failed" yet. Building mental toughness requires you to value the effort over the outcome.

3. Task Aversion

Sometimes, the task is simply unpleasant. It is boring, repetitive, or physically taxing. In these cases, we rely on "Temptation Bundling." You pair the aversive task with something you enjoy, such as listening to a specific podcast only while doing a chore.

4. Impulsivity

Some individuals are biologically more prone to distraction. High levels of impulsivity mean your "bottom-up" attention system is constantly scanning for novelty. For you, the battle is won or lost in the environment. You cannot rely on willpower; you must rely on physical barriers.

5. Perfectionism and Anxiety

As discussed earlier, the fear of not being perfect is a major driver of delay. We will use the "B-Minus Work" strategy. By intentionally aiming for a "good enough" first draft, you lower the emotional stakes and allow yourself to enter a state of flow.

6. Lack of Meaning

If you do not see why a task matters, your brain will struggle to allocate resources to it. We will explore "Value Alignment," where you connect even the most boring administrative tasks to your larger life goals.

The Role of Chronic Stress and Cortisol

We often blame ourselves for a lack of character when we procrastinate. However, chronic stress plays a massive role in our ability to stay disciplined. When you are under high levels of stress, your body produces cortisol. High cortisol levels can actually shrink the prefrontal cortex over time and make the amygdala (the fear center of the brain) more reactive.

This means that the more stressed you are, the harder it is for your brain to choose the long-term benefit over the short-term escape. This is why "just trying harder" rarely works for chronic procrastinators. If your biology is in "survival mode," your brain will always choose the safest, easiest path. You have to lower your baseline stress levels through sleep, nutrition, and movement.

Self-Compassion as a Productivity Tool

One of the most surprising findings in procrastination research is the role of self-forgiveness. A study of university students found that those who forgave themselves for procrastinating on their first exam actually procrastinated less on their second exam.

When you beat yourself up for wasting time, you create more negative emotions. Since procrastination is a way to avoid negative emotions, the guilt of having procrastinated actually makes you *more* likely to procrastinate again to escape the guilt. It is a self-perpetuating cycle of shame. By practicing self-compassion, you lower the emotional stakes and move back into action without the heavy weight of self-loathing.

The Structure of This Book

This section is designed to move you from understanding to execution. We will start by identifying your specific procrastination style. Understanding your specific triggers is essential for applying the right solutions.

From there, we will move into practical, daily tools. You will learn:

- **The Two-Minute Rule:** How to overcome the initial hurdle of starting.
- **Micro-Tasking:** How to dismantle large, intimidating projects.
- **Energy Management:** How to align your hardest work with your peak biological hours.
- **The Power of Environment:** How to make the right choices automatic.
- **The Art of the Reset:** How to recover when you have a bad day.

The Neurochemistry of Action vs. Avoidance

To truly master your time, you must understand the neurochemical landscape of your brain. Two main chemicals dictate your level of discipline: Dopamine and Norepinephrine. While dopamine is often called the "pleasure" chemical, it is actually the chemical of "anticipation." It is what makes you want to check your phone or eat a snack. It drives the "craving."

Norepinephrine, on the other hand, is released when we are under a small amount of stress or when we are intensely focused. It is what allows us to stay on task. The procrastinator's brain is often stuck in a "Dopamine Loop" where it seeks the quick hit of novelty to avoid the "effortful" release of norepinephrine. In the following chapters, we will learn how to "prime" your brain for the right neurochemical balance, ensuring you have the mental fuel to stay focused.

The Historical Precedent of Self-Mastery

History is full of examples of high-achievers who struggled with the same urges we feel today. Victor Hugo, the famous author, famously asked his valet to take away all his clothes so he could not leave his house until he finished writing *The Hunchback of Notre Dame*. He forced himself into a state of "environmental lockdown" because he knew his willpower alone was not enough.

This teaches us that even the greatest minds throughout history were not immune to delay. They simply became masters of creating systems that forced them to act. We will use these historical "forcing functions" and adapt them for our digital world. Whether it is using app blockers or social accountability, you will learn to build a structure that makes action inevitable.

CHAPTER 1

IDENTIFY YOUR PROCRASTINATION STYLE AND TRIGGERS

Most people treat procrastination as a monolithic character flaw. They say, "I am a procrastinator," as if it is a single, unchangeable trait. In reality, procrastination is a symptom of various underlying emotional and cognitive triggers. Just as a doctor cannot treat a fever without knowing if the cause is a virus, an infection, or heatstroke, you cannot cure your delay until you diagnose your specific "Procrastination Style."

Self-awareness is the first step toward mental toughness. If you do not know why you are stopping, you cannot build a system to keep yourself going. In this chapter, we will dismantle the myth of the "lazy person" and replace it with a clear, scientific framework for identifying what triggers your specific desire to avoid work. We will explore the biology of the brain, the psychology of the ego, and the environmental factors that dictate your daily output.

The Cognitive Architecture of Avoidance

Procrastination is often a "misregulation" of emotion. When you look at a task, your brain performs a lightning-fast assessment of the emotional "cost" of that task. This happens in the amygdala, the brain's emotional processing center. If the task feels boring, difficult, or scary, your brain treats it as a threat.

The amygdala triggers a surge of anxiety, often before your conscious mind even realizes what is happening. This is what neuroscientists call an "amygdala hijack." To calm this anxiety, your brain seeks an immediate escape. This escape usually takes the form of a "low-stakes" activity, like checking your phone or cleaning your desk. These activities provide a temporary hit of relief, which reinforces the habit of avoidance.

This process is a primitive survival mechanism. Your limbic system is designed to prioritize immediate safety and comfort over long-term abstract goals. When you procrastinate, you aren't failing a logic test; you are losing a battle to an ancient part of your brain that thinks a difficult spreadsheet is a literal predator. To break this, we must look at the specific psychological profiles that lead to this cycle.

The Deep Dive into the Six Procrastination Styles

To solve the problem, you must first name it. Most individuals oscillate between these six styles depending on the nature of the task. Identifying which one is active in a given moment allows you to apply the correct counter-strategy.

1. The Perfectionist (The Fear-Based Avoider)

The Perfectionist is not someone who does everything perfectly. Rather, they are someone whose self-worth is tied entirely to their performance. Because they fear being judged as "less than," they view every task as a test of their value.

If they cannot guarantee an A+ result, they would rather not start at all. By delaying, they preserve the fantasy that they *could* have been perfect if they only had more time. For the Perfectionist, procrastination is a shield against the pain of being "average." They are often paralyzed by the "blank page" because the first word represents the end of a perfect idea and the beginning of an imperfect reality.

2. The Dreamer (The Ambiguity Avoider)

The Dreamer loves the "idea" of a project but hates the "logistics" of it. They have big visions and grand plans, but they struggle with the boring, granular details required to execute those plans.

Dreamers often procrastinate because the actual work feels mundane compared to the exciting fantasy. They struggle with "executive function"—the mental processes that allow us to plan, focus attention, and juggle multiple tasks. They often tell themselves they are "waiting for inspiration," but in reality, they are avoiding the cognitive friction of organized effort.

3. The Defier (The Autonomy Avoider)

The Defier procrastinates as a form of rebellion. This often stems from a childhood where they felt over-controlled by authority figures. As adults, they view deadlines, requests from bosses, or even their own to-do lists as an attack on their freedom.

By delaying the task, they feel they are "taking back power." It is a self-sabotaging form of independence. They are essentially saying, "You can't make me do this," even when the person "making" them do it is their own future self. The Defier thrives on the feeling of being the bottleneck.

4. The Worrier (The Safety Avoider)

The Worrier lacks confidence in their ability to handle change. They procrastinate because they are afraid that finishing the task will lead to more responsibility, more visibility, or more potential for failure.

They prefer the "uncomfortable comfortable"—the state of being stressed about an unfinished task is safer to them than the "unknown" of a finished one. They fear that success will change their life in ways they cannot control, so they stay stuck in the purgatory of "almost starting."

5. The Crisis-Maker (The Adrenaline Addict)

This individual believes they "work better under pressure." They intentionally delay tasks until the last possible second to trigger a massive spike in cortisol and adrenaline. While this force-starts the brain, it is a dangerous strategy.

The adrenaline rush provides a temporary focus, but the quality of work is usually lower, and the cost to the body is higher. Crisis-Makers are often addicted to the "heroic save," enjoying the rush of finishing a week's worth of work in a single night, unaware that they are burning out their adrenal glands in the process.

6. The Over-Doer (The Priority Avoider)

The Over-Doer stays incredibly busy but ignores the most important tasks. They will answer fifty unimportant emails to avoid the one difficult phone call that actually matters. This is "productive procrastination."

By staying busy, they avoid the guilt of doing nothing, but they also avoid the discomfort of the "Big Task." They confuse activity with achievement. They are the people who clean the entire house when they should be studying for an exam.

The Biology of Executive Function and Sequencing

While personality plays a role, we must also look at the biology of executive function. This refers to the set of cognitive processes that include working memory, flexible thinking, and self-control. These functions are primarily located in the prefrontal cortex (PFC).

The PFC is responsible for "sequencing"—the ability to break a large goal into a series of small, logical steps. If you have executive function challenges (common in those with ADHD or high chronic stress), your brain struggles to organize information. You might look at a messy room or a complex project and literally not know where to start.

This is not laziness; it is a "sequencing" error. When the brain cannot see a clear step-by-step sequence, the amygdala perceives the task as a chaotic, overwhelming mass and triggers the flight response. This leads to "paralysis by analysis," where the mental effort of trying to organize the task is so high that you have no energy left to actually perform it.

The Intertemporal Choice Model: Hyperbolic Discounting

To understand your procrastination style, you must understand how your brain values time. Neuroscientists use a model called "Hyperbolic Discounting." This theory suggests that humans are hardwired to prefer smaller, immediate rewards over larger, delayed rewards. The closer a reward is in time, the more "valuable" it feels to your brain.

When you procrastinate, you are suffering from a high "discount rate." You are viewing the comfort of the next ten minutes as more valuable than the success of the next ten years. Your brain treats your "Future Self" like a stranger. FMRIs show that when people think about their future selves, the brain activity looks identical to when they think about a complete stranger.

Building mental toughness requires "Future Self Continuity"—the ability to feel an emotional connection to the person you will be in a week, a month, or a year. If you don't care about that stranger, you will continue to "borrow" their time to pay for your current comfort.

The Dopamine Baseline: The Novelty Trap

Many people struggle because their dopamine baseline is dysregulated. Dopamine is not just about pleasure; it is about the "drive" to seek a reward. In a world of constant notifications, endless video streams, and high-stimulation digital environments, our baseline for what feels "exciting" has been pushed too high.

When you sit down to do a "boring" task like data entry or deep research, your brain looks at the dopamine potential of that task and compares it to the instant gratification of your phone. The task feels "painful" simply because it isn't as stimulating. This is why you feel the urge to check your email every few minutes; you are looking for a "dopamine hit" to bring your brain back to its elevated baseline. You aren't lazy; you are "over-clocked."

The Advanced Environmental Audit

Your environment acts as the match that lights the fire of procrastination. We call these "situational triggers." Most of us try to fight these with willpower, but willpower is a finite resource. A better strategy is to audit your environment to remove the triggers before they hit your amygdala.

1. Digital Friction and the "Brain Drain"

A study from the University of Texas at Austin showed that the mere presence of a smartphone reduces "available cognitive capacity," even if it is off and face down. A part of your brain is constantly working to *not* check the phone. This is "attentional drain." To solve this, the phone must be in a different room.

2. Visual Clutter and Open Loops

Every unfinished object in your peripheral vision—like a pile of laundry, a stack of bills, or a cluttered desktop—acts as an "open loop." These loops drain your mental energy because your brain is constantly "pinging" them as tasks that need completion. This leads to the "Over-Doer" style, where you clean to quiet the visual noise.

3. Lighting and Circadian Rhythms

Dim, warm lighting (like evening lamps) signals your brain to produce melatonin and rest. If you try to do high-focus work in a cozy, dimly lit room, you are fighting your own biology. Using bright, "cool" white light during work sessions keeps your cortisol levels at a functional high, signaling to the brain that it is time for "alert action" rather than "rest and digest."

The "Mood-First" Fallacy and Self-Perception Theory

The biggest trigger for procrastination is the belief that you need to be "in the mood" to start. We have been conditioned to believe that motivation leads to action. In reality, the reverse is true: **Action leads to motivation.**

The science of "Self-Perception Theory" suggests that our minds look at our behavior to decide how we feel. If you sit down and start typing—even if the words are terrible—your brain thinks, "I guess I am in a productive mood today," and begins to release the neurochemicals required for focus. If you wait until you feel ready, you are giving your limbic system permission to keep you on the couch.

This is the "Five-Minute Rule" in action: tell yourself you will only work for five minutes. This lowers the "threat" level of the task, allowing you to start. Once started, the Zeigarnik Effect takes over—your brain naturally wants to finish what it has begun.

We are social creatures, and our habits are often a reflection of our "tribe." If you spend time with people who view deadlines as suggestions and celebrate "slacking off," your brain will adopt those norms to fit in. This is "social proof."

Conversely, being in an environment of high-performers creates a "positive pressure." This isn't about competition; it's about the subconscious mirroring of behaviors. We will explore how to curate your "Social Architecture" to ensure that your peers are pulling you toward action rather than pushing you toward delay.

How to Conduct Your Personal Trigger Audit

To end this chapter, you must become a researcher of your own life. For the next 72 hours, you are not a worker; you are a scientist observing a subject. Keep a "Resistance Log" (digital or physical) and record every instance of delay.

Record the following four data points:

1. **The Task:** What were you supposed to be doing? (Be specific).
2. **The Feeling:** What was the dominant emotion the moment you decided to look away? (Boredom, fear of failure, confusion about the first step, resentment?)
3. **The Style:** Which of the six styles were you acting out? (e.g., Were you "Over-Doing" by cleaning the kitchen?)
4. **The Escape:** What did you do instead? (Social media, snacking, checking email?)

By the end of this audit, you will have a map of your minefield. You will know that you don't procrastinate on "everything"—you only procrastinate when a task hits a specific emotional nerve or occurs in a specific environment. You will see that your "laziness" is actually a predictable response to specific triggers.

Once these triggers are visible, they lose their power. In the following chapters, we will begin the work of disarming them using the "Two-Minute Rule," "Micro-Tasking," and "Environmental Design." You have the map; now it's time to navigate the terrain.

CHAPTER 2

APPLY THE TWO-MINUTE RULE TO GAIN MOMENTUM

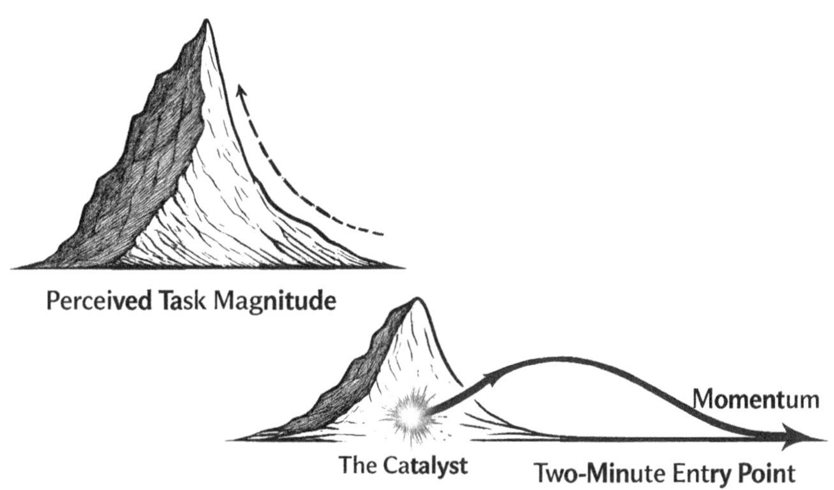

If Chapter 1 was about diagnosing the "why" of your delay, Chapter 2 is about the "how" of your escape. The most difficult moment of any task is not the middle or the end; it is the transition from a state of rest to a state of motion. In physics, this is known as **static friction**—the force that resists the initiation of movement. Once an object is sliding, the kinetic friction is significantly lower.

The human brain operates under a similar law of cognitive physics. The **Two-Minute Rule** is not a simple productivity hack; it is a surgical tool designed to bypass the amygdala and lower the **Activation Energy** required to start. To master this, we must understand the bio-chemical barriers that keep us stationary and the neurological pathways that facilitate the "first inch" of progress.

The Science of Activation Energy and Chemical Catalysts

In chemistry, **activation energy** is the minimum amount of energy required to trigger a chemical reaction. A match does not strike itself; it requires a specific amount of friction to ignite the phosphorus on the head. In the context of human behavior, every task on your to-do list has an activation energy cost. The problem is that our brains, influenced by stress, fatigue, and the "Perfectionist" or "Worrier" styles we identified in Chapter 1, often overestimate this cost.

When you think about "writing a ten-page report," your brain calculates the energy required for the *entire* project all at once. This perceived cost is so high that your brain refuses to provide the "spark" to start. The Two-Minute Rule works as a **biological catalyst**. By telling your brain, "I am only going to open the document and write for two minutes," you reduce the energy hump to a level that is almost impossible to refuse. You are not tricking yourself; you are realigning the task with your brain's current capacity for effort.

The Cognitive Switching Penalty and the Loading Phase

Moving from a state of relaxation or "productive procrastination" to high-focus work requires the **Prefrontal Cortex (PFC)** to recruit massive neural resources. It must load the context of the task into your working memory, suppress distractions, and activate the motor pathways for action. This "loading" phase is physically uncomfortable. It feels like mental strain or a "fog" in the front of the head.

Most procrastinators interpret this discomfort as a sign that they "aren't in the mood." By applying the Two-Minute Rule, you accept that the first two minutes will feel clunky and difficult, but you commit to it because the "load" is small. This is similar to a computer "booting up." You wouldn't expect a machine to run complex software the millisecond you hit the power button; you must give your brain the 120-second "boot-up" period it requires to reach operational efficiency.

The Basal Ganglia vs. The Prefrontal Cortex

The brain is essentially a dual-process system. The **basal ganglia** handle habits and automatic behaviors—the "auto-pilot"—while the **prefrontal cortex** handles conscious decision-making and willpower. Procrastination occurs when the PFC is too exhausted to override the basal ganglia's desire for the "status quo" of rest.

The Two-Minute Rule acts as a **neurological wedge**. It is small enough that the basal ganglia don't perceive it as a threat to your current state of comfort. Once you have been moving for two minutes, the PFC begins to "prime" the basal ganglia to accept the new activity as the current state, making the rest of the hour feel significantly easier. You are essentially slipping the work "under the radar" of your brain's resistance mechanisms.

The Zeigarnik Effect and Cognitive Loop Closure

The **Zeigarnik Effect** is the psychological phenomenon where our brains remember uncompleted tasks better than completed ones. This creates **Task Tension**. Once you start a task—even for just two minutes—you create a "mental itch" that the brain wants to scratch. By opening the file and writing the first sentence, you have opened a cognitive loop.

Your brain now feels a subconscious pressure to close that loop. The Two-Minute Rule uses this effect to create **momentum**. Most people wait until they feel "motivated" to start. The pro knows that **starting creates the motivation**. The moment you are "in" the task, the brain's focus shifts from *avoiding the pain of starting* to *the desire to finish what was begun.*

The Law of Diminishing Resistance

The first two minutes of a task represent 80% of the total resistance you will feel. This is a non-linear relationship. Imagine pushing a car; the hardest part is getting the tires to rotate for the first foot.

- **Minute 0–1 (Static Friction):** Peak resistance. The brain is screaming for an escape. This is where most people quit.
- **Minute 2–5 (Kinetic Friction):** Resistance drops by 50%. The "loading" phase is complete. You have established a "rhythm."

- **Minute 10+ (Flow State):** Resistance is nearly zero. The task becomes self-sustaining.

By committing only to the first two minutes, you are essentially agreeing to endure the peak resistance phase with the knowledge that it is temporary. You are "budgeting" your willpower for the only part of the task that actually requires it.

Scaling the Rule: The Entry Point Strategy

The Two-Minute Rule is about identifying the **Entry Point**. Every habit or project has a gateway. If you can master the gateway, the rest follows automatically. To apply this, you must "scale down" your goals until they have zero friction.

For example, if the goal is to **Exercise for an hour**, the Two-Minute Entry Point is "Put on workout clothes and shoes." If the goal is to **Write a 3,000-word chapter**, the Entry Point is "Open the laptop and write one sentence." You cannot improve a habit that doesn't exist; therefore, your only job is to show up for the first 120 seconds. Once the shoes are tied or the laptop is open, the "cost" of not doing the work actually becomes higher than the "cost" of continuing.

The Biology of Flow and the "Just Start" Threshold

Neurochemically, the state of "Flow"—where time disappears and work feels effortless—is characterized by a specific cocktail of dopamine, endorphins, and anandamide. However, these chemicals are not released *before* you start. They are the reward for the struggle.

By using the Two-Minute Rule, you are essentially buying a ticket to the "Flow" lottery. If you don't start, your neurochemistry remains in a baseline state of stasis. By starting, you initiate the process of **Autotelic Movement**, where the work itself becomes its own reward. The struggle of the first two minutes is the toll you pay to enter the highway of productivity.

Overcoming the Wall of Awful and Task-Based Shame

The **"Wall of Awful"** describes the emotional barrier that builds up around a task you have avoided for a long time. Every time you think about the task and feel guilty, you add another "brick" of shame to the wall. Eventually, the task itself isn't the problem—the wall of fear is.

The Two-Minute Rule is a way to **climb the wall** without needing to knock it down. You don't have to deal with the whole wall; you just have to deal with one brick. By focusing only on the next two minutes, you make the emotional barrier irrelevant. This is the essence of mental toughness: the ability to act in spite of your emotional state.

The Hard Stop Strategy for Chronic Aversion

For those with deep-seated task aversion, I recommend the **Hard Stop**. Tell yourself: "I will work on this for exactly two minutes, and then I am *obligated* to stop." Ninety percent of the time, once you start, you will want to keep going.

But for the other ten percent, if the task is truly grueling, you give yourself permission to quit after 120 seconds. This builds **trust** with your brain. If your brain knows that "starting" doesn't mean "being trapped for five hours," the resistance to starting will vanish. Paradoxically, the permission to quit is what gives you the strength to stay.

The Physics of Ritual: Priming the Pump

Great performers don't just start; they use **rituals** to slide into the Two-Minute Rule. A ritual is a pre-determined set of actions that signals to your brain that "Deep Work" is about to begin. This lowers the cognitive load of decision-making.

An effective ritual involves a **Physical Trigger** (like making a specific cup of tea), an **Environmental Anchor** (like sitting in a "work-only" chair), and the **Two-Minute Launch**. By repeating this ritual, you create an associative link in your brain. Eventually, the act of putting on your "focus" headphones will automatically trigger the release of focus-oriented neurochemicals.

Decision Fatigue and the Burden of Choice

One of the primary reasons we fail to start is **Decision Fatigue**. When we look at a complex project, our brain is forced to make hundreds of micro-decisions: *Where do I begin? What font should I use? Which email should I reply to first?* Each decision drains a small amount of our glucose and willpower.

The Two-Minute Rule eliminates decision fatigue by pre-ordaining the first move. You no longer have to decide *what* to do; you only have to execute the "two-minute version." By removing choice from the initiation phase, you conserve your mental energy for the actual work that follows.

The Social and Identity Impact of the Start

Every time you execute the Two-Minute Rule, you are casting a vote for the person you want to become. Procrastination is not just a loss of time; it is a loss of **Identity Capital**. When you say you will do something and then don't, you lose trust in yourself.

Conversely, completing a two-minute start—even if you stop immediately after—proves that you are someone who follows through on their intentions. Over time, this builds a **"Bias for Action."** You stop being a "Procrastinator" and start being a "High-Initiative Individual." This shift in identity is more valuable than any single task completed, as it dictates your behavior for the rest of your life.

Chapter 2 Summary and Action Plan

The Two-Minute Rule is the antidote to "all-or-nothing" thinking. It acknowledges that the hardest part of any journey is the first step and provides a low-stakes way to take that step. By mastering the start, you take away procrastination's greatest weapon: the ability to keep you stationary.

Your Action Plan:

1. **Identify your Lead Domino:** Pick the most important task you've been avoiding.
2. **Scale it down:** Define the two-minute version—the physical "first inch" of movement.
3. **Set a Starting Ritual:** Choose a time and a physical cue that leads directly into the task.
4. **Execute the 120 Seconds:** Start a timer. Focus entirely on the movement, not the quality of the work.
5. **Evaluate:** After two minutes, decide if you want to continue. If the resistance is still too high, stop guilt-free. You have succeeded in your primary goal of *starting*.

CHAPTER 3

DISMANTLE LARGE PROJECTS WITH MICRO-TASKING

The Monolithic Project

The Micro Tasking Architecture

The primary reason ambitious projects fail is not a lack of talent or resources; it is a failure of **scale**. When we look at a complex objective—writing a book, launching a startup, or mastering a new language—our brain does not see a series of steps. It sees a monolithic, impenetrable wall. This perception triggers a state of "Cognitive Freeze," where the sheer magnitude of the task overwhelms the prefrontal cortex, leading to the path of least resistance: procrastination.

To regain control, we must master the art of **Micro-Tasking**. This is the process of deconstructing a macro-objective into its smallest possible units of action. In this chapter, we will learn how to dismantle the "monolith" and replace it with a high-velocity sequence of micro-wins that build their own momentum.

The Planning Fallacy and the Burden of the Monolith

Psychologically, we are prone to the **Planning Fallacy**, a phenomenon where we chronically underestimate the time and effort required to complete a task. We view the future with an optimistic lens, assuming that "Future Me" will have more energy and focus than "Present Me." When a large project is left in its monolithic state, the Planning Fallacy makes it feel manageable in the abstract but terrifying in the concrete.

By dismantling a project, we force ourselves to confront the reality of the work. If you say you want to "Build a Website," your brain treats it as one item. If you list the **forty individual micro-tasks** required to build that website, the Planning Fallacy is stripped away. You are no longer looking at an idea; you are looking at a manufacturing process. This granularity is the first step toward mental toughness because it removes the ambiguity that feeds anxiety.

Cognitive Load Theory and the Mental Workbench

Your working memory is essentially a "mental workbench." According to **Cognitive Load Theory**, this workbench has a very limited capacity. When you attempt to manage a large project in your head, you are cluttering that workbench with every "what if" and "how to" associated with the goal.

Micro-tasking serves as a **Cognitive Offload**. When you break a project down into micro-tasks and put them on paper or a digital tool, you are clearing the workbench. You no longer have to remember *all* the steps; you only have to focus on the *one* micro-task currently in front of you. This focus reduces "Executive Strain" and allows you to apply 100% of your cognitive power to a single, manageable action.

The Neurobiology of the Micro-Win

Every time you cross an item off a list, your brain's reward system releases a small pulse of **dopamine**. This is the "Completion High." If your task is "Write Book," you only get that dopamine hit once—months or years from now. This creates a "Dopamine Desert," where your motivation withers because the reward is too distant.

Micro-tasking creates a "Dopamine Oasis." By breaking the project into 100 micro-tasks, you create 100 opportunities for success. This constant feedback loop trains your brain to associate the project with progress rather than pain. You are essentially "hacking" your neurochemistry to keep your motivation high through the long, difficult middle phase of a major project.

The Anatomy of Task-Dependency

One of the most paralyzing aspects of a large project is not knowing the **order of operations**. We often feel stuck because we are trying to do Task B before Task A is finished. In project management, this is known as a **Dependency**.

When you dismantle a project, you create a "Value Stream." You begin to see which tasks are "Blockers" and which are "Open Lanes." For example, you cannot "Design a Logo" until you have "Chosen a Brand Name." By identifying these dependencies, you remove the mental friction of choosing what to do next. The path becomes a logical progression rather than a chaotic scramble.

The Rule of Granularity: When is a Task Small Enough?

The most common mistake in dismantling a project is stopping too soon. A task is not "micro" until it is **actionable without further thought**. If a task requires you to sit and think for ten minutes before you can act, it is still too large.

- **The Macro Goal:** Launch a marketing campaign.
- **The Weak Task:** Write copy for the ad. (Too vague; requires several sub-decisions).
- **The Micro-Task:** Write a three-word headline for the Facebook ad. (Specific, actionable, and low-friction).

The goal of granularity is to reach a state of **Zero-Decision Action**. You want your to-do list to be a set of instructions so clear that you could follow them even when you are exhausted or unmotivated. This is the ultimate defense against the "I don't feel like it" reflex.

Visual Mapping and the Hierarchy of Action

To manage micro-tasks, you need a visual system that maintains the connection between the tiny steps and the big picture. Without this, you risk "Micro-Task Blindness," where you are busy doing small things but losing sight of the objective.

A **Work Breakdown Structure (WBS)** or a **Gantt Chart** helps maintain this hierarchy. It allows you to see the "Forest" (the goal) while you are focusing on a single "Tree" (the micro-task). This dual perspective is essential for long-term endurance. It reminds you *why* the small task matters, preventing the feeling that you are just performing busy work.

The Neuro-Economics of Task Saliency

Your brain constantly performs a "Cost-Benefit Analysis" on every task. If the perceived cost (effort) is higher than the immediate benefit (dopamine/progress), the brain will choose to procrastinate. This is **Hyperbolic Discounting** in action.

Micro-tasking changes the "Economic Value" of the work. By making the task tiny, you reduce the perceived cost to near zero. Suddenly, even a small benefit makes the task worth doing. You are essentially making it "cheaper" for your brain to work than to avoid work. This shift in the internal economy is what allows high-performers to maintain a high "Velocity of Output" over long periods.

The Strategy of the "Lead Domino"

In any complex project, not all tasks are created equal. Some tasks are **Lead Dominos**—actions that, once completed, make the rest of the project easier or even unnecessary. Micro-tasking allows you to identify these dominos.

By dismantling the project, you can see the dependencies clearly. You might realize that "Choosing a Brand Color" is a distraction, while "Interviewing Three Potential Customers" is the Lead Domino that validates your entire business model. Mental toughness is not just about doing work; it is about having the discipline to do the *right* work first.

Managing Project Fatigue and the 10% Rule

Large projects often fail at the **70% mark**. This is where the initial excitement has faded, and the finish line is still too far away to provide motivation. Micro-tasking protects you from this slump by allowing you to focus only on the **"Next 10%."**

When you feel overwhelmed, stop looking at the mountain. Look at the next three micro-tasks on your list. Commit to finishing those, and nothing else. This "Tunnel Vision" is a survival mechanism for high-performers. It prevents the scale of the project from becoming an emotional burden. You aren't finishing a project; you are just finishing the next ten minutes.

The Psychology of "Done" and the Momentum Effect

There is a profound psychological difference between "90% finished" and "Done." In our brains, a task that is 90% finished still occupies space on the mental workbench. It creates **Cognitive Residue**.

Micro-tasking allows you to reach the state of "Done" multiple times a day. Each time you finish a micro-task, you clear that residue. This creates a "clean slate" effect that allows you to move to the next task with fresh energy. This is the **Momentum Effect**: the more "Dones" you accumulate, the faster you move.

Precision Deconstruction: The 15-Minute Rule

If you are struggling to break a task down, use the **15-Minute Rule**. If a task will take longer than 15 minutes, it is not a micro-task; it is a "Mini-Project."

For example, "Researching competitors" is a Mini-Project. To turn it into micro-tasks, you must deconstruct it:

1. Find three competitor websites.
2. List their top three features.
3. Screenshot their pricing pages.

Each of these can be done in under 15 minutes. This level of precision removes the "vagueness" that causes the brain to hesitate. You are giving your brain a narrow, clear target.

Overcoming the "Thinking is Working" Trap

We often procrastinate by "over-planning." We spend hours creating beautiful spreadsheets and lists, convinced that this is the same as progress. This is a form of **Productive Procrastination.**

Micro-tasking fights this by making the "Action" the unit of measurement. A task is not a task unless it results in a tangible change in the project. If your list is full of "Think about X" or "Research Y," you are in the thinking trap. Change those to "Write 5 bullet points on X" or "Download one paper on Y." This shifts the focus from internal processing to external output.

Conclusion: The Architecture of Success

Dismantling a large project is an act of **Architectural Intelligence**. It is the process of taking a dream and turning it into a blueprint. By mastering micro-tasking, you are no longer at the mercy of your "mood" or your "motivation." You are a builder, following a set of precise instructions that lead inevitably to completion.

Mental toughness is not about having a stronger will; it is about having a better system. When the path is broken down into small, clear steps, the "will" required to take those steps is minimal. You don't need to be a hero to finish a micro-task; you just need to be a person who can do one thing at a time.

Action Plan for Chapter 3

1. **The Brain Dump:** Write down every single thing you need to do for your current large project. Don't worry about order or size yet.

2. **The Dismantling Phase:** Take each item from your brain dump and break it down until no task takes longer than 15 minutes to complete.

3. **Identify the Lead Domino:** Highlight the one micro-task that, if finished today, would provide the most momentum for tomorrow.

4. **The "One-at-a-Time" Rule:** Hide your master list. Only keep your current three micro-tasks visible to avoid cognitive overwhelm.

5. **Audit Your Tasks:** If you find yourself hesitating on a task for more than 5 minutes, it is too big. Break it down again.

CHAPTER 4

ESTABLISH A DISTRACTION-FREE ENVIRONMENT

In the modern age, focus is not merely a mental discipline; it is an act of environmental engineering. We have evolved to be highly sensitive to our surroundings—a survival mechanism that once allowed our ancestors to detect predators in the brush. Today, however, that same sensitivity is weaponized against us by a multi-billion-dollar "Attention Economy" designed to exploit our biological vulnerabilities.

If you attempt to use willpower alone to resist the lure of a smartphone or the chaos of a cluttered room, you are fighting a losing battle against your own biology. Mental toughness is not about having a stronger shield; it is about choosing to stand where the arrows aren't flying. To achieve elite-level productivity, you must stop treating your environment as a neutral backdrop and start treating it as a **Cognitive Extension** of your brain.

The Neuro-Biology of Environmental Priming and Associative Triggering

Our brains are governed by **Associative Learning**, a process often summarized by Hebb's Law: "Neurons that fire together, wire together." Every environment you enter sends a "pre-stimulus" signal to your neurons, telling them which pathways to activate. This is known as **Contextual Cueing**. When you enter a kitchen, your brain primes the neural pathways associated with hunger and consumption. When you enter a bedroom, it primes the pathways for rest.

The crisis of modern productivity is the "Multi-Purpose Space." If you work in the same place where you sleep, watch movies, or eat, your brain is in a state of **Functional Ambiguity**. It is receiving conflicting signals: *Should I be focused or should I be resting?* This ambiguity creates **Attentional Friction**. When you sit at a desk cluttered with household bills, toys, or reminders of unfinished errands, your brain must use a portion of its glucose-driven energy just to *suppress* those visual cues. This is known as **Background Tasking**. Your brain is essentially running a dozen background applications that drain your battery before you've even opened your primary work file.

The Physics of Visual Saliency and the Superior Colliculus

In the realm of focus, **Saliency** is the degree to which an object stands out from its neighbors. Your brain is a saliency-detecting machine, constantly scanning for anomalies. This is handled by the **Superior Colliculus**, a primitive structure in the midbrain that directs your gaze toward anything that moves, flashes, or contrasts with its environment. This was life-saving when an anomaly meant a snake in the grass; it is life-ruining when an anomaly is a "New Email" notification.

To counter this, we apply the **Principle of Negative Space**. A distraction-free environment is not defined by what is in it, but by what is *absent*. The "Frictionless Desk" is a space where the only salient objects are the tools required for the immediate micro-task. Everything else—cables, pens you don't use, old notes—is visual noise. By removing this noise, you lower the **Threshold of Initiation**, making it biologically easier for your brain to "lock in" to the work. When your visual field contains nothing but your work, the brain naturally defaults to that work as its primary stimulus.

The Digital Panopticon: Weaponizing Choice Architecture

We currently live in a **Digital Panopticon**, where our devices are designed to keep us in a state of constant, shallow engagement. The "Notification Loop" is a sophisticated psychological trap based on **Variable Ratio Reinforcement**—the same mechanism that makes slot machines addictive. You check your phone not because you know there is something important, but because there *might* be. This creates a state of **Continuous Partial Attention**, which is the antithesis of mental toughness.

To establish focus, you must implement **Radical Digital Sanitization**. This involves manipulating your **Choice Architecture**—the way in which choices are presented to you. If your phone is on your desk, your brain is using executive function to *not* check it. This is a "Cognitive Tax." If the phone is in another room, that energy is reclaimed.

- **The Gray-Scale Shift:** Colors on a screen are designed to trigger dopamine. Red notification bubbles are specifically tuned to the frequency that triggers our "Alert" response. By removing the color, you strip the apps of their **Incentive Salience**.

- **The 20-Second Rule:** Procrastination is often a path-of-least-resistance choice. If you make a distraction 20 seconds harder to access (e.g., putting your phone in a timed lockbox), your brain will often choose the work instead because the energy cost of the distraction has become too high.

Sensory Architecture: The Sonic Cocoon and Cognitive De-coupling

Focus is a multi-sensory experience. While visual distraction is the most obvious, **Auditory Overload** is often the most insidious because the ears have no "eyelids." High-frequency or unpredictable sounds—such as a conversation in the next room or a sudden door slam—trigger the brain's **Orienting Response**. This causes a spike in cortisol and shatters the state of **Flow**.

To protect your focus, you must build a **Sonic Cocoon**. This isn't just about silence; it's about **Acoustic Masking**. Using pink noise, brown noise, or specific binaural beats creates a consistent, low-information auditory background. This allows the brain to engage in **Cognitive De-**

coupling, where your internal thoughts become more vivid and salient than the external world. Research into **Neural Entrainment** suggests that certain rhythmic frequencies can actually coax the brain into Alpha or Theta wave states, which are associated with deep relaxation and creative problem-solving.

Circadian Alignment and the Ergonomics of Alertness

The environment also dictates your biological "readiness" through light and temperature. Your **Suprachiasmatic Nucleus** (the brain's master clock) reacts to the "color temperature" of light. Blue-rich light (above 5000K) suppresses melatonin and boosts cortisol, making it ideal for the "Lead Domino" tasks described in Chapter 3. Conversely, warm, dim lighting triggers the release of adenosine, preparing the body for rest.

Furthermore, the **Ambient Temperature** of your workspace acts as a cognitive regulator. Studies from Cornell University suggest that in cold offices (under 20°C), employees make 44% more errors than in rooms at an optimal temperature (around 22°C). When you are cold, your brain diverts energy to thermoregulation—energy that should be used for complex synthesis. By controlling these invisible variables, you are essentially "tuning" your biology for peak performance.

Territoriality and the Shrine of Deep Work

Human beings are territorial creatures. We perform best when we have a "home base" where we feel safe and dominant. In psychology, this is known as **Place-Identity**. You can weaponize this by creating a "Focus Shrine"—a physical space that is used for *nothing else*.

By strictly guarding the sanctity of this space, you create a powerful **Habit Anchor**. Eventually, the mere act of sitting in that specific chair or lighting a specific candle will trigger a "Pre-Focus State." You are no longer fighting for focus; you are sliding into it as a Pavlovian response. This is the difference between "trying to work" and "being in work mode." This shrine should be treated with reverence; if you find yourself wanting to browse social media, you must physically leave the shrine. This maintains the neural purity of the environment.

The Social Engineering of Focus: Defense and Signaling

Human interruptions are the "High-Saliency" distractions that are hardest to ignore because we are evolutionarily hard-wired to respond to social cues. A tap on the shoulder is a **Tactile Interrupt** that can take up to 23 minutes to fully recover from in terms of deep-work depth. This is because of **Context Switching Cost**—the mental energy required to "reload" the complex rules and data of your task.

Establishing a distraction-free environment requires **Social Engineering**. This involves the creation of clear "Visibility Cues" (such as a closed door, a specific light, or large over-ear headphones) that signal to others that you are in a "Deep Work" state. More importantly, it requires the mental toughness to set and defend these boundaries. You are not being "rude"; you are protecting the limited cognitive resources you have to offer the world. You must train those around you to respect the "Sanctity of the Deep Work Block."

The Attention Residue and the Environmental Buffer

Even with a perfect environment, you cannot instantly move from the chaos of life to the stillness of focus. As discussed in Chapter 2, **Attention Residue** means that a part of your brain is still processing the last stimulus it received. If you just finished a stressful phone call and sit down to write, your brain is still "in" that phone call.

A distraction-free environment must include a **Transitional Buffer Zone**. This is a physical or ritualistic space that separates "Life" from "Work." It might involve a five-minute "Desk Clearing Ritual," where you physically remove every item not related to the task at hand. This act of manual cleaning serves as a psychological signal that the transition is complete. By the time you sit down, the "residue" of the outside world has been washed away.

The Clean Slate Protocol: Closing the Loop for Tomorrow

The final component of environmental mastery is the **Shut-Down Protocol**. A distraction-free morning begins with a "Sanitized Evening." By clearing your workspace, closing all browser tabs, and laying out the tools for your next task the night before, you remove the **Decision Friction** of the following morning.

When you walk into your workspace the next day, the environment is already "pointing" toward the work. This is an application of **Priming Theory**: by seeing your notebook open to the correct page and your pen ready, your brain begins to load the relevant "Work Schema" before you even sit down. This is how the mentally tough operate: they don't rely on willpower to start; they rely on an environment that makes starting the only logical option.

Action Plan for Chapter 4

1. **The Visual Audit:** Take a photo of your current workspace. Look at it as a stranger would. Every item you see is a potential "Attention Thief." Remove 50% of what you see.

2. **The Digital Sanitization:** Turn your phone to grayscale. Move all distracting apps into a folder labeled "Time Wasters" on the third page of your home screen.

3. **The Sonic Mask:** Download a pink noise or binaural beats app. Use it consistently to build a "Sonic Anchor" for work.

4. **The Light and Temp Check:** Ensure your morning work is done in bright, cool light (5000K+). Set your thermostat to 21°C.

5. **The 20-Second Rule:** Identify your biggest environmental distraction (e.g., the TV remote or your phone) and place it 20 seconds away from your "Shrine of Focus."

6. **The Shutdown Ritual:** Spend the last 10 minutes of your workday clearing your physical and digital desktop. Set out the "Lead Domino" for tomorrow.

CHAPTER 5

SET DAILY INTENTIONS AND PRIORITIES

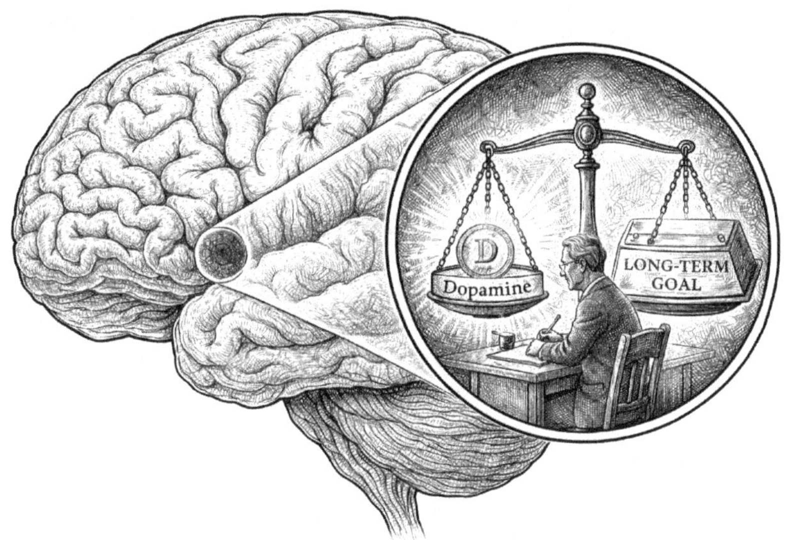

If the previous chapters were about clearing the path and sharpening the blade, Chapter 5 is about selecting the target. Without a rigorous system of intention and prioritization, even the most focused individual becomes a "high-efficiency wanderer"—someone who is very good at doing things that don't actually matter. In the landscape of modern work, the volume of tasks will always exceed your capacity to complete them. Mental toughness, therefore, is not the ability to do *everything*; it is the disciplined refusal to do the *wrong things*.

The Neuro-Economics of Choice and the Ventromedial Prefrontal Cortex

Every time you decide what to do next, your brain performs a **Neuro-Economic Calculation**. The **Ventromedial Prefrontal Cortex (vmPFC)** acts as a biological accountant, weighing the "Expected Value" of a task against its "Metabolic Cost." This is not a conscious process; it is a rapid-fire assessment of potential dopamine reward versus the energy required from the body's glucose stores.

The problem is that our brains are evolutionarily biased toward **Immediate Gratification**. We are hard-wired to prefer a small, certain reward now (like clearing five easy emails) over a large, uncertain reward later (like finishing a difficult project). This is known as **Hyperbolic Discounting**. When you don't set a conscious priority, your brain will naturally default to the "Lowest Metabolic Cost" tasks—the trivial, low-value activities that make you feel busy but leave your goals untouched. Setting a daily intention is the act of manually overriding this biological bias. It is a "top-down" executive intervention that forces the brain to assign value to long-term survival and success rather than short-term comfort.

The Physics of Decision Fatigue and Ego Depletion

Prioritization is a high-energy activity. Every choice you make—from what to wear in the morning to which email to answer first—drains a finite resource known as **Willpower Capital**. In social psychology, this is referred to as **Ego Depletion**. When your willpower is depleted, your vmPFC loses its ability to calculate long-term value, and your brain defaults to impulsivity.

This is why the most successful individuals set their intentions the night before. By deciding your "Big Three" before the day begins, you bypass the "Morning Choice Tax." You wake up with your cognitive battery at 100%, and instead of spending 20% of that energy deciding what to do, you spend 100% of it *doing* the work. Mental toughness is recognizing that your ability to choose is a depreciating asset throughout the day. You must protect it by automating the trivial and front-loading the critical.

The Planning Fallacy and the "Priority Dilution" Trap

We are all victims of the **Planning Fallacy**, a cognitive bias that causes us to chronically overestimate our future efficiency. Because we view "Future Me" as a more disciplined, energized version of ourselves, we pack our daily lists with "Ideal Self" tasks. However, when the reality of the day hits—interruptions, physical fatigue, and the inevitable "decision fatigue"—the high-value, difficult tasks are the first to be sacrificed.

This leads to **Priority Dilution**. By trying to make everything a priority, nothing becomes a priority. You end up in a state of **Cognitive Fragmentation**, where you touch twenty different tasks but complete none of them. Mental toughness requires you to accept the **Brutal Reality of Trade-offs**. To say "Yes" to your Lead Domino, you must have the courage to say "No" (or "Not Today") to ten other legitimate requests for your time. This is the "Omission Strategy": the realization that your productivity is defined more by what you *don't* do than what you do.

The Eisenhower Matrix: Reclaiming the "Important but Not Urgent"

One of the most powerful frameworks for daily intention is the **Eisenhower Matrix**. Most people spend their lives in the "Urgent and Important" quadrant (Crisis Management) or the "Urgent but Not Important" quadrant (Interruption Management). These quadrants are high-stress and high-adrenaline, which can create a false sense of productivity.

The secret to elite productivity lies in the **Second Quadrant: Important but Not Urgent**. These are the tasks that build long-term value: strategy, relationship building, skill acquisition, and deep work. Because these tasks lack a screaming deadline, the brain will deprioritize them indefinitely unless they are anchored by a **Binding Intention**. Your daily priority must include at least one "Quadrant Two" task to ensure you are not just surviving the day, but building a future. Mental toughness is the ability to ignore the "Urgency Signal" of an incoming email in favor of the "Importance Signal" of your long-term goals.

The Architecture of the "Big Three" and the Rule of One

To fight the "Monolith" of the to-do list, we apply the **Rule of Three**. Research into working memory suggests that the brain can effectively track and maintain focus on approximately three major objectives at once. This is governed by the **Dorsolateral Prefrontal Cortex (dlPFC)**, which holds information in a "ready state" for execution. Beyond three items, the "Overload Effect" kicks in, and performance degrades across all tasks due to **Interference**.

However, even within the Big Three, there is a **Primary Lead Domino**. This is the one task that, if completed, would make the other two easier or even unnecessary. Elite-level intention setting involves identifying this "One Thing" and scheduling it for your period of **Peak Cognitive Alertness**. For most, this is the first two to four hours of the day. By winning the "Battle of the One," you create a psychological ripple effect. You prove to yourself that you are in control, which triggers the release of **Serotonin**, increasing your confidence and making the rest of the day feel like a downhill sprint.

The Psychology of Opportunity Cost and The "Fear of Missing Out" (FOMO)

At its core, prioritization is the management of **Opportunity Cost**. Every minute spent on Task A is a minute that can never be spent on Task B. For the high-achiever, this reality often leads to **Analysis Paralysis**—the fear that choosing one path means missing a better one.

Mental toughness requires the cultivation of **JOMO (The Joy of Missing Out)**. You must reach a psychological state where you are comfortable ignoring 99% of the world's noise because you are 100% committed to your 1%. This requires a shift from a "Scarcity Mindset" (I need to do everything) to an "Essentialist Mindset" (I only need to do what matters). When your daily intentions are clear, the Opportunity Cost of saying no to a distraction becomes zero, because the distraction has no value relative to your goal.

Temporal Discounting and the "Future-Self" Bridge

Why is it so hard to prioritize the difficult work in the morning? It comes down to **Temporal Discounting**—the tendency for rewards to lose value the further they are in the future. To your brain, "Future You" (the one who gets the promotion or the finished book) is a stranger. Functional MRI scans show that when people think about their future selves, the brain areas associated with "self" often go quiet, and the areas associated with "stranger" activate.

To bridge this gap, your daily intentions must be **Visceral**. Instead of writing "Work on project," which is abstract, you must write "Finalize the three core arguments of the executive summary." By making the intention specific and outcome-oriented, you help the brain visualize the completion reward. This "Simulated Reward" makes the long-term task more competitive against the immediate dopamine hit of checking social media. You are essentially "tricking" your brain into valuing the future as much as the present.

The Decision-Action Gap and the Implementation Intention

Setting a priority is useless if it doesn't translate into action. Psychologists call this the **Decision-Action Gap**. To close it, we use **Implementation Intentions**, also known as "If-Then" planning. This technique leverages our brain's natural ability to recognize environmental cues without using conscious willpower.

Instead of saying "I will prioritize the report," you say, "**If** it is 9:00 AM and I have my coffee, **then** I will open the report file and write for 90 minutes." This simple linguistic shift moves the task from the "Conscious Willpower" system (which is easily exhausted) to the **Situational Cue** system. You are essentially "pre-programming" your brain to act when the environment meets the criteria. This reduces the **Activation Energy** required to start, making the execution of your priorities nearly automatic.

The Neuro-Physics of Momentum: The Reticular Activating System

A daily intention is not just a plan; it is a **Neurological Prime**. When you declare a priority, you are activating the **Reticular Activating System (RAS)** in your brainstem. This system acts as a high-level filter, highlighting information and opportunities that align with your declared goal while filtering out the irrelevant noise of the world.

Furthermore, the **Progress Principle** states that the single most powerful motivator for high-level work is the "Sense of Progress" in meaningful work. By setting micro-intentions that you can actually achieve within the day, you trigger a "Success Spiral." Each small win provides the dopamine necessary to tackle the next task. Mental toughness is the recognition that momentum is not something you "find"—it is something you build, brick by brick, through the completion of intentional priorities.

Social Compliance and the "Priority Sabotage"

Environment isn't just physical; it's social. Often, our daily intentions are sabotaged by the "Priorities of Others." When you start your day by checking email or Slack, you are handing over your vmPFC to the world.

You are allowing other people's emergencies to dictate your neuro-economic value.

To protect your intentions, you must establish **Proactive Boundaries**. This means "Dark Time"—periods where you are unreachable. By signaling that your time is high-value, you teach others to respect your priorities. Mental toughness is the social courage to be unavailable. If you don't prioritize your life, someone else will.

The Audit and the "Inhibitory Control" Phase

The final stage of prioritization is the **Daily Audit**. At the end of the day, the mentally tough individual does not just walk away; they perform a "Post-Mortem" on their intentions. This involves a rigorous comparison between the **Intended Priority** and the **Actual Execution**.

- *Did I hit my Big Three?*
- *If not, what was the specific "Interrupt" that pulled me away?*

This develops **Inhibitory Control**—the ability to suppress impulses and stay the course. Over time, this audit refines your ability to estimate task difficulty and strengthens your "Prioritization Muscle." You begin to see patterns in your own behavior, allowing you to build "Defensive Intentions" against your most common distractions. Your intentions become more accurate, and your results become more predictable.

The "Deep Stop" Ritual and Parkinson's Law

Just as we must set a start-time intention, we must set an **End-Time Intention**. Chronic "Priority Overspill"—where work leaks into evening hours—leads to **Neural Burnout** and the erosion of focus. When the brain knows there is no "hard stop," it loses the sense of urgency, leading to a phenomenon called **Parkinson's Law**: "Work expands so as to fill the time available for its completion."

By setting a strict intention to stop at a specific hour, you force your brain to prioritize more ruthlessly throughout the day. You create a "Constraint-Based Focus" that increases your efficiency. This "Hard Stop" protects your cognitive battery, ensuring that you wake up the next day with a full store of glucose and norepinephrine to tackle the next set of priorities.

Conclusion: The Architecture of Intent

Prioritization is not a clerical task; it is a **Moral Decision**. It is the act of deciding what your life is worth and where your limited energy will be invested. By setting daily intentions with neurological precision, you cease being a victim of your circumstances and start being the architect of your destiny.

Mental toughness is the ability to maintain the "Long View" while executing the "Short Step." It is the marriage of vision and action, powered by the discipline of the daily start. When you master your intentions, you master your time, and when you master your time, you master your life.

Action Plan for Chapter 5

1. **The Evening Brain-Dump:** Before bed, write down every "Open Loop" in your mind. Get it out of your head and onto paper to clear your mental workbench.

2. **The Selection of the Big Three:** From your dump, select exactly three tasks that will move the needle on your most important projects.

3. **Identify the Lead Domino:** Circle the one task among the three that is the most difficult and the most valuable. This is your "Non-Negotiable."

4. **Create an Implementation Intention:** Write down the "If-Then" statement for your Lead Domino: "If it is [Time], then I will [Action]."

5. **The Shutdown Ritual:** Set a hard-stop time for your workday. Execute a "Digital Blackout" at that hour to allow for the neural recovery required for tomorrow's performance.

6. **The Five-Minute Audit:** At the end of the day, review your Big Three. Score yourself on execution and identify the primary reason for any missed targets.

CONCLUSION

MAINTAIN YOUR SPEED AND CONSISTENCY

You have reached the final threshold of this first book. We have dismantled the myth that productivity is a byproduct of inspiration and replaced it with a rigorous, biological framework for action. We have addressed the physics of starting, the architecture of task-deconstruction, the engineering of the environment, and the neuro-economics of priority. However, the most difficult phase of mental toughness is not the "Start"—it is the **Maintenance**.

The world is characterized by **Entropy**, a thermodynamic certainty that systems, when left to themselves, tend toward disorder. Your discipline is no different. Without a deliberate strategy for maintaining speed and consistency, the friction of daily life—the "Static Friction" of reality—will inevitably erode your progress. This conclusion is the blueprint for ensuring that the systems you have built become permanent fixtures of your identity rather than temporary spikes in effort.

The Neuro-Plasticity of Habituation: From the PFC to the Basal Ganglia

The ultimate goal of every technique in this book is to move your productivity from the **Prefrontal Cortex** (PFC) to the **Basal Ganglia**. The PFC is the "CEO" of the brain; it is responsible for logical reasoning, complex decision-making, and conscious willpower. However, the PFC is incredibly energy-expensive. It runs on glucose and norepinephrine, and it fatigues rapidly. This is why "trying hard" feels exhausting.

Conversely, the **Basal Ganglia** is the brain's "Automation Center." It manages repetitive, habitual behaviors—like driving a car or brushing your teeth—with almost zero conscious effort. This transition from conscious effort to automaticity is known as **Habituation**.

When you first apply the Two-Minute Rule or Time-Blocking, your brain is in a state of **High Cognitive Load**. You are manually overriding your old, ingrained patterns. However, through the principle of **Long-Term Potentiation (LTP)**, the synaptic connections associated with your new routines strengthen every time they are repeated. Neurons that fire together, wire together.

Eventually, you reach the **Crossover Point**, where *not* doing the work feels more uncomfortable than doing it. This is because the brain hates "broken patterns." Consistency is the fuel that drives this neural transformation. If you stop for a week, the process of **Synaptic Pruning** begins—the brain, ever-efficient, starts to dissolve the connections you aren't using. To maintain your speed, you must keep the "wires hot."

The Physics of Constant Velocity and the "Stop-Start" Tax

In classical mechanics, the energy required to accelerate an object from zero to one is significantly higher than the energy required to keep it moving at a constant velocity. In the psychology of work, this is the **Stop-Start Tax**. Every time you take a "week off" or allow your systems to collapse entirely, you are resetting your momentum to zero. You are forcing yourself to pay the massive "Activation Energy Tax" all over again.

Mental toughness is the recognition that **Consistency is a Multiplier**. A person who works with 70% intensity every single day will eventually outperform the "Heroic Worker" who works with 110% intensity for three days and then collapses for four. By maintaining a constant, sustainable speed, you avoid the "Activation Energy Hump" we discussed in Chapter 2. You aren't just working; you are maintaining a state of **Kinetic Readiness**. You are staying "in the flow," which makes the work feel lighter and the progress more inevitable.

The Entropy of Discipline and the "Broken Window" Theory of the Mind

In urban sociology, the **Broken Window Theory** suggests that visible signs of disorder (like a broken window or graffiti) encourage further disorder and neglect. Your productivity system works on the same principle. If you allow one micro-task to slide, or if you ignore your environment for one day, you send a signal to your brain that the "Standard of Excellence" has been lowered.

This creates a "slippery slope" effect. Once you allow yourself to skip the shutdown ritual once, the second time becomes easier. Maintaining speed requires a **Zero-Tolerance Policy for Systemic Drift**. This doesn't mean you must be perfect; it means you must be quick to repair. If a "window" breaks—if you miss a day of time-blocking or ignore your priorities—you must apply the **24-Hour Repair Rule**. Fix the system within 24 hours to prevent "The Slide," where a single exception becomes a new, lower-quality habit. Consistency is not the absence of failure; it is the presence of rapid recovery.

The Neuro-Biology of Burnout and the Recovery-to-Stress Ratio

Consistency is often misunderstood as "working without ceasing." Biologically, this is a recipe for catastrophic failure. Real consistency is a rhythmic cycle of **Stress and Recovery**. The **Sympathetic Nervous System** (the "Gas Pedal") must be balanced by the **Parasympathetic Nervous System** (the "Brake").

High-performers do not maintain speed by pushing harder; they maintain speed by recovering more intelligently. Consistency requires you to treat your sleep, nutrition, and mental "Dark Time" as high-priority tasks. If you do not schedule recovery, your body will eventually schedule an illness or a burnout for you. This is the **Entropy of the Body**. To fight it, you must implement **Deliberate Decompression**. Mental toughness is having the discipline to stop when the system requires a recharge, ensuring that the "battery" is full for the next day's Lead Domino. You are not "taking a break" from the work; you are "fueling" the maintenance of your speed.

The Identity Shift: Moving from "Doing" to "Being"

The final, most profound stage of maintaining speed is the **Identity Shift**. Most people view productivity as something they *do*—a set of chores or external requirements. This is "Outcome-Based Habituation," and it is fragile. To achieve permanent consistency, you must move toward **Identity-Based Habits**.

When you say, "I am a person who never misses a morning deep-work session," you are leveraging **Cognitive Consonance**. The human brain has a deep-seated need for its actions to match its self-image. By consistently showing up—even on days when you produce very little—you provide "evidence" to your brain of your new identity.

Once the identity is locked in, consistency no longer requires "willpower." It becomes a path of least resistance. You don't "choose" to work; you simply *are* a person who works. This is the ultimate peak of mental toughness: when the struggle to start is replaced by the ease of existence. You have terraformed your internal world to support your external goals.

The Architecture of the Long View: The 1% Compounding Principle

Maintaining consistency is the act of betting on **Compound Interest**. In finance, a 1% daily gain leads to an astronomical increase over a year. In cognitive output, the same rule applies. If you improve your focus, your environment, or your prioritization by just 1% each week, the cumulative effect is a total transformation of your life's trajectory.

Consistency allows you to stop worrying about "Big Wins" and start focusing on "Small Constants." When you maintain your speed, the Big Wins happen as a natural byproduct of the system. You are no longer chasing success; you are attracting it through the sheer gravity of your consistency.

The "Deep Stop" and the Sanctity of the Void

A system that cannot stop cannot be maintained. To protect your consistency, you must protect your "Void"—the time where you are not productive, not thinking, and not striving. This is the **Decoupling Phase**. By setting a hard-stop time for your work, you allow your brain to enter the **Default Mode Network (DMN)**, where it can synthesize information and perform the "Maintenance" of your creative and logical faculties.

A person who never stops is like a car that never changes its oil; eventually, the engine seizes. Maintaining speed over years requires the wisdom to embrace the void every night. This is the **Sustainable Velocity** that separates the greats from the "flashes in the pan."

Conclusion: The Unending Start

Mental toughness is not a destination; it is a **Continuous State of Readiness**. You have the tools. You understand the neurology. You have the physics of focus at your disposal. Now, the task is simply to **Stay in the Game**.

The "Start" is not something that happened at the beginning of this book; the "Start" happens every morning when you sit at your desk and apply the Two-Minute Rule. The "Start" happens every time you choose your Lead Domino over a trivial distraction. Consistency is just a long string of "Correct Starts" woven together into a life of purpose.

Go back to the beginning if you must. Refine your environment. Re-calibrate your priorities. But above all, keep moving. The momentum you have built is your most valuable asset. Protect it with your life.

REFLECTION QUESTIONS
EVALUATE YOUR PROGRESS AND RESISTANCE

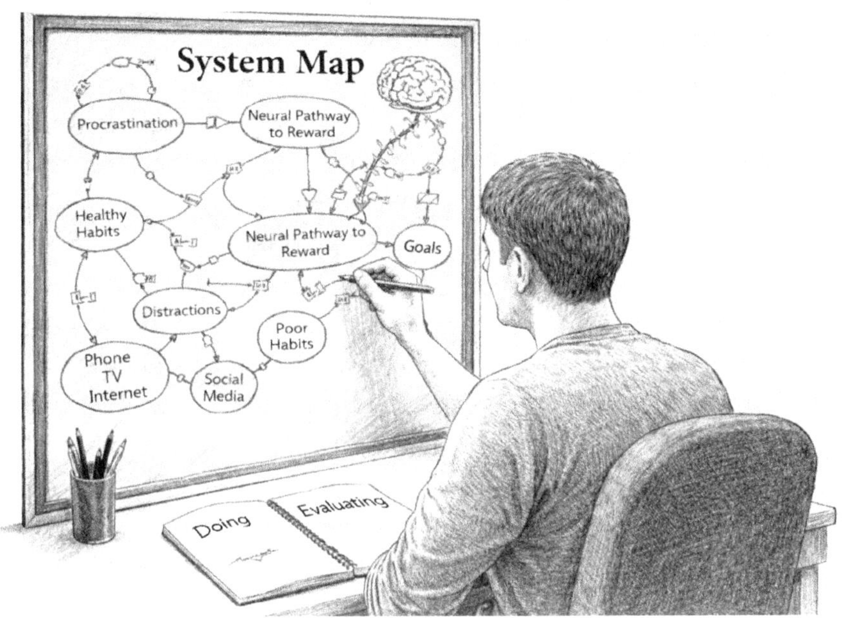

The transition from theory to mastery requires a process of **Active Reflection**. In the preceding chapters, we have laid out the neurological and physical architecture of mental toughness. However, the human brain is a master of **Cognitive Dissonance** and "Self-Deception." We often believe we are following a system when, in reality, we are merely performing the "Theater of Productivity"—going through the motions to appease our ego while avoiding the high-stakes work that actually moves the needle.

To ensure the systems of Book 1 are truly integrated into your biology, you must perform a **Systemic Audit**. These reflection questions are designed to bypass your protective ego and force a confrontation with your actual behaviors. This is where we identify the "Leaks" in your cognitive energy and the "Friction" in your focus.

The Two-Minute Rule is not about the two minutes; it is about the **Neuro-Chemical Physics of Transition**. Every time you move from a state of rest (or distraction) to a state of work, your brain must overcome **Static Friction**. If you are still struggling to begin your Lead Domino, you have a failure in your "Launch Sequence."

- **1.1. The Resistance Threshold:** Think of the last time you procrastinated on a major task. What was the *exact* moment of hesitation? Was it the moment you looked at the screen, or the moment you thought about the entire project?

- **1.2. Micro-Task Accuracy:** When you applied the Two-Minute Rule this week, did you actually start a task that took two minutes, or did you start a task that "felt" like it would take two minutes but actually required twenty? If it requires a sub-decision (e.g., "I'll start by researching..."), it is too big. Did you fail because the task was still a "Monolith" in disguise?

- **1.3. The Sensory Trigger:** What is the physical sensation of your "Starting Ritual"? Can you describe the specific tactile or auditory cue that tells your brain "The Launch has Begun"? If you cannot, your start is still accidental rather than intentional. Are you waiting for "motivation" to strike, or are you triggering it?

Section 2: Architectural Deconstruction (The Chapter 3 Audit)

Complexity is the primary fuel for anxiety. If you feel overwhelmed, your "Dismantling Process" has failed. You are still looking at the mountain instead of the next three inches of the climb.

- **2.1. The Monolith Check:** Look at your current to-do list. How many items are "Verbs" (Write, Call, Buy) and how many are "Projects" (Launch, Organize, Fix)? Any item that is a "Project" is a Monolith that will trigger your amygdala's fear response. How many "Fear-Triggers" are currently on your list?

- **2.2. The Lead Domino Identification:** Out of every task you completed today, which one *actually* lowered the pressure for tomorrow? If you cannot identify one, you are "Productively Procrastinating"—doing easy work (like clearing an inbox) to avoid the work that matters. Are you staying busy to avoid being effective?

- **2.3. Dependency Mapping:** When you get stuck, is it because you lack motivation, or because you haven't identified the "Hidden Blocker"? What is the one task you are waiting for someone else to do, and how can you circumvent that dependency today?

Your environment is either a **Cognitive Catalyst** or a **Biological Burden**. There is no middle ground. Every object in your field of vision is a "background process" running in your brain.

- **3.1. The Visual Saliency Audit:** Sit in your workspace and close your eyes. When you open them, what is the *first* thing you see that is not related to your work? That object is "Attention Residue." Why is it still there? Is your workspace a shrine to your future or a museum of your past distractions?

- **3.2. Digital Barrier Effectiveness:** In the last 48 hours, how many times did you check a notification that was not urgent? What was the "Friction Level" of that distraction? Was the phone in your hand, on the desk, or in another room? If your phone is in the same room as your deep work, you have already lost 20% of your cognitive capacity to the effort of *not* checking it.

- **3.3. The Social Signal Test:** Have you clearly communicated your "Deep Work" boundaries to the people in your life? If you are still being interrupted, is it because they are being disrespectful, or because your "Signal" (closed door, headphones, light) is inconsistent? Do people know that interrupting you carries a "Social Cost"?

Section 4: The Intentionality Gap (The Chapter 5 Audit)

Priority is a zero-sum game. Your time is a finite currency. If you add one thing, you must remove another. There is no such thing as "finding" time; there is only "allocating" it.

- **4.1. The Morning vs. Evening Choice:** Do you decide your priorities in the morning (when decision fatigue is low but urgency is high) or the night before (when perspective is high)? How does the quality of your choices differ between these two states?

- **4.2. The Eisenhower Quadrant Reality:** Look at your calendar for the last seven days. What percentage of your time was spent in **Quadrant 2 (Important but Not Urgent)**? If it is less than 20%, you are not building; you are just maintaining. Are you a firefighter or an architect?

- **4.3. The Implementation Intention "If-Then":** Write down your "If-Then" plan for tomorrow's Lead Domino. Is the "If" a specific environmental cue (e.g., "If I close my laptop from the morning meeting...") or a vague time (e.g., "If it's around 10 AM...")? Vague cues fail because they require a decision. Are your plans automated or manual?

Section 5: The Consistency and Identity Audit (The Conclusion Audit)

Consistency is the proof of identity. If you are inconsistent, you have an "Identity Mismatch." You are trying to act like someone you don't yet believe you are.

- **5.1. The 24-Hour Repair Check:** When was the last time you "fell off the wagon"? How long did it take you to get back on? Was it 24 hours, or did the lapse turn into a "Slumping Week"? The mentally tough person doesn't avoid failure; they avoid the *prolongation* of failure.

- **5.2. The Language of Identity:** How do you describe your work to others? Do you say "I'm trying to be more productive" or "I am a person who prioritizes deep work"? Notice how the first version seeks permission, while the second version states a fact. Which one triggers your brain to protect its self-image?

- **5.3. The Recovery-to-Stress Balance:** Are you "resting" or are you just "distracting"? (Recall: Resting is active recovery for the Parasympathetic system; Distraction is just shallow stimulation for the Dopamine system). How do you feel 30 minutes after your "rest" ends? If you feel depleted, you weren't resting—you were leaking energy.

Section 6: Identifying the "Root Resistance"

Every person has a "Primary Resistance Mode"—a specific way their brain likes to sabotage progress to keep them in the "Safety Zone" of the status quo.

- **6.1. The Perfectionist Loop:** Do you delay starting because the conditions aren't "perfect"? (This is a fear of judgment disguised as a standard of quality).
- **6.2. The "Busy-Brag" Loop:** Do you fill your day with small, urgent tasks so you can tell yourself you were "too busy" to do the hard work? (This is a fear of failure disguised as a work ethic).
- **6.3. The "New Idea" Loop:** Do you abandon a project at the 70% mark because a "better" or "more exciting" idea came along? (This is a fear of completion and the responsibility that comes with success).

Section 7: Final Synthesis and The Road Ahead

- **7.1. The 1% Compounding Question:** If you changed *nothing* about your current habits, where will you be in five years? If that image is uncomfortable, what is the **single 1% change** in your environment or schedule that you will commit to for the next 30 days?
- **7.2. The Legacy of the Start:** What is the one thing you have learned in Book 1 that you wish you had known ten years ago? Why didn't you know it? And more importantly, now that you *do* know it, what is your excuse for not applying it today?

Section 8: The Neuro-Economics of Future Self-Alignment

- **8.1. The Empathy Gap:** When you set a goal for "Tomorrow Me," are you treating that person like a respected partner or a slave? Do you load "Tomorrow Me" with all the tasks you were too tired to do today? How can you show "Tomorrow Me" more empathy by doing one small task *now* to make their morning easier?
- **8.2. The Sunk Cost Fallacy:** Are you continuing a task or a system just because you've already put time into it, even though

it's no longer your Lead Domino? Mental toughness is the courage to quit the wrong things so you can double down on the right ones. What do you need to stop doing today?

Section 9: The Anatomy of the "Pivot"

- **9.1. Identifying the Drift:** Consistency is not a straight line; it is a series of micro-adjustments. Can you identify the "Early Warning Signs" that your focus is drifting? Is it a certain time of day? A certain person? A certain website?

- **9.2. The Pre-Mortem:** Imagine it is one month from today and you have completely failed to implement Book 1. What was the cause of the failure? By identifying the cause now, you can build a "Defensive Intention" to prevent it.

Section 10: Closing the Cognitive Loop

- **10.1. The Value of the Void:** When was the last time you spent 30 minutes in total silence without a device, a book, or a person? If the answer is "I can't remember," your brain is starving for synthesis time. When will you schedule your next "Void Session"?

- **10.2. The Final Commitment:** You have finished Book 1. This information is now either a "Knowledge Burden" or an "Action Catalyst." Which one will it be? Write down the **one specific system** from this book you will master before moving on to Book 2.

Closing Protocol

The value of these questions is not in the reading, but in the **Writing**. Your brain processes handwritten or typed reflections differently than internal thoughts—a process known as **Externalization**.

To close Book 1, select **three sections** from the list above that made you the most uncomfortable. Write a detailed response to each. That discomfort is the signal that you have found a "Neural Blockage" that needs to be cleared. **Mental toughness is the willingness to look at your own failures without blinking.** You have the tools. You have the audit. Now, perform the maintenance.

BOOK TWO

BUILD GOOD HABITS THAT STICK

INTRODUCTION

THE MECHANICS OF BEHAVIORAL ARCHITECTURE

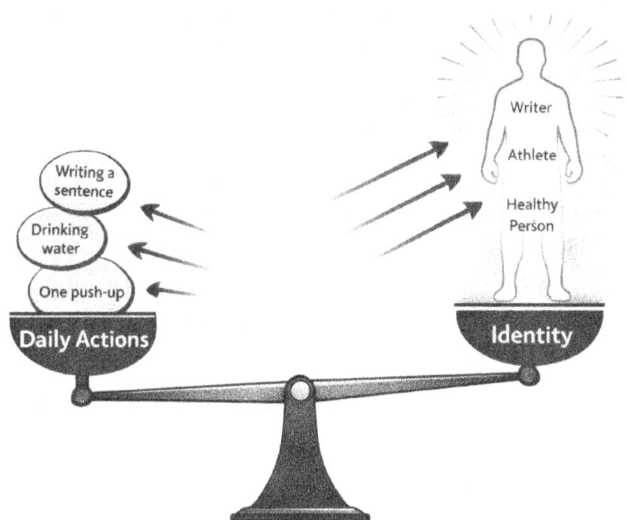

In Book 1, we mastered the "Start." We learned how to dismantle the monolithic projects that paralyze us, how to engineer a physical workspace for focus, and how to ignite momentum using the physics of the Lead Domino. But mental toughness is not merely about the heroic act of starting; it is about the quiet, relentless power of **Automaticity**.

If Book 1 was about the "Launch," **Book 2** is about the **Orbit**.

The most successful individuals on the planet do not have more willpower than you. In fact, research into **Ego Depletion** suggests that high-performers actually use *less* willpower on a daily basis than the average person. They achieve this by offloading the heavy lifting of decision-making to the **Basal Ganglia**—the part of the brain that governs habits. They have transformed the "Start" from a conscious choice into a biological reflex. This is the essence of **Behavioral Architecture**.

The Biological Blueprint: Why the Brain Craves Habits

To understand how to build habits that stick, we must first understand why the brain builds them in the first place. The human brain is a metabolic glutton. Despite making up only 2% of your body weight, it consumes roughly 20% of your daily energy. To ensure survival, the brain is evolutionarily programmed to conserve energy whenever possible. This is the **Principle of Least Effort**.

A habit is simply an energy-saving strategy. When you encounter a problem for the first time—such as learning to drive a car—your **Prefrontal Cortex** is in high gear. You are consciously processing thousands of data points: the pressure on the pedal, the distance to the car ahead, the angle of the mirror. This is exhausting. However, once the brain realizes that "Driving" is a repeatable sequence, it begins to "chunk" these actions. It moves the sequence from the expensive Prefrontal Cortex to the efficient Basal Ganglia.

This process is known as **Neural Consolidation**. Once a behavior is consolidated, it no longer requires a "decision." It requires only a "cue." Mental toughness in Book 2 is the art of deliberately designing these cues so that your success becomes the path of least resistance.

The Anatomy of the Habit Loop: Cue, Craving, Response, Reward

Every habit you possess—from hitting the gym to checking your phone the moment you wake up—is governed by a four-part neurological cycle known as the **Habit Loop**.

1. **The Cue:** This is the "Trigger" that tells your brain to go into automatic mode. It can be a time of day, a location, an emotional state, or the action of another person. It is the bit of information that predicts a reward.

2. **The Craving:** This is the motivational force behind every habit. You don't crave the habit itself; you crave the *change in state* it provides. You don't crave a cigarette; you crave the feeling of relaxation it promises. This is where dopamine performs its primary work.

3. **The Response:** This is the actual habit you perform—the thought or the action. Whether a response occurs depends on how motivated you are and how much friction is associated with the behavior.

4. **The Reward:** This is the end goal. The reward satisfies your craving and, more importantly, teaches your brain which actions are worth remembering for the future.

If any of these four stages are missing or weak, a habit will not stick. In the chapters to follow, we will learn how to manipulate each stage of this loop. We will learn how to make our cues "Obvious," our cravings "Attractive," our responses "Easy," and our rewards "Satisfying." This is not about "trying harder"; it is about **Designing Smarter**.

The Neuro-Chemistry of Progress: The Dopamine Feedback Loop

The "glue" that holds the habit loop together is **Dopamine**. For decades, scientists believed dopamine was about *pleasure*. We now know it is about **Anticipation**. Dopamine is released not just when you receive a reward, but when you *expect* one. This is known as the **Reward Prediction Error** mechanism.

When you first start a new habit, the dopamine spike happens *after* the reward. But as the habit becomes ingrained, the dopamine spike begins to occur *at the moment of the cue*. This is the "Craving" phase. Your brain begins to pull you toward the behavior before you've even started. By understanding this **Dopamine-Driven Feedback Loop**, we can learn to "prime" our brains to anticipate the rewards of our Lead Dominos, making the work feel chemically rewarding even before it is finished.

Cybernetic Control and the Feedback Mechanism

Habitual architecture is essentially a **Cybernetic System**. Cybernetics is the study of communication and control in living organisms and machines. Your habits are the "feedback loops" that keep your life on a specific trajectory. When you set a goal, you are setting a "target state." Your habits are the "error-correction" mechanisms that bring you back to that state when you drift.

Most people have "broken" cybernetic loops. Their targets are set for success, but their feedback loops (habits) are pulling them toward comfort and distraction. In Book 2, we will re-wire these loops. We will turn your daily routines into an autopilot system that constantly corrects your course toward your Lead Dominos.

The Physics of Identity: Outcome vs. Identity-Based Habits

The reason most "New Year's Resolutions" fail is that they are **Outcome-Based**. People focus on *what* they want to achieve (e.g., "I want to lose 20 pounds") rather than *who* they want to become. This creates a psychological gap where the person feels like they are "faking it" until they reach the goal.

In Book 2, we shift to **Identity-Based Habits**. Every action you take is a "vote" for the type of person you wish to become. If you write one page, you are a writer. If you work out for ten minutes, you are an athlete. Mental toughness is the accumulation of these votes. When your behavior is aligned with your identity, consistency no longer feels like a struggle. You are no longer "trying" to be productive; you are simply acting in accordance with who you are. This is the difference between saying "I am trying to quit smoking" and "I am a non-smoker."

The Threshold of Automaticity: The "Hebb's Law" of Consistency

We have all heard the myth that it takes 21 days to form a habit. In reality, the time required reaches a wide range—from 18 to 254 days—depending on the complexity of the behavior. What matters is not the *time*, but the **Repetitions**.

This is governed by **Hebb's Law**: "Neurons that fire together, wire together." Each repetition of a habit strengthens the synaptic connection. You are physically re-wiring your brain. In this introduction, we establish the **Threshold of Automaticity**—the point where the habit becomes easier to do than not to do. Book 2 is the guide to reaching that threshold in every area of your life.

The Ethology of Habits: Overcoming Fixed Action Patterns

In biology, a **Fixed Action Pattern** is an instinctive behavioral sequence that is relatively invariant within the species and almost inevitably runs to completion once triggered. Humans have cognitive versions of these.

When we feel stressed, we reach for comfort food. When we feel bored, we reach for a screen. These are "Bad Habits" that have become Fixed Action Patterns.

To architecturalize your behavior, you must learn to "Interrupt" these patterns at the cue level. We are not just building new habits; we are **De-conditioning** old ones. This requires a high level of **Metacognitive Awareness**—the ability to watch your own brain respond to a cue and choose a different response before the loop closes.

The Economics of Habit Scaling: The 1% Principle

Behavioral Architecture is not a "quick fix." It is a structural overhaul of your daily existence. We use the **1% Principle of Marginal Gains**. If you improve your habits by just 1% each day, you will be 37 times better by the end of a year. Conversely, if you decline by 1% each day, you will decline nearly to zero.

As we move through the chapters of Book 2—from **Habit Stacking** to **Environment Design** to **Visual Tracking**—you will learn to build a "Fortress of Routine" that protects your goals from the volatility of your emotions and the chaos of the world.

Synaptic Decay and the Entropy of Discipline

Just as neurons wire together through repetition, they "prune" through neglect. This is the **Synaptic Decay** of inconsistency. Every time you skip a day of a new habit, you are allowing the neural bridge you've built to weaken. This is why the first few weeks are critical. You are not just "doing work"; you are preventing the decay of your neural infrastructure. Consistency is the preservative of progress.

Discipline, in its raw form, is subject to **Entropy**. It tends toward decay. Architecture, however, is structural. By building habits, you are moving from a system that relies on the "energy" of willpower to a system that relies on the "structure" of routine. Structure does not decay as fast as energy depletes.

Mental toughness is the recognition that **Small Wins Compounded Over Time** create an unstoppable force. You don't need a massive breakthrough; you need a massive amount of "Micro-Consistency." In Book 1, you learned how to win the battle of the morning. In Book 2, you will learn how to win the war of the decade.

You have the "Start" from Book 1. Now, let's build the "Forever." We are moving beyond discipline and into **Nature**. When your habits are aligned with your goals, you no longer need to "force" yourself to be great. Greatness becomes your default setting.

Action Plan for the Introduction to Book 2

1. **The Habit Audit:** For the next 24 hours, write down every "Automatic" action you take. Label them as Positive (+), Negative (-), or Neutral (=) based on your long-term goals.

2. **The Identity Translation:** Choose one goal and translate it into an identity statement. (e.g., "I want to be debt-free" $\rightarrow$ "I am a financially disciplined person").

3. **The One-Rep Rule:** Choose one habit you want to build and commit to performing just one "Rep" of it tomorrow. The goal is not the work; the goal is the *activation of the loop*.

4. **Reward Analysis:** For your most persistent "Bad Habit," identify the *actual* reward your brain is seeking. Is it the snack, or is it the dopamine of a distraction?

5. **Identify the Cue:** For the next three days, when you perform a bad habit, immediately stop and write down what triggered it. Was it a time? A place? A feeling?

CHAPTER 1

USE HABIT STACKING TO LINK NEW ACTIONS

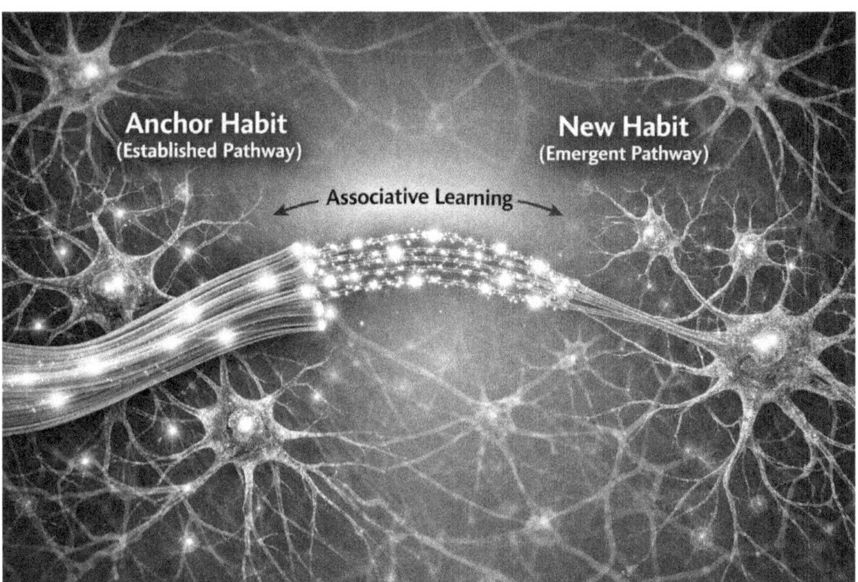

If the Introduction established that habits are the "Orbit" of your life, Chapter 1 provides the propulsion system for entering that orbit. Most people fail to build new habits not because they lack willpower, but because they lack **Contextual Integration**. They attempt to inject a new behavior into a vacuum, hoping that sheer desire will sustain it. But the brain does not operate in a vacuum; it operates in a dense web of interconnected neurons. To build a new habit effectively, you must learn to "hitch a ride" on the neural highways that are already established. This is the science of **Habit Stacking**.

The Neuro-Biology of Associative Learning

At the heart of Habit Stacking lies **Associative Learning**, a principle discovered by the Russian physiologist Ivan Pavlov and refined by modern neuroscience. Your brain is a "pattern-matching machine." It is constantly looking for relationships between stimuli and responses. When two events happen in close temporal proximity, the brain creates a "Synaptic Bridge" between them.

In your brain right now, there are thousands of "Neural Superhighways"—habits so ingrained that they require zero metabolic energy to initiate. These include activities like brushing your teeth, pouring your morning coffee, or checking the deadbolt on your front door. These are **Anchor Habits**. Habit Stacking is the process of identifying these high-traffic neural pathways and "stacking" a new, desired behavior directly on top of them. You are leveraging the momentum of the old habit to carry the weight of the new one.

The Physics of the "Stack": The Formula of Integration

Habit Stacking follows a rigid, almost mathematical formula developed by BJ Fogg and popularized by James Clear:

After [CURRENT HABIT], I will [NEW HABIT].

This simple linguistic structure is a "Top-Down Executive Order" for your brain. By using the word "After," you are providing your brain with an explicit **Temporal Cue**. You are removing the need for a decision. Instead of saying "I will meditate today," which requires you to constantly scan your environment for a "good time," you say "After I pour my morning coffee, I will meditate for one minute."

The coffee becomes the "Start" signal. The brain no longer needs to use the Prefrontal Cortex to initiate the meditation; it simply follows the "If-Then" logic of the Basal Ganglia. This reduces the **Activation Energy** required to start the new behavior by nearly 80%.

The Saliency of the Anchor: Choosing the Right Foundation

Not all habits are created equal as anchors. To build a successful stack, the **Anchor Habit** must have **High Saliency** and **Temporal Consistency**.

- **High Saliency:** The habit must be something you do without fail, every single day. If your anchor is "After I go to the gym," but you only go to the gym three times a week, your new habit will be intermittent and fragile.

- **Temporal Consistency:** The anchor should happen at the same time and in the same environment every day.

For example, "After I sit down for dinner" is a strong anchor because it happens daily and involves a specific physical transition. "After I feel inspired" is a weak anchor because it is internal and volatile. Mental toughness involves the disciplined selection of anchors that are "unshakeable."

The Neuro-Economics of "Micro-Stacking"

A common mistake in Habit Stacking is attempting to stack a "Monolith" onto an "Anchor." If you say, "After I brush my teeth, I will write 2,000 words of my novel," the stack will collapse. The "Weight" of the new habit is too heavy for the anchor to support during the initial phase of neural consolidation.

We apply the **Principle of Cognitive Weight**. The stacked habit should initially be so small that it is "impossible to fail."

- *After I close my laptop for the day, I will do one push-up.*
- *After I put on my pajamas, I will think of one thing I am grateful for.*

By keeping the "Rep" small, you are focusing on the **Synaptic Connection** rather than the **Task Magnitude**. Once the "Bridge" between the two neurons is strong, you can scale the task magnitude (from one push-up to fifty) without breaking the link.

The Ethology of "Sequencing": Building the Behavioral Chain

In animal behavior studies, researchers use a process called **Chaining**. This is how a dolphin is trained to perform a complex series of jumps and flips. The trainer doesn't teach the whole sequence at once; they teach the last action first, then the second-to-last, and so on.

In Habit Stacking, we use **Forward Chaining**. You can build an entire "Morning Power Sequence" by stacking multiple habits in a row:

1. After I wake up, I will drink a glass of water.
2. After I drink water, I will make my bed.
3. After I make my bed, I will perform one minute of deep breathing.

Each completed habit serves as the "Cue" for the next one. This creates a **Behavioral Momentum** that makes your entire morning feel automatic. You are no longer managing tasks; you are managing a "Flow State."

The Reward Link: Chemical Reinforcement of the Stack

To ensure the stack "locks in," you must utilize the **Reward Feedback Loop**. When you complete the stacked habit, you must immediately provide a "Micro-Reward." This can be a physical gesture (a "fist pump"), a verbal affirmation ("That's like me!"), or a sensory pleasure (a sip of great coffee).

This micro-reward triggers a small burst of **Dopamine**, which acts as "Neural Cement." It signals to the brain that the link between the Anchor and the Stack is beneficial and should be strengthened during sleep. Without the reward, the brain may view the new habit as "Friction" and attempt to prune the connection.

The "Environment-Cue" Synergy: Strengthening the Signal

Habit Stacking is most effective when combined with the **Environmental Design** principles of Book 1. If your stack is "After I sit at my desk, I will write my Big Three," but your desk is cluttered with distractions, the environmental noise will interfere with the neural cue.

To maximize the stack, you must **Prime the Cue**. If you stack "After I drink coffee, I will take my vitamins," place the vitamin bottle directly next to the coffee maker. You are creating a "Double-Cue"—a temporal cue (the coffee) and a visual cue (the bottle). This redundancy ensures that the habit loop closes every single time.

The Psychology of "Emergency Stacks" and Resilience

Consistency is rarely a straight line. Life will inevitably interrupt your routines. Mental toughness requires **Emergency Habit Stacks**—scaled-down versions of your routines for days when you are traveling, ill, or in crisis.

If your standard stack is "After work, I will run for 30 minutes," your emergency stack might be "After work, I will walk for 2 minutes." By performing the "Emergency Version," you are **Preserving the Neural Pathway**. You are telling your brain, "We still do this." It is much easier to return to a 30-minute run if the "After work" connection is still alive, even if the volume was temporarily reduced.

The Audit: Identifying Your High-Traffic Anchors

Before you can stack, you must perform a **Habit Inventory**. Most people are unaware of the dozens of automatic "Anchor Habits" they perform every day.

- *Waking up*
- *Turning off the alarm*
- *Getting out of bed*
- *Using the bathroom*
- *Looking in the mirror*
- *Turning on the shower*
- *Drying off*
- *Getting dressed*
- *Pouring water/coffee*
- *Checking the phone*

Each of these is a "Neural Hook" waiting for a new behavior. Your task is to select the hooks that align with your highest identity.

Conclusion: The Architecture of the Automatic Life

Habit Stacking is the ultimate tool for the **Behavioral Architect**. It allows you to build a life of high-performance without the constant drain of willpower. By hitching your goals to the established rhythms of your biology, you move from a state of "Striving" to a state of "Being."

You are no longer a person who "tries to meditate" or "tries to exercise." You are a person whose morning coffee *triggers* meditation and whose work shutdown *triggers* movement. You have turned your biology into your ally.

Action Plan for Chapter 1

1. **The Habit Inventory:** Spend 10 minutes listing every automatic habit you perform from 6:00 AM to 10:00 AM.

2. **The Selection:** Choose **one** new habit you want to build (keep it micro—less than 2 minutes).

3. **The Anchor Match:** Match your new habit to the most logical anchor in your inventory. (e.g., "After I brush my teeth, I will do two squats").

4. **The Implementation Statement:** Write your stack in the formula: **"After [Anchor], I will [New Habit]."**

5. **The Physical Prime:** Place a physical reminder of the new habit at the location of the anchor.

6. **The 24-Hour Test:** Execute the stack tomorrow. Immediately following the new habit, give yourself a physical "Micro-Reward" (like a thumbs up in the mirror).

CHAPTER 2

DESIGN YOUR ENVIRONMENT FOR AUTOMATIC SUCCESS

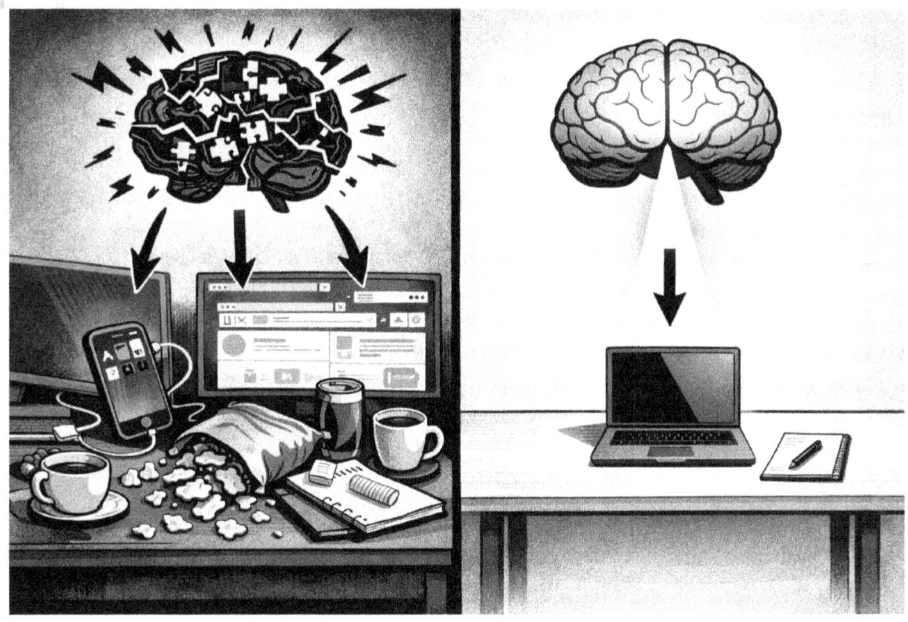

If Chapter 1 was about the internal "Software" of habits (Habit Stacking), Chapter 2 is about the **External Hardware**. Most individuals treat their environment as a static backdrop to their lives, believing that "willpower" is the primary engine of change. However, cognitive science suggests the opposite: **Environment is the invisible hand that shapes human behavior.** We do not choose our actions in a vacuum; we choose them based on the **Cues** available in our immediate surroundings.

If you want to change your results, you must stop fighting your environment and start designing it. Mental toughness is the realization that it is easier to change your room than it is to change your nature.

The human brain is dominated by the **Visual Cortex**. Approximately 50% of the brain's total resources are dedicated to processing visual information. This creates a biological phenomenon known as **Visual Saliency**: the tendency for an object to grab your attention based on its prominence in your field of vision.

Your habits are often a direct response to what you see. This is why you eat a cookie because they are on the counter, or check your phone because it lights up on the desk. Environmental Design is the process of **Intentional Saliency**. You must make the cues for your good habits "unmissable" and the cues for your bad habits "invisible." If you want to practice guitar, do not leave it in the closet; put it in the middle of the living room. If you want to drink more water, place five filled bottles at every station you frequent. You are using the power of the Visual Cortex to bypass the need for the Prefrontal Cortex's willpower.

The Physics of Friction: Managing Activation Energy

In the realm of Behavioral Architecture, the most powerful force is **Friction**. Every action has a "cost" of energy to initiate. By manipulating the physical distance and complexity of a task, you can effectively dictate your own future behavior.

- **The Path of Least Resistance:** Your brain will always choose the path that requires the least amount of metabolic energy. To build a good habit, you must reduce the number of steps required to start it. This is "Greasing the Wheels." Laying out your workout clothes the night before reduces the friction of going to the gym by eliminating the decision of what to wear.

- **The Strategic Barrier:** Conversely, if you want to break a bad habit, you must increase the friction. If you watch too much TV, unplug it and put the remote in a different room. The extra 30 seconds required to set it up provides the "Cognitive Gap" necessary for your Prefrontal Cortex to intervene.

Mental toughness is the discipline to "Stage the Environment" during your periods of high energy so that your low-energy self is forced into the correct behavior. You are essentially "pre-loading" your success.

The Psychology of "Context Cues" and The One-Space-One-Use Rule

The brain associates specific environments with specific behaviors through a process called **Contextual Anchoring**. If you work in bed, your brain associates the bed with stress and alertness, leading to insomnia. If you eat at your desk, your brain associates work with snacking.

To achieve "Automatic Success," you must implement the **One-Space-One-Use Rule**.

1. **The Deep Work Zone:** A space where *only* high-value work happens. No phones, no casual browsing.

2. **The Recovery Zone:** A space where *only* rest happens. No work emails, no laptop.

By strictly segregating your environments, you allow the "Context Cue" to do the heavy lifting. When you sit in your Deep Work Zone, your brain recognizes the physical triggers and automatically shifts into a state of **Focus**. You are leveraging the **Basal Ganglia's** ability to recognize patterns to trigger your professional "Flow State."

Choice Architecture and Nudge Theory

Nobel Prize winner Richard Thaler introduced the concept of **Choice Architecture**—the idea that the way choices are presented to us significantly influences our decisions. In your home and office, you are the architect.

If the "Default Option" in your environment is the healthy or productive one, you will choose it 90% of the time. This is the **Power of Defaults**.

- **Default:** Your computer opens only the software needed for your Lead Domino.

- **Default:** The only snacks in your house require preparation (increasing friction).

- **Default:** Your phone is set to "Do Not Disturb" automatically at 8:00 PM.

By automating your defaults, you remove the "Decision Tax" from your day. You are no longer "choosing" to be productive; you are simply existing in a world where productivity is the easiest possible outcome.

The Impact of Physical Clutter on Cognitive Load

There is a direct correlation between **Physical Clutter** and **Cognitive Load**. Every object in your field of vision that is out of place or represents an "unsolved problem" (like a stack of mail or a tangled cord) acts as a "Micro-Stressor." These objects trigger the **Amygdala**, causing a low-level background noise of anxiety that drains your focus.

Environmental Sanitization must be maintained as a habit. A "Clean Desk" is not about aesthetics; it is about **Neural Clarity**. By removing visual complexity, you allow the brain to dedicate all its "Primary Processing Power" to the task at hand. You are creating a "High-Signal, Low-Noise" environment.

Digital Environmental Design: The Portable Environment

In the 21st century, your environment is no longer just physical; it is digital. Your smartphone is a "Portable Environment" that follows you everywhere. If your home screen is filled with social media icons, you are living in an environment designed by engineers to hijack your dopamine system.

Digital Environmental Design involves:

- **The "Grey Scale" Trick:** Removing the color from your phone to reduce the visual saliency of icons.

- **The One-Folder Rule:** Hiding all non-essential apps in a single folder on the second page of your phone.

- **The Notification Blackout:** Disabling all non-human notifications.

Your digital environment should be as sparse and intentional as your physical one. If your digital environment is chaotic, your mental toughness will be consistently eroded by the "Algorithmic Pull" of distraction.

Sensory Priming: Sound and Scent as Cognitive Anchors

Beyond visual cues, you can use **Auditory** and **Olfactory** cues to prime your brain for success. This is known as **Sensory Priming**.

- **Sound:** Using a specific "Deep Work Playlist" that you *only* listen to when performing your Lead Domino.

- **Scent:** Using a specific candle or essential oil (like peppermint or rosemary) during work sessions.

Over time, these sensory cues become "Anchors." Your brain learns that the smell of peppermint + the sound of lo-fi beats = "Time for High-Intensity Focus." This allows you to enter "The Zone" in seconds rather than minutes.

The Socio-Biological Impact of Proximity

We are social creatures, and our environment includes the people around us. Proximity is a powerful driver of habit. If you sit next to high-performers, you will naturally adopt their work ethics through **Mirror Neurons**. If you sit near the office kitchen, you will eat more.

Designing your environment means choosing your **Proximity**. Position yourself in places where the "average" behavior is the one you want to emulate. This is the "Social Environment" of success.

Behavioral Geography: Mapping Your Daily Routes

Most of our movements are habitual. We take the same path through the office, the same route home, and the same walk to the kitchen. **Behavioral Geography** is the study of how these routes influence our choices.

If your route to your desk passes the breakroom with free donuts, you are exposing yourself to a high-risk cue every day. Designing your environment includes mapping your physical routes to avoid "Trigger Zones" and maximize "Success Zones."

The "Sunk Cost" of Maintenance

A poorly designed environment requires constant "Willpower Maintenance." You have to *force* yourself not to check the phone, *force* yourself to find your gym shoes, and *force* yourself to focus in a noisy room.

By investing the time to architect your environment once, you remove this maintenance cost forever. You are moving from a "Manual" life to an "Automatic" life. Mental toughness is the intelligence to build a system that makes "toughness" unnecessary.

Environmental Design is the final step in moving from a life of "Willpower" to a life of "Systems." By architecting your physical and digital world, you create a **Fortress of Routine** that protects you from your own impulses.

Mental toughness is not about being a "superhero" who can resist any temptation. It is about being a "strategist" who ensures that temptation never enters the room in the first place. You are the architect. Build a world that makes you great.

Action Plan for Chapter 2

1.   **The Visual Audit:** Stand in your workspace. Identify the three most prominent "Bad Cues" (e.g., phone, messy pile, snacks). Move them out of sight or into another room.

2. **The Friction Flip:** Identify one good habit you want to start. Reduce the friction by two steps (e.g., put your book on your pillow). Identify one bad habit to stop. Increase friction by two steps (e.g., put batteries for the remote in a high cabinet).

3. **The One-Space Assignment:** Designate one chair or desk area where *only* deep work is allowed. If you feel the urge to browse the web, you *must* physically move to a different location.

4. **Digital Sanitization:** Move all social media and news apps to a single folder on the last page of your phone. Turn off all notifications except for phone calls and direct texts.

5. **Sensory Anchor:** Select one specific scent or playlist to use *exclusively* during your Lead Domino session tomorrow.

CHAPTER 3

TRACK YOUR WINS WITH VISUAL PROGRESS CUES

In the architecture of mental toughness, there is a pervasive enemy often referred to as the **"Valley of Disappointment."** This is the psychological chasm that exists between the moment you start a new habit and the moment you see tangible, external results. During this phase, the metabolic cost of the habit is high, but the biological reward—the "payoff"—is low. Most people quit here because the brain, which is evolutionarily wired for immediate feedback, assumes the effort is being wasted.

Chapter 3 provides the solution: **Visual Progress Cues**. By making your progress visible and tangible, you provide your brain with the "Synthetic Dopamine" it needs to bridge the gap between starting and mastering. You are not just tracking work; you are providing your nervous system with evidence of its own evolution.

The Neuro-Biology of Feedback Loops and Reward Prediction Error

The human brain is a **Difference Engine**. It is designed to notice changes in state rather than static conditions. When you work toward a long-term goal—such as writing a book or losing weight—the daily change is often too microscopic for the naked eye to detect. This lack of perceived movement triggers the **Amotivational Syndrome**, where the brain reduces the release of norepinephrine and dopamine because it no longer perceives a path to a reward.

This is governed by the **Reward Prediction Error (RPE)**. Your brain constantly predicts the value of an action. If the actual value (the result) is less than the prediction, dopamine levels drop, and your motivation evaporates.

Visual tracking creates an artificial feedback loop that hacks the RPE. Every time you record a "win," you are providing a visual stimulus that the brain interprets as a **Progress Signal**. Even if the scale hasn't moved or the book isn't finished, the act of checking a box triggers a small burst of dopamine in the **Nucleus Accumbens**. You are rewarding the *process* rather than the *outcome*, which keeps the engine running until the external rewards finally catch up.

The "Paperclip Strategy": The Power of Physical Representation

One of the most effective forms of visual tracking is the **Physical Representation of Volume**. This technique, famously utilized by a successful stockbroker to stay motivated during grueling cold-calling sessions, involves moving physical objects to represent completed tasks.

- **The Kinetic Mechanism:** Place two glass jars on your desk. Fill one with 100 paperclips (or marbles). Every time you complete a micro-task (a sales call, a page of writing, a set of exercises), move one paperclip to the empty jar.

- **Proprioceptive Satisfaction:** The brain experiences a sense of "Sensory Satisfaction" from the tactile and visual movement. You can *see* the jar filling up, which provides a concrete measurement of effort that a digital spreadsheet cannot replicate.

Mental toughness is the discipline to value the "Paperclip" as much as the "Profit." When you focus on the movement of the clips, you decouple your motivation from external results and attach it to your own consistency. You are turning "Doing the Work" into a physical game of accumulation.

The Seinfeld Strategy: "Don't Break the Chain"

The **Seinfeld Strategy** is perhaps the most famous method of visual progress tracking. It utilizes a large wall calendar and a red marker. Every day you complete your Lead Domino, you put a big red "X" over that date.

- **The Zeigarnik Effect:** Humans have a deep-seated psychological aversion to "Incompleteness." This is known as the **Zeigarnik Effect**. Once a chain of red X's is established, your brain begins to perceive the "Chain" as a unified object.

- **The Cognitive Shift:** Eventually, your motivation shifts from "Doing the Habit" to "Not Breaking the Chain." The pain of seeing a gap in your progress becomes greater than the friction of the work itself.

This is the **Inertia of Consistency**. A visual chain is a physical manifestation of your momentum. It allows you to see the "Mass" of your work, making it harder for temporary emotions to stop your progress.

The Physics of the "Visual Scoreboard"

In sports, athletes play harder when the scoreboard is visible. This is because the scoreboard provides a **Real-Time Performance Audit**. In your personal and professional life, you must create your own "Visual Scoreboard" to maintain **Cybernetic Control**.

- **Saliency and Proximity:** The scoreboard must be in your immediate field of vision. If it is buried in an app on page three of your phone, it does not exist in your "Active Environmental Architecture."

- **High-Signal, Low-Noise:** It should track only one or two "Key Performance Indicators" (KPIs). Tracking too many variables leads to **Cognitive Dilution**, where the importance of the Lead Domino is lost in a sea of trivial data.

A visual scoreboard serves as a **Biological Reminder** of your priorities. When you feel the "Entropy of Focus" (the tendency to drift toward trivial tasks), one glance at the scoreboard re-aligns your Prefrontal Cortex with your long-term identity.

Leading vs. Lagging Indicators: Tracking the Action, Not the Result

A common mistake in tracking is focusing exclusively on **Lagging Indicators**—results that happen after the work is done (e.g., the number on the scale, the dollars in the bank, the "Likes" on a post). Lagging indicators are often influenced by variables outside your control, leading to frustration and the "Illusion of Failure."

Mental toughness requires tracking **Leading Indicators**—the specific, high-leverage behaviors that *produce* the results.

- *Lagging*: Losing 10 pounds.
- *Leading*: Tracking 30 minutes of zone-two cardio.
- *Lagging*: Getting a promotion.
- *Leading*: Completing 90 minutes of Deep Work before 10:00 AM.

When you track leading indicators, you are tracking your **Execution**. This gives you a sense of agency and "Locus of Control," which is the primary psychological defense against burnout and learned helplessness. You are rewarding yourself for the only thing you can actually control: your effort.

The Gamification of Effort: Levels, Streaks, and Symbolic Progression

Modern digital habits are designed using **Gamification Principles** to hijack the brain's reward centers. You can use these same principles to protect your productivity.

- **Sunk Cost Streaks:** The power of a "100-day streak" is a psychological weight. It creates a "Sunk Cost" where you feel you have too much "Progress Equity" invested to quit.
- **Leveling Up:** Divide your habits into levels.
    - *Level 1:* The "2-Minute Version" (Establishing the Loop).
    - *Level 2:* The "20-Minute Version" (Building Capacity).

- *Level 3*: The "Deep Mastery Version" (Maximum Intensity). By "leveling up," you provide yourself with a sense of growth and novelty, preventing the boredom that often kills consistency in the "Intermediate Plateau."

The "Never Miss Twice" Rule: Resiliency over Perfection

The greatest threat to a visual tracking system is the first "Missing X." This often triggers the **"What the Hell" Effect**, where one failure leads to a total collapse of the system because the "Perfection" of the chain is ruined. This is a failure of **Cognitive Flexibility**.

To maintain mental toughness, you must implement the **"Never Miss Twice" Rule**.

- Missing one day is an accident (or a necessary recovery).
- Missing two days is the start of a new, destructive habit.

Your visual tracker should allow for "Repair Marks." If you miss a day, acknowledge it with a different color, but ensure the very next box is filled with double intensity. This shifts the focus from "Being Perfect" to "Being Resilient." In the long run, the person who misses 5 days out of 100 but never misses twice always outperforms the person who stays perfect for 20 days and then quits forever.

Proprioceptive Feedback: The Power of the Physical Log

There is a unique cognitive benefit to **Handwriting** your progress. The physical act of moving a pen across paper involves more neural circuitry—including the motor cortex and the somatosensory system—than clicking a mouse or tapping a screen.

This is a form of **Proprioceptive Feedback**. A physical journal or habit-tracker acts as a "Hard Drive" for your successes. On days when you feel like a failure, flipping back through 50 pages of completed tasks provides the **Objective Evidence** necessary to silence your inner critic. It is a biological "Proof of Concept" for your potential. You aren't just "thinking" you are productive; you are looking at a physical artifact that proves it.

The Social Component of Tracking: Public Accountability

While most tracking is internal, the **Socio-Biological Impact** of public tracking can be immense. When you share your "Visual Scoreboard" with a partner or a community, you leverage the **Social Evaluative Threat**. Your brain's desire to maintain status within the tribe becomes a powerful motivator to keep the "X's" moving. However, use this cautiously; the goal is to build an identity-based habit, not just a performance for others.

Conclusion: The Evidence of Transformation

Visual progress tracking is the final layer of **Behavioral Architecture**. It turns the invisible internal struggle of discipline into a visible external reality. It provides the "Fuel of Feedback" that keeps your momentum moving forward when your emotions fail you.

Mental toughness is the realization that **What Gets Measured, Gets Managed.** By tracking your wins, you are not just recording history; you are designing your future. You are providing your brain with the map, the fuel, and the destination. You have moved from "Hoping" for success to "Engineering" it.

Action Plan for Chapter 3

1. **Select Your Metric:** Choose **one** leading indicator (the Lead Domino) to track.

2. **Choose Your Physical Medium:** Avoid digital apps for this initial phase. Use a Wall Calendar, a Physical Journal, or the Two-Jar Paperclip method.

3. **Establish the Scoreboard:** Place your tracker in a location that forces a "Visual Confrontation" every morning.

4. **The 60-Second Entry:** Record your win immediately after the task is done. The shorter the gap between the action and the "X," the stronger the dopamine reinforcement.

5. **The Repair Protocol:** If you miss a day, your only priority for the next 24 hours is to "Resume the Chain." No excuses.

CHAPTER 4

REPLACE BAD PATTERNS WITH POSITIVE SUBSTITUTES

One of the greatest fallacies in the history of self-improvement is the idea that habits can be "broken." In the realm of neuroscience, a habit is not a physical object that can be shattered; it is a **Neural Pathway**—a physical ridge burned into the brain's architecture. To attempt to simply "stop" a bad habit is to fight against the very laws of physics that govern your nervous system.

The brain abhors a vacuum. If you remove a behavior but leave the **Cue** and the **Craving** intact, your biology will eventually find the path of least resistance to satisfy that itch. Usually, it returns to the old pattern with renewed intensity. This is known as **Spontaneous Recovery**. To master your behavior, you must learn the art of **Neural Substitution**: you do not break a habit; you replace it.

The Neuro-Pathology of the "Bad Habit" Loop

Every "bad" habit—whether it is mindless scrolling, emotional eating, or chronic procrastination—is essentially a maladaptive solution to a biological problem. Your brain isn't trying to sabotage you; it is trying to satisfy a need.

Most bad habits are fueled by **Dopaminergic Spikes** in the **Ventral Tegmental Area (VTA)**. When you feel a negative emotion (stress, boredom, loneliness), your brain searches for a "Response" that has previously provided a "Reward" (a shift in state).

- **Stress** (Cue) $\rightarrow$ **Smoke/Drink** (Response) $\rightarrow$ **Relaxation** (Reward).

- **Boredom** (Cue) $\rightarrow$ **Social Media** (Response) $\rightarrow$ **Novelty** (Reward).

If you remove the response without addressing the cue or providing an alternative reward, the "Craving" will grow until it overrides your Prefrontal Cortex. Substitution is the process of hijacking the loop and inserting a new, productive response that provides a similar chemical reward.

The Law of Displacement: Nature Abhors a Void

In physics, displacement occurs when one object takes the place of another. In behavioral science, the **Law of Displacement** states that a habit can only be permanently removed if a new behavior is funneled into the same "Cue-Reward" channel.

Mental toughness is the ability to perform a **Behavioral Audit** to identify the underlying reward. If you realize your "afternoon snack" habit isn't actually about hunger, but about a "Break from the Desk," you can replace the snack with a five-minute walk. The "Reward" (a break) remains the same, but the "Response" changes from a health-negative to a health-positive one.

Identifying the "Ghost Cues" and Emotional Triggers

Substitution fails when we do not understand the **Cue**. Most people think the cue for their bad habit is "desire," but desire is actually the *craving*. The cue is the environmental or internal spark. We categorize these as **Ghost Cues**:

1. **Location:** Does the habit only happen when you are at your desk? On the couch?
2. **Time:** Is it the "3:00 PM Slump"? The "Late Night Boredom"?
3. **Emotional State:** Are you feeling overwhelmed, neglected, or undervalued?
4. **Other People:** Does the habit trigger when you are around a specific social circle?
5. **Immediately Preceding Action:** Does checking one email always lead to an hour of YouTube?

By mapping these cues, you can predict when the "Urge" will strike. Mental toughness is not about resisting the urge; it is about **Predicting the Urge** and having a substitute ready before it arrives.

The Technique of "Response Inhibition" and the 10-Second Gap

The moment between the **Cue** and the **Response** is the "Battleground of the Mind." This is where the Basal Ganglia (automatic) and the Prefrontal Cortex (conscious) compete for control. To substitute a habit, you must expand this gap.

We use **The 10-Second Gap Rule**. When you feel the urge to engage in a bad pattern, you must count to ten. During these ten seconds, you are performing **Response Inhibition**. You are forcing the brain to move the signal from the impulsive midbrain to the analytical forebrain.

Once the signal is in the forebrain, you execute your **Implementation Intention**: *"I feel the urge to [Bad Habit], but instead, I am going to [Positive Substitute]."*

The Architecture of "Friction Symmetry"

To successfully replace a pattern, you must apply the principles of **Friction** (from Chapter 2) with mathematical precision. You must make the bad habit **High Friction** and the substitute **Zero Friction**.

- **Bad Habit:** Scrolling in bed. *Friction:* Put the phone in the kitchen (High Friction).
- **Substitute:** Reading a book. *Friction:* Place the book on the pillow (Zero Friction).

Substitution is a game of **Path of Least Resistance**. If the positive substitute is even slightly harder to perform than the bad habit, your brain will revert to the old pathway under stress. You must "Grease the Groove" for the new action so that it feels like the easiest way to get the reward.

The Power of "Incompatible Behaviors"

One of the most effective ways to replace a pattern is to choose a substitute that is **Physically Incompatible** with the bad habit.

- If you tend to snack while watching TV, start a hobby that requires your hands (knitting, drawing, puzzles). You cannot eat mindlessly if your hands are occupied.
- If you tend to procrastinate by sitting on the couch, make your substitute "Putting on your running shoes." You cannot easily lounge in compression gear and sneakers.

By choosing incompatible behaviors, you are using the **Physics of the Body** to support the **Psychology of the Mind**.

The "Dopamine Taper": Managing the Withdrawal Period

When you replace a high-dopamine bad habit (like junk food or social media) with a lower-dopamine substitute (like a piece of fruit or a book), your brain will initially feel a sense of "Deprivation." This is a chemical withdrawal.

Mental toughness is the understanding of **Down-regulation**. Your brain has "muted" its dopamine receptors to handle the flood of the bad habit. As you substitute, your brain will slowly "up-regulate," making the smaller rewards of the positive substitute feel satisfying again. This transition period usually lasts 14 to 21 days. During this time, you must rely on the **Visual Tracking** from Chapter 3 to provide "Synthetic Dopamine" until your natural receptors recover.

The Social Substitution: Changing the "Tribe"

Many of our worst patterns are **Socio-Biological**. We adopt the habits of our "Tribe" to ensure belonging. If your social circle's default pattern is complaining, drinking, or laziness, substitution is nearly impossible if you remain in that proximity.

Substitution often requires **Tribal Re-alignment**. You must find a new group where the "Positive Substitute" is the default behavior. If you want to replace "Happy Hour" with "Fitness," you must join a running club. In this new environment, the social reward of "Belonging" is tied to the positive habit, making the substitution permanent.

Dealing with the "Extinction Burst"

Just as you are about to successfully replace a habit, your brain will often stage a "Final Protest." This is known in psychology as the **Extinction Burst**. The old neural pathway, sensing its own "death," will trigger an incredibly intense craving to see if the old response still works.

Most people interpret this burst as a sign that they "failed" or that the new habit "isn't working." In reality, the Extinction Burst is the sign that the **Substitution is Succeeding**. If you can hold the line during this 24-48 hour window, the old pathway will begin to wither (Synaptic Pruning), and the new substitute will become the dominant default.

Conclusion: The New Default Mode

Replacing bad patterns is not an act of self-flagellation; it is an act of **Neural Engineering**. You are a behavioral architect, redirecting the flow of your internal energy from paths that destroy to paths that build.

Mental toughness is the realization that **You are the master of the loop.** By identifying the cue, understanding the reward, and meticulously placing a substitute, you turn your "Weaknesses" into the very foundations of your strength. You have moved from being a victim of your impulses to being the designer of your destiny.

1. **The Pattern Audit:** Identify one bad habit you want to change. Write down the **Cue** (What triggers it?) and the **Reward** (What feeling does it give you?).

2. **The Substitution Selection:** Choose a positive behavior that provides a similar reward. (e.g., Boredom $\rightarrow$ Podcast instead of Social Media).

3. **The Incompatibility Check:** Is your substitute physically incompatible with the bad habit? If not, how can you make it so?

4. **The Friction Flip:** Increase friction for the bad habit by 3 steps. Decrease friction for the substitute to 0 steps.

5. **The 10-Second Commitment:** For the next 48 hours, commit to the 10-second gap the moment the cue strikes. Use that time to consciously choose the substitute.

CHAPTER 5

SCALE YOUR HABITS FOR LONG-TERM GROWTH

In the previous chapters, we focused on the architecture of *establishment*—how to start, how to stick, and how to track. If you have followed the protocols of Book 2 thus far, you have successfully built a "Maintenance Engine." You are showing up. You are consistent. You are no longer fighting the daily battle of "Willpower vs. Couch."

However, consistency is not the destination; it is merely the entry fee.

There is a dangerous trap that awaits the consistent individual: **The Trap of Stagnation.** In psychology, this is known as the **"Ok Plateau."** It occurs when a behavior becomes so automatic that your brain stops paying attention to the details of execution. You go to the gym, but you don't get stronger. You write every day, but your prose doesn't get sharper. You have mistaken "Repetition" for "Improvement."

Chapter 5 is about **Scaling**. It is about taking the stable foundation of your habits and building a skyscraper of mastery upon it. We will explore how to transition from **Naive Practice** (doing it again) to **Deliberate Practice** (doing it better), ensuring that your habits compel you toward exponential, rather than linear, growth.

The Physics of Compounding: The Math of 1%

We often hear the phrase "get 1% better every day," but few people grasp the mathematical violence of this concept. It is not a poetic sentiment; it is a statistical reality governed by the laws of **Compound Interest**.

If you improve by 1% every day for one year, the math looks like this:

$$1.01^{365} = 37.78$$

You end the year 37 times better than you started.

Conversely, if you degrade by 1% every day:

$$0.99^{365} = 0.03$$

You decline nearly to zero.

The gap between the "Maintenance Thinker" and the "Scaling Thinker" is the understanding of the **Aggregations of Marginal Gains**. In the beginning, the difference between a scaler and a maintainer is invisible. On Day 1, the difference is negligible. On Day 30, it is barely noticeable. But by Day 365, the scaler is operating at a level of proficiency that looks like "magic" to the maintainer.

Mental toughness in this phase is the patience to trust the **Exponential Curve**. You must be willing to endure the "flat" part of the curve (the early days of scaling) to reach the vertical spike of mastery.

The Three Levers of Scaling: Volume, Intensity, Complexity

How do you actually scale a habit? You cannot simply "do more" forever, or you will run out of time. You must manipulate three distinct variables to force adaptation in your nervous system.

1. Volume (The Capacity Lever)

This is the most basic form of scaling. You increase the **Duration** or **Frequency** of the habit.

- *Phase 1:* Read 10 minutes/day.
- *Phase 2:* Read 30 minutes/day.

Volume is necessary to build **Work Capacity**—the biological tolerance for effort. However, volume has a ceiling. You cannot read for 24 hours a day. Once you max out your volume, you must switch levers.

2. Intensity (The Efficiency Lever)

This involves doing the same amount of work in less time, or with higher focus, or with heavier load.

- *Phase 1:* Run 5 miles in 60 minutes.
- *Phase 2:* Run 5 miles in 50 minutes.
- *Phase 1:* 60 minutes of "distracted" work.
- *Phase 2:* 60 minutes of "Deep Work" (zero interruptions).

Intensity forces the brain to optimize its neural firing rates, recruiting more muscle fibers or cognitive resources per second. This is where **Efficiency** is born.

3. Complexity (The Skill Lever)

This is the highest form of scaling. You add layers of difficulty or new constraints to the habit.

- *Phase 1:* Write a journal entry (Free flow).
- *Phase 2:* Write a persuasive essay (Structure + Logic).
- *Phase 1:* Basic Scales on guitar.
- *Phase 2:* Improvisation over complex chord changes.

Complexity forces **Neuroplasticity**. It requires the brain to forge entirely new connections, rather than just strengthening old ones. To scale for the long term, you must constantly oscillate between these three levers.

The Goldilocks Rule: Engineering the "Flow State"

How do you know *when* to scale? If you scale too fast, you hit anxiety and burnout. If you scale too slow, you hit boredom and apathy.

You must navigate the **Goldilocks Zone**. Research in cognitive psychology determines that human beings experience peak motivation when working on tasks that are right on the edge of their current abilities. This is the **Yerkes-Dodson Law** of arousal.

- **Too Easy:** The habit becomes boring. Dopamine drops. Attention wanders.
- **Too Hard:** The habit becomes threatening. Cortisol rises. Avoidance behavior triggers.
- **Just Right:** The habit is roughly **4% harder** than your current skill level.

This "Just Right" zone is the gateway to **Flow**—the mental state where action and awareness merge. Mental toughness is the discipline to constantly adjust your habits to stay in this channel. When a habit feels "easy," that is not a signal to coast; it is a signal to increase the Intensity or Complexity immediately.

Naive Practice vs. Deliberate Practice

The psychologist Anders Ericsson, the father of the "10,000 Hour Rule," made a critical distinction that most people miss. **Experience does not equal expertise.**

- **Naive Practice:** Doing the same thing over and over, expecting to improve. (e.g., Driving a car for 20 years but remaining a mediocre driver).
- **Deliberate Practice:** A focused, systematic effort to improve performance. It requires specific goals, immediate feedback, and intense focus on technique.

To scale your habits, you must inject **Deliberate Practice** into your routine.

- *Naive:* "I will practice tennis for an hour."
- *Deliberate:* "I will practice my backhand volley for an hour, aiming to hit the target 8 out of 10 times, and adjusting my footwork after every miss."

Automaticity is the enemy of Deliberate Practice. Habits are designed to be automatic (unconscious), but mastery requires you to make them conscious again. This creates a paradox: *You need habits to be automatic to start, but you need them to be conscious to grow.*

The solution is **"Habitual Reviews."** You let the habit run on autopilot for 90% of the time, but schedule specific "Audit Sessions" where you break the habit down and analyze the mechanics, looking for micro-inefficiencies.

The Plateau of Latent Potential: Trusting the Lag

When you begin scaling, you will inevitably hit a period where you are working harder (increasing intensity/complexity) but seeing *zero* external results. This is the **Plateau of Latent Potential**.

Imagine heating an ice cube.

- -10 degrees to -5 degrees: No melting.
- -5 degrees to -1 degrees: No melting.
- 0 degrees: **Melting begins.**

During the temperature increase from -10 to -1, energy was being stored, not wasted. The "Phase Transition" only happens at the tipping point. In your habits, this lag time is where 99% of people quit. They say, "I've been working harder for a month and nothing has changed."

Mental toughness is the understanding that **progress is not linear; it is stored.** You are storing potential energy. If you persist through the plateau, you trigger the phase transition, and the results come in a flood (the exponential spike).

Periodization: The Cycle of Expansion and Recovery

Biological systems cannot grow linearly forever. If you try to scale your habits indefinitely without rest, you will suffer **Systemic Failure** (burnout or injury). We must borrow the concept of **Periodization** from elite athletics.

- **Macro-Cycles:** The Big Picture (The Yearly Goal).
- **Meso-Cycles:** The Monthly Block (Focus on one specific Lever— e.g., "This is a Volume Month").
- **Micro-Cycles:** The Weekly Routine.

Crucially, you must schedule **"Deload Weeks."** Every 6 to 12 weeks, you should deliberately *reduce* the volume or intensity of your habits by 50%. This allows your "Dopamine Receptors" to re-sensitize and your nervous system to recover.

A "Deload" is not quitting. It is a strategic retreat to allow for super-compensation. When you return to full intensity after a deload, you will often find that you have broken through your previous plateau. Growth happens during the *rest*, not the *stress*.

The Sorites Paradox: When Does a Heap Become a Heap?

The **Sorites Paradox** asks: If you have a heap of sand and remove one grain, is it still a heap? Yes. If you remove another? Yes. At what specific grain does it cease to be a heap? There is no clear line.

The same applies to your growth.

- Does one workout make you an athlete? No.
- Do two? No.
- At what point do you become an athlete?

There is no specific day where you cross the line. This ambiguity is painful for the logical brain. However, scaling requires you to ignore the need for a specific "Crossing Line." You must accept that identity is an **Emergent Property**. It emerges slowly from the heap of your daily actions. You scale your habits not to "cross a line" today, but to ensure the heap is undeniable in a decade.

Breaking the "Upper Limit Problem"

In his book *The Big Leap*, Gay Hendricks describes the **Upper Limit Problem**. We all have an internal "thermostat" for how much success, wealth, or happiness we allow ourselves to feel. When we scale our habits and exceed this setting, our subconscious often self-sabotages to bring us back down to our "familiar" zone.

- You get in the best shape of your life, then suddenly get "lazy" or "injured."
- You reach a new level of productivity, then pick a fight with your spouse that ruins your focus.

This is a **Homeostatic Response**. Your ego wants to keep you safe (familiar). Scaling requires you to reset your thermostat. You must consciously visualize yourself at the new level and affirm, "This is my new normal." You must acclimate to the higher altitude of performance, or your brain will force you back down the mountain.

Conclusion: The Infinite Game

Ultimately, scaling habits is about shifting from a **Finite Game** (playing to win/end) to an **Infinite Game** (playing to keep playing).

- *Finite Goal:* "I want to lose 20 pounds." (Once you lose it, the game ends, and often the habits end too).
- *Infinite Goal:* "I want to be an athlete." (There is no end. There is only scaling).

True mental toughness is the love of the infinite game. It is the realization that there is no finish line. There is only the next level of complexity, the next layer of depth, and the next 1% improvement. You scale your habits not because you want to be "done," but because you want to see how far the human organism—*your* organism—can go.

Action Plan for Chapter 5

1. **The Lever Audit:** Look at your primary habit (Lead Domino). Which lever have you been pulling? (Volume, Intensity, or Complexity). Identify the lever you have neglected.

2. **The 4% Challenge:** Design next week's routine to be roughly 4% harder.

3. **Schedule the Deload:** Mark a week 8 weeks from now as "Deload Week." Commit to reducing volume by 50% that week.

4. **The Deliberate Practice Protocol:** Choose one session next week to perform a "Form Check." Record yourself doing it, or critique your output immediately.

5. **Re-set the Thermostat:** Spend 5 minutes visualizing yourself operating at the "Next Level" of your habit. Feel the comfort of it. Tell your brain, "This is where we belong."

CONCLUSION

TURN SMALL ACTIONS INTO PERMANENT IDENTITY

We have arrived at the end of Book 2. Together, we have traversed the landscape of human behavior, from the microscopic firing of a dopamine neuron in the Basal Ganglia to the macroscopic architecture of your daily environment. We have learned how to stack habits like Lego bricks, how to design rooms that compel success, how to track progress with the precision of a scientist, and how to scale our efforts into the realm of elite mastery.

But if you close this book and think that "Habits" are simply tools you use to get things, you have missed the point.

Habits are not just the method by which you achieve success; they are the method by which you **become** success. The ultimate goal of Mental Toughness is not to have a "Productive Day." It is to have a "Productive Soul." It is the shift from *doing* the right thing to *being* the person who does the right thing.

This conclusion is about that final, alchemical shift. It is about the death of "Discipline" and the birth of "Nature." When your habits are fully integrated, you no longer need willpower. You no longer need to "force" yourself to work, or train, or create. You simply do these things because they are who you are. This is the **Identity-Based Life**.

The Architecture of Being: From "I Do" to "I Am"

Most people operate on the level of **Outcome-Based Habits**.

- *Outcome:* "I want to lose 20 pounds."

- *Outcome:* "I want to write a bestseller."

- *Outcome:* "I want to have a million dollars."

The problem with outcomes is that they are external and transient. If your motivation is to "lose 20 pounds," what happens when you lose them? The motivation evaporates. You are left with a vacuum, and usually, the weight returns. This is the **Yo-Yo Effect** of outcome-oriented thinking.

True Mental Toughness operates on the level of **Identity-Based Habits**.

- *Identity:* "I am an athlete."

- *Identity:* "I am a writer."

- *Identity:* "I am a financier."

When you shift to identity, the goal is no longer a finish line; it is a state of being. You don't run to "lose weight"; you run because *that is what runners do*. You don't write to "finish a book"; you write because *you are a writer*.

The beauty of this shift is that it eliminates the "Decision Tax." An athlete doesn't wake up and ask, "Should I train today?" The question is irrelevant. It would be like asking, "Should I be myself today?" The action flows naturally from the identity.

The Cognitive Dissonance of Growth

To reach this state, you must navigate a psychological phenomenon known as **Cognitive Dissonance**. This occurs when your actions and your beliefs are in conflict.

When you first start a new habit—say, going to the gym—there is high dissonance.

- *Belief:* "I am lazy and out of shape."
- *Action:* "I am lifting weights."

This conflict is uncomfortable. Your brain hates it. It wants alignment. Usually, people resolve this by quitting the action to align with the belief. "I'm just not a gym person," they say, and they quit.

However, if you possess the mental toughness to **sustain the action**, the brain is forced to resolve the dissonance in the *opposite direction*. It cannot deny the evidence of your actions. So, it changes the belief.

- *Action:* "I have lifted weights every day for 60 days."
- *New Belief:* "I must be an athlete."

This is **Self-Perception Theory**. We do not just act because of who we are; we know who we are by observing how we act. You are the sculptor and the clay. Every repetition of a habit is a chisel strike that reshapes your self-image.

The Sorites Paradox: The Accumulation of Self

In philosophy, the **Sorites Paradox** (or the Paradox of the Heap) asks a simple question: *If you have a heap of sand and remove one grain, is it still a heap? Yes. If you remove another? Yes. If you continue until only one grain remains, is it a heap? No. So at what specific grain did it cease to be a heap?*

There is no answer. There is no line. The "Heap" is an emergent property.

Your identity works the same way.

- Does writing one page make you a writer? No.
- Does writing two? No.
- Does writing for ten years? Yes.

So when did you become a writer? You didn't become one in a "moment." You became one through **Accumulation**.

Most people are looking for the "Transformation Moment"—the epiphany, the lightning bolt. They want to cross a finish line and say, "Now I am changed." But Book 2 teaches us that there is no line. There is only the pile of sand.

Mental toughness is the willingness to add a grain of sand to the pile every single day, even when it looks like nothing is changing. It is the understanding that **Identity is a lagging measure of your habits.** You are not who you say you are; you are who your habits prove you are.

The Ship of Theseus: The Biological Reality of Change

There is another paradox that explains the biology of your transformation: **The Ship of Theseus**. If you have a ship, and over time you replace every single plank of wood, every sail, and every nail, is it still the same ship?

Biologically, you are the Ship of Theseus. Every cell in your body has a lifespan. Your skin cells are replaced every few weeks. Your red blood cells every few months. Your skeleton every few years. Even your neural pathways—the physical structures of your thoughts—are constantly being pruned and re-wired through neuroplasticity.

You are literally not the same person you were when you started Book 1. The "You" that struggled to get out of bed no longer exists. That version of you has been cellularly and neurologically overwritten by the habits you have built.

This is why "Bad Habits" are so hard to break—they are physical parts of your ship. And it is why "Good Habits" eventually become effortless— they become the structural keel of your new vessel.

You must stop clinging to your old identity. Stop saying "I've always been a procrastinator" or "I've always been bad with money." That person is dead. You have replaced their planks. You are a new ship. Sail like one.

The Social Mirror: The External Validation of Identity

We are social animals. Our identity is not formed in a vacuum; it is reflected back to us by our tribe. This is the **Looking-Glass Self**.

As your habits change, your social signal changes. People start to treat you differently. They stop offering you junk food because "you're the healthy one." They start asking you for book recommendations because "you're the reader."

This external validation is a powerful reinforcement loop. When the tribe acknowledges your new identity, it solidifies it. It raises the cost of regression. To quit your habits now would not just be a personal failure; it would be a "Social Lie."

However, this also means you must be prepared for **Social Friction**. The people who knew the "Old You" may resist the "New You." Your change shines a light on their stagnation. This is the **Crab Bucket Theory**—when one crab tries to escape, the others pull it back down.

Mental toughness is the courage to outgrow your environment if necessary. It is the realization that to fully inhabit your new identity, you may need to find a new tribe that reflects your future, not your past.

The Entropy of Identity: Why Maintenance is Growth

In physics, **Entropy** is the tendency of a system to move from order to disorder. A clean room becomes messy. A hot coffee becomes cold. A disciplined life becomes chaotic.

There is no such thing as "Standing Still." If you stop putting energy into your system, you do not stay the same; you decay.

Many people achieve a goal—they run the marathon, they save the money—and then they stop. They think they have "crossed the finish line." But because of entropy, the moment they stop, they begin to slide backward.

Maintenance is not stagnation; maintenance is the active fight against entropy.

To keep your identity, you must continue to cast votes for it. You don't stop being a writer once the book is published; you start the next one. You don't stop being an athlete once the race is over; you train for the next season.

This is the **"Forever" Mindset**. You are not building a habit for 21 days or 66 days. You are building a habit for *life*. This sounds exhausting to the amateur, but to the master, it is liberating. It means you stop rushing. You stop looking for shortcuts. You settle into the rhythm of the work, knowing that the work is the destination.

The Masterpiece: Life as a Work of Art

In the end, Book 2 asks you to view your life not as a series of chores, but as a **Masterpiece**.

A painter does not complain about the brushstrokes. The brushstrokes are the art. A sculptor does not complain about the chipping away of stone. The chipping is the art.

Your habits—your morning routine, your deep work, your diet, your sleep—these are your brushstrokes. They are the millions of tiny actions that, when viewed from a distance, form the portrait of your life.

If you paint with erratic, lazy, distracted strokes, you will paint a blur. If you paint with intentional, disciplined, focused strokes, you will paint a masterpiece.

Behavioral Architecture is the art form of the self. You are the architect, the builder, and the inhabitant of your own potential.

The Final Synthesis: The Unified Theory of Mental Toughness

Let us look back at the journey of Book 2:

1. **Chapter 1 (Habit Stacking):** We learned that we cannot rely on motivation; we must rely on *connection*. We hitch new actions to old anchors, weaving a web of automaticity.

2. **Chapter 2 (Environment Design):** We learned that we are products of our space. We stopped fighting temptation and started removing it. We built a fortress where success is the default setting.

3. **Chapter 3 (Visual Tracking):** We learned that the brain needs evidence. We hacked our dopamine loops by making the invisible visible, turning the grind into a game.

4. **Chapter 4 (Substitution):** We learned that energy cannot be destroyed, only transferred. We stopped trying to "break" bad habits and started replacing them, hijacking the loop for our own gain.

5. **Chapter 5 (Scaling):** We learned that good is the enemy of great. We refused to settle for the "Ok Plateau," pushing into the discomfort of deliberate practice to achieve exponential growth.

And now, here in the Conclusion, we realize that all of these tools serve one singular purpose: **To rewrite the story of who you are.**

You are no longer a victim of your impulses. You are no longer a slave to your environment. You are no longer a leaf blowing in the wind of your emotions.

You are a **Machine of Consistency**. You are a **Vessel of Discipline**. You are the master of your own "Start," and the architect of your own "Forever."

The Torch is Passed

The knowledge is now yours. The science has been explained. The protocols have been laid out. The rest is simply... **Execution.**

The world is filled with people who "know" what to do. They have read the books. They have listened to the podcasts. But they remain unchanged because they refuse to pay the price of action.

Do not be one of them. Be the anomaly. Be the one who does the work when no one is watching. Be the one who values the "X" on the calendar more than the "Like" on the screen. Be the one who understands that the only easy day was yesterday.

Go build your habits. Go build your identity. Go build your life.

Final Action Plan for Book 2

1. **The Identity Contract:** Write a formal contract to yourself. "I am a [New Identity]." List the three "Non-Negotiable Standards" that this identity upholds. Sign it. Frame it.

2. **The Purge:** Take one final look at your environment. Anything that contradicts your new identity must go. Donate the junk food. Delete the apps. Cancel the subscriptions. Burn the ships.

3. **The 10-Year Vision:** Fast forward 10 years. Imagine the "Accumulation" of your current habits. If you stay on this path, who will you be? If you don't like the answer, change the habit today.

4. **The "Forever" Vow:** Choose one habit—just one—that you vow to perform for the rest of your life. Not for a challenge. Not for a result. But because it is *you*.

5. **Turn the Page:** You have mastered the Start (Book 1) and the Orbit (Book 2). You are ready.

REFLECTION QUESTIONS
AUDIT YOUR DAILY ROUTINES

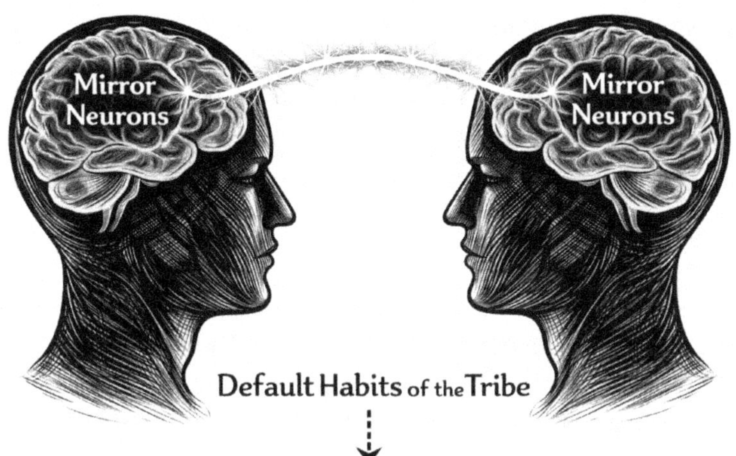

The transition from a disciplined individual to an integrated identity requires constant, clinical monitoring. In systems engineering, any system lacking a feedback mechanism is destined for **Entropy**—the inevitable slide into disorder. You cannot simply "set and forget" your habits. The human brain is a master of "Habitual Decay," a process where we slowly cut corners, reduce intensity, and allow environmental triggers to drift.

This chapter is your **Behavioral Inventory**. Approach these sections as a forensic investigator examining the "Crime Scene" of your daily productivity. We are looking for the leaks in your energy, the friction in your systems, and the lies in your identity.

Section 1: The Habit Stacking Architecture (The Chapter 1 Audit)

A habit stack is a neural chain. If one link is weak, the entire sequence collapses. This audit focuses on the **Connectivity** and **Logic** of your behavioral chains.

1.1. The Reliability and Purity of the Anchor: A habit stack is only as strong as the foundation it sits upon. Analyze your primary **Anchor Habit**. Is it a **Fixed Biological Constant** (e.g., the first time your feet touch the floor, the first sip of water, the sound of your alarm) or is it a **Contextual Variable** (e.g., "when I feel like starting work" or "after I check my phone")?

If your anchor is variable, your stack will be intermittent. You must ask: Does this anchor occur with 100% frequency regardless of my location or emotional state? If you are traveling, does the anchor still exist? If the anchor is compromised by external factors, your "If-Then" neural programming will fail to fire. How can you tighten the temporal and physical boundaries of your anchor to ensure the brain never has to "decide" if the sequence has begun?

1.2. The Spatial Flow and Kinetic Friction: Map the physical movement required by your stack. This is the **Kinetic Audit**. When you finish your Anchor Habit, what is the exact physical distance to the tools required for the next action? If you finish your coffee (Anchor) in the kitchen, but your journal (New Habit) is upstairs in the bedroom, you have introduced **Spatial Friction**.

Every meter of distance and every second of transition is a "Decision Point" where your brain can choose distraction over discipline. Does the completion of the Anchor Habit place you in the immediate physical vicinity of the tools required for the next step? If not, how can you relocate your environment so that the transition feels like a singular, unified motion? Your goal is to make the move from Anchor to Stack feel like a downhill slide.

1.3. The Temporal Window of Neuro-Chemical Reinforcement: Identify the exact millisecond you provide yourself with a reward after completing the stack. The **Basal Ganglia** requires a reward signal within a very narrow window—typically less than 60 seconds—to effectively "stamp in" the new neural circuit.

Are you delaying your reward (e.g., "I'll relax tonight because I worked this morning")? If so, you are effectively cooling the circuit before it can be cemented. The reward must be **Biologically Immediate**. Does your stack end with a visceral "Win"? This could be a physical gesture, a specific scent, or a verbal affirmation. Are you successfully hijacking your own dopamine system, or are you leaving your brain "unpaid" for its effort?

Your environment is the **Invisible Hand** that guides your behavior. This audit examines the "Physical Logic" of your home and office.

2.1. The 5-Second Saliency Diagnostic: Imagine a total stranger—a "Behavioral Consultant"—enters your primary workspace. They are allowed only five seconds of observation. Based purely on the visual cues, could they identify your **Lead Domino** (your most important task)?

If your environment is "Neutral" (e.g., a clean desk with a closed laptop and a lamp), you have failed the saliency test. A high-performance environment is not "neat"; it is **Directional**. The tools for your success should be so visually prominent that they "scream" for your attention, while the tools for your distractions are hidden or removed. What is the most visually "loud" object in your room right now? If it isn't the tool for your Lead Domino, you are fighting a losing battle against your own visual cortex.

2.2. The Friction Ratio and Asymmetry of Choice: Select your most persistent maladaptive pattern (e.g., junk food, social media, news binging). Now, calculate the **Friction Ratio**. How many physical steps or "clicks" are required to initiate that behavior? If the phone is in your pocket, the friction is **Zero-Step**.

To dismantle this pattern, you must achieve **Friction Asymmetry**. You must make the bad habit a **3-Step Process** at minimum. (e.g., Phone is in a different room + inside a drawer + requiring a 20-digit password). Simultaneously, you must reduce your positive substitute to a **0-Step Process**. Where is the friction currently working *against* your goals? Are you making it too easy to fail and too hard to succeed?

2.3. The Sanitization of Contextual Anchors: Analyze your "Deep Work Zone." This is a **Contextual Audit**. The brain associates specific chairs, lighting levels, and even smells with specific mental states. Has your work zone become "Contaminated"? If you answer casual emails, scroll through news, or eat snacks in the same chair where you perform your high-intensity focus, you have created **Neural Cross-Talk**.

When you sit down, your brain doesn't know whether to release "Focus Neurotransmitters" (Acetylcholine) or "Entertainment Neurotransmitters" (Dopamine). Are you currently fighting your environment to get into "The Zone"? If you have contaminated your space, you must perform an **Environmental Reset**. How will you re-establish the singular, sacred association of that space?

Section 3: Feedback Loops and Momentum (The Chapter 3 Audit)

You cannot manage what you do not measure, but measuring the wrong things leads to **Systemic Despair**.

3.1. Input-Centric vs. Output-Centric Metrics: Examine your tracking data. What is the ratio of **Leading Indicators** (inputs you control) to **Lagging Indicators** (outputs you don't)? If you are tracking "Money Earned" or "Pounds Lost," you are tracking the past. If you are tracking "Minutes of Deep Work" or "Grams of Protein," you are tracking the future.

Mental toughness is the ability to ignore the lagging indicator while obsessing over the leading indicator. Does your current scoreboard reward you for things you can actually influence today? If you are only tracking results, you are setting yourself up for the "Valley of Disappointment." How can you shift your metrics so that 90% of your "Wins" are based purely on your **Execution**?

3.2. The Gravity and Saliency of the Scoreboard: Is your progress tracker an **Active Provocateur** or a **Passive Record**? A tracker buried in a notebook or hidden in a phone app is passive. It has no "Visual Gravity." An active scoreboard is one that you are forced to confront as you move through your day.

Does your scoreboard cause a sense of "Positive Guilt" or "Urgency" when you see a gap? If you can go an entire day without being reminded of your current streak, your feedback loop is broken. Where can you place your tracking data so that it serves as a constant, silent coach, pulling you back toward your goals whenever you drift?

3.3. The Resilience and "Floor-Level" Audit: Recall your last "Miss." What was the **Primary Failure Point**? Was it a breakdown in the stack, an environmental temptation, or an emotional collapse? More importantly, what was your **Recovery Velocity**?

The "Never Miss Twice" rule is the gold standard of consistency, but it requires a **Floor-Level Routine**. Do you have a "2-Minute Version" of your habit for days when you are sick, traveling, or overwhelmed? If you don't have a plan for your "Worst Days," your system is fragile. How will you design your minimum viable performance to ensure the "Chain" is never broken, even when life becomes chaotic?

Section 4: Substitution and The Taper Diagnostic (The Chapter 4 Audit)

Habits are not broken; they are replaced. This audit identifies the **Neural Vacuums** in your behavior change process.

4.1. The Reward Matching Test: When you replaced a bad habit with a positive substitute, did you ensure the "Reward" was chemically similar? The brain engages in habits to achieve a specific state shift. If you replaced "Social Media" (Novelty/High Dopamine) with "Stretching" (Calm/Serotonin), the brain will likely reject the swap during times of high stress because the "Need" for novelty isn't being met.

Are you trying to satisfy a hunger with a glass of water? Analyze the neurochemical payoff of your old habit. Was it a sedative effect or a stimulant effect? If your positive substitute doesn't hit the same receptor profile, your substitution is structurally weak.

4.2. The Ghost Cue Identification: Identify the environmental or emotional "Ghost Cues" that trigger your old patterns. Most habits are triggered by micro-cues we aren't consciously aware of—a specific lighting level, a scent, or a certain person entering a room.

If you haven't mapped these triggers, you are playing defense. How can you preemptively "Sanitize" the cue before it strikes? Are there specific locations where you are "weaker"? Why? What is the physical object in that location that acts as the Ghost Cue for your regression?

4.3. The Withdrawal and Extinction Burst Awareness: In the last 14 days of habit change, have you experienced an "Extinction Burst"—a sudden, intense urge to return to old ways? The brain often stages a final "protest" when a neural pathway is being pruned.

Did you recognize this as a sign of progress, or did you interpret it as a personal failure of willpower? Mental toughness is the ability to recognize biological withdrawal symptoms without attaching emotional meaning to them. Are you respecting the 21-day "Dopamine Taper," or are you expecting your brain to enjoy "Low-Dopamine" activities immediately?

Good is the enemy of great. This audit prevents you from settling for the **"Ok Plateau."**

5.1. The Three Levers Check: Which lever have you been pulling to scale your habit: **Volume, Intensity, or Complexity**? Most people only use Volume (doing it longer), which eventually hits a ceiling of time and energy.

If you have been doing the same routine for 30 days without increasing the Intensity (speed/quality) or Complexity (difficulty), your brain has stopped adapting. You are in "Maintenance Mode." How can you pull a different lever this week to force new neuroplasticity?

5.2. The Goldilocks and Flow Channel Evaluation: Is your current routine roughly **4% harder** than it was last month? Human peak performance occurs in the narrow channel between boredom and anxiety.

If the habit feels "easy," you have stopped growing. If it feels "terrifying," you will eventually avoid it. Are you actively seeking the "Anxiety-Boredom" channel, or have you become a "Maintenance Thinker" who is afraid to disturb the status quo of a comfortable habit?

5.3. The Periodization and Deload Plan: When was your last "Deload Week"? Biological systems cannot scale linearly forever. If you have been scaling without strategic recovery, you are courting **Systemic Failure** (burnout or injury).

Have you scheduled a 50% reduction in volume for every 8-12 weeks of progress to allow for super-compensation? Remember: Growth happens during the rest, not the stress. Is your calendar built for a marathon or a sprint to exhaustion?

The ultimate goal of Book 2 is to move from **"Doing" to "Being."** This audit examines the internal code of your self-image.

6.1. The Linguistics of Self-Categorization: Pay close attention to your internal and external dialogue. Are you still using **Permission-Based**

Language (e.g., "I'm trying to be a runner," "I'm attempting to wake up early")? Or have you transitioned to **Identity-Based Language** (e.g., "I am a runner," "I am an early riser")?

Language is not just a reflection of reality; it is a **Constructor of Reality**. When you say "I'm trying," you are signaling to your brain that the behavior is optional and external to your nature. What is one "Legacy Phrase" you are still using that anchors you to your old, lower-performing self?

6.2. The Evidence of the Ledger Identity is an **Emergent Property** of your actions. If you claim the identity of a "Leader," but your habit tracker shows zero time spent on team development or strategic thinking, your brain recognizes the **Cognitive Dissonance**.

You are effectively lying to yourself, which erodes your **Self-Efficacy**. Which of your claimed identities is currently "Bankrupt" of evidence? What specific "Daily Vote" (habit) can you cast tomorrow to provide your brain with the undeniable, physical proof it needs to believe in your new identity?

6.3. The 10-Year Linear Extrapolation: This is the most sobering part of the audit. Perform a **Mathematical Projection** of your current daily routines. If you change absolutely nothing about your current habits—your diet, your consumption of digital media, your work intensity, your sleep hygiene—where will you be in exactly ten years?

Will you be a **Masterpiece** of accumulated marginal gains, or will you be a **Cautionary Tale** of accumulated marginal decays? Does the "Future You" look back at your current choices with gratitude or with resentment? If you do not like the 10-year destination, which specific habit must be course-corrected today to change the trajectory of the entire decade?

Section 7: Final Synthesis and The Road Ahead

7.1. The Maintenance vs. Growth Question: Are your current habits designed to keep you where you are, or to take you where you want to go? Most habits are **"Defensive"**—they prevent us from falling behind. **"Offensive"** habits are those that aggressively move the needle toward a new reality.

What is the one "Offensive" habit you have been neglecting because it feels too difficult to automate? Why is it not currently in your stack?

7.2. The Integration and Willpower Score: On a scale of 1-10, how much willpower is required to perform your Lead Domino? If the answer is above a 3, your environmental architecture or habit stack is flawed.

The goal of Book 2 is to make the right thing the **Path of Least Resistance**. What is the one specific "Friction Point" you will remove in the next 24 hours to bring that score down to a 1?

Closing Protocol

The value of these questions is not in the reading, but in the **Writing**. Your brain processes handwritten or typed reflections through the **Prefrontal Cortex**, whereas internal thoughts often remain trapped in the emotional **Limbic System**.

To close Book 2, select three sections from the list above that caused you the most discomfort or where you felt the most "Resistance" while reading. Write a detailed, **500-word response** for each, outlining the current systemic failure and the specific **Architectural Fix** you will implement.

That discomfort is the signal that you have found a **Neural Blockage**. Mental toughness is the willingness to look at your own failures without blinking. You have the tools. You have the audit. Now, perform the maintenance.

Book 2: The Architecture of the Automatic Life is now complete. You have moved from the "Spark" of Book 1 to the "System" of Book 2. Your habits are no longer a chore; they are your infrastructure.

BOOK THREE
GROW WILLPOWER AND SELF-CONTROL

INTRODUCTION

STRENGTHEN YOUR MENTAL MUSCLE

Welcome to the third pillar of your transformation.

If you have followed the journey through Book 1 and Book 2, you have achieved something rare: you have mastered the **Start**, and you have mastered the **Orbit**. You have learned how to bypass the initial friction of change and how to build an environment that automates your success. You have optimized your external world to be a "high-performance playground."

But there is a final, darker territory we must now traverse. It is the territory of the **Internal Engine**.

In the life of every high-performer, there comes a moment where the "system" is not enough. There is a day when the habit stack fails because of a family crisis. There is a night when your environment is compromised because you are traveling in a foreign city and have no control over your surroundings. There is a season where the "automation" of your life is stripped away by chaos, grief, or sheer exhaustion, and you are left with nothing but the raw, naked strength of your own mind.

This is where the average person breaks. They have built a "fair-weather" discipline. They are consistent when their routine is perfect, but they are fragile when the world becomes volatile. They rely on their environment to *be* their discipline.

Book 3 is about becoming Unbreakable.

We are moving away from the "Architectural" approach of Book 2 and entering the **"Fortification"** phase. This book is dedicated to the development of **Willpower**—not as a vague, mystical concept or a moral virtue, but as a biological, measurable, and expandable mental muscle. We are going to treat your self-control like a bicep: we will feed it, we will exercise it through intentional stress, we will learn how to prevent it from fatiguing, and we will study the neurochemistry that allows it to grow.

The Civil War Within: The Dual-Process Theory

To master willpower, you must first understand the anatomy of the struggle. Every time you face a choice—to hit the snooze button or to stand up, to eat the kale or the cake, to focus on the work or check the phone—a civil war is being fought inside your skull. This is known in psychology as the **Dual-Process Theory**.

On one side, you have **System 1**: The Limbic System. This is the ancient, reptilian part of your brain that has remained largely unchanged for millions of years. It cares only about immediate gratification, survival, and energy conservation. It is the seat of your impulses and your cravings. It operates on the "Pleasure Principle" and the "Path of Least Resistance." When you feel a "pull" toward a distraction, that is System 1 screaming for a dopamine hit.

On the other side, you have **System 2**: The Prefrontal Cortex (PFC). This is the "Executive Center," the most recently evolved part of the human brain. It is the part of the brain that understands the future, calculates long-term consequences, and holds the sacred image of who you want to become. It is the seat of logic, planning, and **Inhibitory Control**.

Willpower is the capacity of the Prefrontal Cortex to exercise dominance over the Limbic System. In the literature, this is often referred to as the **"Prefrontal Governor."** Just like a governor on a high-performance engine limits the top speed to prevent the machine from exploding, your PFC acts as a regulator for your animalistic impulses.

However, there is a catch. The Limbic System is "always on" and requires almost no energy to run. The Prefrontal Cortex, however, is a metabolically expensive organ. It is the "luxury suite" of the brain. It requires massive amounts of glucose and oxygen to function. This brings us to the fundamental challenge of Book 3: **Self-control is a finite, exhaustible resource.**

The "Ego Depletion" Paradox and the Fuel of the Will

For decades, psychological research centered on the concept of **Ego Depletion**—the idea that willpower is like a battery. Every time you resist a temptation or make a difficult decision, you "drain" the battery. This is why, after a day of stressful meetings and complex problem-solving, you find it nearly impossible to resist the junk food in your pantry at 9:00 PM. Your PFC has literally run out of fuel.

Recent science has refined this model. It isn't just that the battery is "empty"; it's that the brain is a **Conservation Machine**. When the PFC senses that energy levels (glucose) are dipping, it enters a "power-saving mode." It stops spending energy on difficult tasks (like self-control) and reverts to automatic, low-energy behaviors (like habits and impulses).

In **Chapter 1: Feed Your Brain for Better Decision Making**, we will dive into the thermodynamics of the will. You cannot build mental toughness on a foundation of biological instability. We will explore the **Glucose Model of Willpower** and how to maintain "High-Octane" blood sugar levels to ensure your Prefrontal Governor never loses power during a crisis.

The Mythology of "Natural" Discipline

One of the most damaging lies in our culture is the idea that some people are simply "born" with discipline while others are not. We look at the elite—the Navy SEAL, the concert pianist, the stoic CEO—and we assume they possess a mystical quality of "character" that we lack.

This is a fundamental misunderstanding of **Neuroplasticity**.

When you observe someone with elite self-control, you are not looking at a "natural." You are looking at someone who has undergone **Neuro-Chemical Hardening**. Through a process called **Myelination**, the neural pathways associated with inhibitory control become thicker and more efficient over time. Every time you say "No" to a distraction and "Yes" to your mission, you are physically insulating the "cables" of your willpower.

Just as a physical muscle grows micro-tears under the strain of a heavy weight and heals back stronger, the Prefrontal Cortex becomes more resilient when it is repeatedly pushed to its threshold of resistance. In Book 3, we stop treating willpower as a personality trait and start treating it as a **Skill**. We will apply the principles of **Progressive Overload** to your mind.

In **Chapter 2: Practice Intentional Discomfort to Build Grit**, we will explore the concept of "Voluntary Suffering." This isn't about being a martyr; it's about **Callousing the Mind**. By seeking out small, controlled doses of discomfort—cold water, fasting, extended focus—you are training your brain to stay calm and executive-focused when involuntary stress inevitably hits.

The Decision Fatigue Epidemic

We live in a world designed to drain your willpower. The average modern human makes roughly **35,000 decisions a day**. In the ancestral environment, choices were limited: *Where is the water? Is that a predator? Should I eat this berry?* Today, every notification, every email subject line, every choice of coffee, and every "skip ad" button is a micro-tax on your Prefrontal Cortex. By the time you reach your most important work, you have already paid thousands of "Decision Taxes." This is **Decision Fatigue**.

In **Chapter 4: Reduce Decision Fatigue through Daily Systems**, we move from the "mental" to the "systemic." We will show you how to build a **Choice-Minimal Life**. High-performers do not have more willpower than you; they simply *use* it less on trivialities. They wear the same clothes, eat the same breakfasts, and follow the same morning algorithms. They preserve their "Mental Gold" for the 5% of decisions that actually move the needle of their destiny.

Implementation Intentions: The "If-Then" Neural Script

Even a hardened mind can be ambushed. The world is full of "Limbic Traps"—highly palatable foods, addictive algorithms, and social pressures designed to bypass your logic and hit your pleasure centers.

Relying on "white-knuckle" willpower in the moment of temptation is a losing strategy. It's like trying to build a dam while the flood is already hitting. Instead, we use **Chapter 3: Use Implementation Intentions to Fight Temptation**.

This is the most scientifically validated tool in the history of self-regulation. We move the decision from the *moment of stress* to the *moment of planning*. By creating "If-Then" scripts (e.g., *"If I feel the urge to check my phone, then I will take one sip of water and do 10 deep breaths"*), you are "pre-loading" a neural response. You are effectively "outsourcing" your discipline to a pre-recorded program, allowing your PFC to remain idle while the system handles the threat.

The Stoic Shift: Cognitive Reframing

The final frontier of self-control is not the avoidance of stress, but the **Transformation of Stress**.

When your heart starts racing and your palms sweat before a high-stakes event, your Limbic System is screaming "Danger!" Most people interpret this as anxiety and try to suppress it, which only drains more willpower.

In **Chapter 5: Apply Cognitive Reframing to High-Stress Situations**, we will learn the art of **Cognitive Appraisal**. We will study the science of how your body's "Stress Response" can be reframed as a "Challenge Response." By changing the narrative—viewing the pounding heart as "blood preparing my brain for battle" rather than "panic"—you change the very neurochemistry of your blood. You move from **Cortisol (The Stress Hormone)** to **DHEAS (The Growth Hormone)**.

This is the "Special Forces" level of mental toughness. It is the ability to stay "Cool-Blooded" when the world is on fire. It is the transition from being a victim of your emotions to being the **Director of your Neurochemistry**.

The Evolution of the "Will"

To truly appreciate the power of what we are about to build, we must look at where this concept came from. The Greeks called it **Enkrateia**—the power over oneself. The Stoics viewed it as the only thing we truly "own" in this life. Everything else—your money, your reputation, your health—can be taken from you by fate. But your ability to choose your response to a situation is the "Invincible Fortress."

In the 20th century, the "Marshmallow Test" revolutionized our understanding of this power. Children who could delay gratification—resisting one marshmallow now to get two later—showed significantly higher success rates in every metric of life: SAT scores, BMI, income, and relationship stability.

Self-control is the **Master Virtue**. It is the multiplier of every other talent you possess. Without willpower, your intelligence is just potential energy that never turns into kinetic work. Without self-control, your kindness is just a fleeting emotion that never turns into consistent service.

The Journey Ahead: The Hardened Mind

The ultimate goal of Book 3 is the **Conclusion: Live with Discipline as a Default**.

We are aiming for a state of **"Effortless Effort."** This is the paradox where you are working harder than anyone else, but it no longer feels like "work" in the traditional sense. It has become your baseline. You have hardened your mind to the point where the things that used to be "hard"—the cold showers, the 5:00 AM starts, the deep work sessions, the rejection of sugar—are now the most comfortable parts of your day.

You are no longer a person "trying" to be disciplined. You are no longer "wrestling" with your impulses. You have achieved **Identity Alignment**.

In Book 1, we learned to **Start**. In Book 2, we learned to **Automate**. In Book 3, we learn to **Endure**.

The journey through Book 3 is not easy. It will require you to face your weaknesses, audit your biology, and intentionally step into the fire. But on the other side of this fire is a version of you that is no longer a slave to impulse. You are about to build the "Mental Muscle" that will carry you through the rest of your life.

It is time to stop being a leaf blowing in the wind of your emotions and start being the wind itself.

The Three Pillars of the Willpower Engine

1. **Biological Fueling:** Ensuring the brain has the glucose and stability required for the Prefrontal Cortex to function. (The "Matter")

2. **Psychological Hardening:** Using intentional stress and discomfort to increase the threshold of what the mind can endure. (The "Spirit")

3. **Systemic Preservation:** Using "If-Then" logic and choice architecture to preserve willpower for the high-stakes moments. (The "Method")

The Book 3 Mindset Shift

- **From:** "I don't have enough willpower."
- **To:** "I haven't trained my willpower muscle yet."
- **From:** "I failed because I was tempted."
- **To:** "I failed because my Prefrontal Governor ran out of fuel."
- **From:** "Discipline is a chore."
- **To:** "Discipline is my biological baseline."
- **From:** "I need to feel motivated."
- **To:** "I need to trigger my executive function."

Action Plan for the Introduction

1. **The Impulse Audit:** For the next 24 hours, do not try to change anything. Simply carry a small notebook and mark every time you feel a "pull" from System 1 (the impulse) that contradicts your System 2 (your goal). Notice when the pull is strongest. Is it after a long meeting? Is it when you are hungry? This is your "Baseline of Resistance."

2. **The Decision Inventory:** Count how many "Useless Decisions" you make before noon tomorrow. (What to wear, what to eat, which route to take). We will be eliminating these in Chapter 4.

3. **The "Governor" Visualization:** When you feel the urge to procrastinate or indulge, visualize your Prefrontal Cortex as a steady, calm "Governor" sitting at the controls of a high-speed engine. Your job is not to kill the engine (the passion/impulse), but to regulate it so the machine stays on the track.

CHAPTER 1

FEED YOUR BRAIN FOR BETTER DECISION MAKING

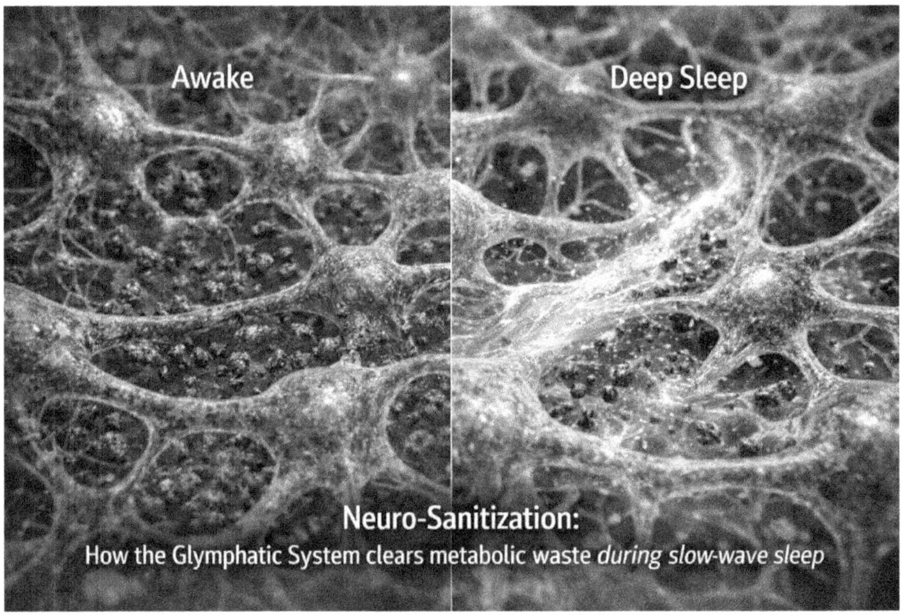

If you walked into a Formula 1 pit garage and watched the mechanics pour low-grade, diluted gasoline into a multimillion-dollar engine, you would call them incompetent. You understand intuitively that a high-performance machine requires high-performance fuel. The tolerances are too tight, and the demands are too high for anything less than premium chemistry.

Yet, most high-performers treat their own biology with a level of negligence they would never accept in their vehicles. They expect their Prefrontal Cortex (PFC)—the most complex, energy-demanding piece of organic machinery in the known universe—to function at an elite level while running on caffeine, processed sugar, and four hours of sleep.

They view willpower as a "software" issue. They believe that if they just try harder, read more books, or grit their teeth, they can override their biology.

This is a fundamental error. **Willpower is not just software; it is hardware.**

Your ability to say "no" to a distraction, to regulate your emotional outbursts, and to maintain deep focus is strictly limited by the metabolic state of your brain. When your biological fuel gauge hits empty, your "Executive Governor" shuts down, and your animalistic "Limbic System" takes over. This is not a moral failing; it is a physiological safety mechanism.

In this chapter, we are going to perform a **Biological Audit** of your willpower. We will move beyond the vague advice of "eat healthy" and look at the specific neurochemistry of self-control. We will explore the **Glucose Model of Depletion**, the **Hydration-Cognition Link**, and the **Glymphatic System** of sleep.

You are about to learn how to bio-hack your way to better decisions.

The Thermodynamics of Willpower

To understand why you fail, you must understand the "energy budget" of the brain. The brain comprises roughly 2% of your total body weight, yet it consumes a staggering **20% to 25% of your total glucose and oxygen intake**. It is a metabolic furnace.

However, not all parts of the brain consume energy equally.

- **The Basal Ganglia (Habits)** and **The Brain Stem (Survival)** are efficient. They run on "autopilot" and require very little fuel to function.

- **The Prefrontal Cortex (Willpower/Decisions)** is an energy hog. It is evolutionarily new, and it is inefficient.

This creates a dangerous dynamic known as the **"Self-Control Trade-Off."** When your blood glucose levels drop—even slightly—the brain senses a resource scarcity. To preserve energy for essential life functions (breathing, heart rate, scanning for danger), the brain aggressively cuts power to "non-essential" systems. Unfortunately, from a survival standpoint, your ability to focus on a spreadsheet or resist a donut is considered "non-essential."

When fuel is low, the PFC is the first system to go offline.

This phenomenon was famously illustrated in a study of parole judges. Researchers analyzed over 1,000 judicial rulings and found a disturbing pattern. Judges were significantly more likely to grant parole (a difficult, high-stakes decision requiring active analysis) early in the morning or immediately after a food break.

As the session wore on and their glucose levels (and willpower) depleted, the rate of granting parole dropped to nearly **zero**. The tired, hungry judges defaulted to the "Status Quo" decision: deny parole. Denying parole is the "safe," low-energy choice. It requires no active risk assessment.

This is the **Physiology of the Default**. When your brain is under-fueled, you do not become "stupid"; you become "conservative." You stop taking risks. You stop innovating. You stop resisting impulses. You revert to your basest instincts.

If you want to maintain elite self-control from 8:00 AM to 8:00 PM, you cannot rely on three square meals. You must treat your blood sugar like a thermostat, keeping it in a narrow, high-performance range.

The Insulin Rollercoaster: Why Sugar Kills Discipline

If glucose is the fuel of willpower, the amateur solution is to "eat more sugar." This is a trap.

While it is true that a spike in glucose can temporarily restore willpower (studies show a quick hit of sugar can reverse decision fatigue for about 15 minutes), the long-term cost is catastrophic. This is the **Insulin Rollercoaster**.

When you consume simple carbohydrates (bagels, sugary coffee, candy), your blood glucose spikes rapidly. You feel a surge of energy and focus. But the body panics at this toxic level of sugar and releases massive amounts of **Insulin** to clear it out.

The result is a **Hypoglycemic Crash**. Your blood sugar plummets below the baseline.

In this crash state, your self-control doesn't just dip; it vanishes. The brain perceives the rapid drop in fuel as a survival threat. It activates the Amygdala (the fear and aggression center) and releases stress hormones like cortisol and adrenaline. You become irritable, anxious, and impulsive. You are "Hangry."

In this state, your Prefrontal Governor is offline. You are physically incapable of making a disciplined, long-term choice because your brain is screaming for immediate, high-calorie relief to survive the "famine."

The Protocol: The Steady-State Fueling Strategy To build a brain that can endure, you must switch from "Dirty Fuel" (simple carbs) to "High-Octane Fuel" (proteins, healthy fats, and complex fiber).

1. **The Protein Anchor:** Never eat a carbohydrate without a protein or fat "anchor." Protein slows the absorption of sugar into the bloodstream, flattening the glucose curve. A bagel is a sedative; a bagel with salmon and cream cheese is fuel.

2. **The 4-Hour Rule:** The brain's glycogen stores begin to dip after roughly four hours of cognitive exertion. Do not wait until you are hungry to eat. Hunger is a lagging indicator; by the time you feel it, your cognitive performance has already dropped by 10-15%. Schedule "fueling stops" as religiously as you schedule meetings.

3. **The MCT Oil Advantage:** Many high-performers utilize Medium-Chain Triglycerides (MCTs) found in coconut oil. Unlike glucose, which causes an insulin response, MCTs are converted directly into ketones, which can cross the blood-brain barrier and provide a "clean burning" energy source for the brain that doesn't result in a crash.

Hydration: The Hydraulic Pressure of Thought

If glucose is the electricity, water is the coolant.

The human brain is roughly **75% water**. The structural integrity of your neurons and the fluidity of the neurotransmitters firing across your synapses depend entirely on your hydration status.

Most people live in a state of chronic, low-grade dehydration. Research shows that a drop in body water of just **1-2%** (which is often not enough to trigger thirst) leads to a measurable decline in cognitive function.

The Symptoms of "Dry Brain":

- **Reduced Short-Term Memory:** You walk into a room and forget why you are there.
- **Impaired Psychomotor Speed:** Your reaction times slow down.
- **Focus Fragmentation:** You cannot hold a single train of thought for more than a few minutes.

When the brain is dehydrated, the tissue literally shrinks. The fluid-filled cavities (ventricles) expand to compensate, putting mechanical stress on the brain matter. You are trying to perform elite work with a shriveled engine.

Furthermore, water is the delivery mechanism for the glucose and oxygen your PFC needs. If your blood volume is low due to dehydration, the delivery system slows down. You could eat the perfect diet, but without water, the fuel never reaches the engine.

The Protocol: The First Liter Rule You lose roughly a liter of water every night simply through breathing and sweat. You wake up in a biological deficit.

- **Step 1:** Do not touch coffee until you have consumed **one liter (32oz)** of water. Coffee is a diuretic; if you drink it while dehydrated, you are accelerating the deficit.
- **Step 2:** The "Visual Line." Keep a large water bottle on your desk. If it is not in your visual field, you will not drink it. We are creatures of visual cues (as learned in Book 2).
- **Step 3:** Electrolyte Balance. Water alone isn't enough if you are stripping your body of salts. A pinch of sea salt or an electrolyte packet ensures the water is actually absorbed into the cells rather than passing straight through you.

The Glymphatic System: Why Sleep is Non-Negotiable

For decades, the "hustle culture" mythos taught us that sleep was for the weak. "I'll sleep when I'm dead" was the mantra of the ambitious.

Neuroscience has now proven that "sleeping when you're dead" is the fastest way to get there. Sleep is not a passive state of rest; it is an active state of **Neuro-Sanitization**.

In 2012, researchers discovered the **Glymphatic System**. Before this discovery, scientists didn't understand how the brain—which is metabolically hyper-active—cleaned up its own waste. The rest of the body uses the Lymphatic system, but the brain doesn't have lymph nodes.

It turns out, the brain has a "night shift" cleaning crew.

During deep, slow-wave sleep, the glial cells (the brain's support cells) shrink by up to 60%. This opens up wide channels between neurons, allowing cerebrospinal fluid to rush through the brain tissue like a high-pressure hose. This fluid washes away the toxic metabolic waste products that accumulate during the day, specifically **Beta-Amyloid** and **Tau proteins**.

If you do not get 7-8 hours of sleep, this cleaning cycle is interrupted. The "trash" remains in your neural pathways.

The Consequences of "Dirty Brain": When you wake up after 4-5 hours of sleep, your brain is literally toxic. The buildup of metabolic waste creates "neural static."

- **Prefrontal Shutdown:** Sleep deprivation hits the PFC harder than any other area. A sleep-deprived brain looks almost identical to a drunk brain on an MRI. Your impulse control is the first thing to collapse.

- **Emotional Volatility:** The connection between the Amygdala (emotion) and the PFC (logic) is severed. You become hyper-reactive to negative stimuli. You snap at your spouse, you rage at emails, and you quit on your goals.

You cannot "will" your way through sleep deprivation any more than you can "will" away being drunk.

The Protocol: Sleep Hygiene as a Performance Discipline

- **The 10-3-2-1 Rule:**
    - **10 hours** before bed: No more caffeine. (It takes 10 hours to clear the adenosine receptors).
    - **3 hours** before bed: No more food. (Digestion raises body temperature; sleep requires a temperature drop).
    - **2 hours** before bed: No more work. (Cortisol suppression).

- o **1 hour** before bed: No screens. (Blue light suppresses melatonin).
- **Temperature Control:** Your core body temperature must drop by roughly 2-3 degrees Fahrenheit to initiate sleep. Keep your room between 65-68°F (18-20°C).

Even with perfect food, water, and sleep, your biology has a rhythm. You are not a machine that operates at 100% output for 16 hours straight. You are a biological organism subject to **Circadian Rhythms**.

Most people have a "Peak," a "Trough," and a "Recovery" period.

- **The Peak (Morning/Early Afternoon):** For roughly 75% of the population (Larks and Third Birds), the morning is when the PFC is most alert, and inhibitory control is highest. This is the **"Decision Window."**
- **The Trough (Early Afternoon):** Around 7 hours after waking, there is a systemic dip in alertness. This is biology, not laziness.
- **The Recovery (Evening):** Mood improves, but analytical capacity remains lower than the morning peak.

The Strategic Error: Most people waste their "Peak" answering emails, sitting in status meetings, or scrolling social media. They then try to do their "Deep Work" or make critical strategic decisions in the "Trough" or "Recovery" periods.

This is a misuse of your biological assets. It is like trying to set a land-speed record in a car that is overheating.

The Protocol: Front-Loading the Hardest Decisions Mental toughness is about **Timing**.

- **The Sacred Hours:** Identify your peak window (usually 8:00 AM – 11:00 AM). Block this time. Protect it with your life. This is when you tackle the tasks that require the highest willpower and the most complex problem-solving.
- **The Administrative Slum:** Move all low-willpower tasks (email, scheduling, data entry) to your Trough. You do not need a high-functioning PFC to reply to a "calendar invite."

- **Never Make "Life Decisions" at Night:** Institute a personal rule: "I do not make decisions about my relationship, my career, or my finances after 9:00 PM." The late-night brain is a tired, emotional, and pessimistic organ. Write the thought down, and review it in the morning when the "Governor" is back online.

Supplementation: The Final 5%

Once—and only once—you have dialed in your glucose, hydration, and sleep, you can look at supplementation. Nootropics (cognitive enhancers) are not magic pills, but they can offer a slight edge in neurotransmitter availability.

- **Omega-3 Fatty Acids (DHA/EPA):** The brain is 60% fat. Omega-3s are the building blocks of cell membranes. High doses (2-3g per day) have been linked to improved executive function and reduced inflammation.

- **Vitamin D3:** There are Vitamin D receptors throughout the brain, specifically in the areas responsible for planning and processing information. Deficiency is rampant and correlates with "Brain Fog."

- **Creatine Monohydrate:** Often viewed as a muscle builder, creatine is also a neuro-fuel. It recycles ATP (energy) in brain cells, helping to sustain focus during tasks that require high cognitive endurance.

Warning: No amount of Alpha Brain or Adderall can out-supplement a diet of donuts and four hours of sleep. Fix the foundation first.

Summary: The Biological Imperative

We often view the "Body" and the "Mind" as separate entities. We treat the body like a vehicle that carries the mind around.

This Cartesian dualism is false. **The Mind *is* the Body.**

Every thought you have, every impulse you resist, and every goal you stick to is a biological event powered by glucose, transmitted by ions, and cleaned by sleep. If you neglect the biology, you are sabotaging the psychology.

You cannot be mentally tough if you are physically compromised. The first step to conquering the world is to conquer your own blood sugar.

1. **Audit Your Fuel:** Are you eating "Anchored" meals? Or are you riding the insulin coaster?

2. **Hydrate First:** Drink 1 liter of water before your first cup of coffee.

3. **Protect the Sleep:** Commit to the 10-3-2-1 rule tonight.

4. **Identify Your Window:** When is your biological peak? Move your hardest work there.

Now that we have fueled the engine, it is time to take it out to the track and see what it can endure.

CHAPTER 2

PRACTICE INTENTIONAL DISCOMFORT TO BUILD GRIT

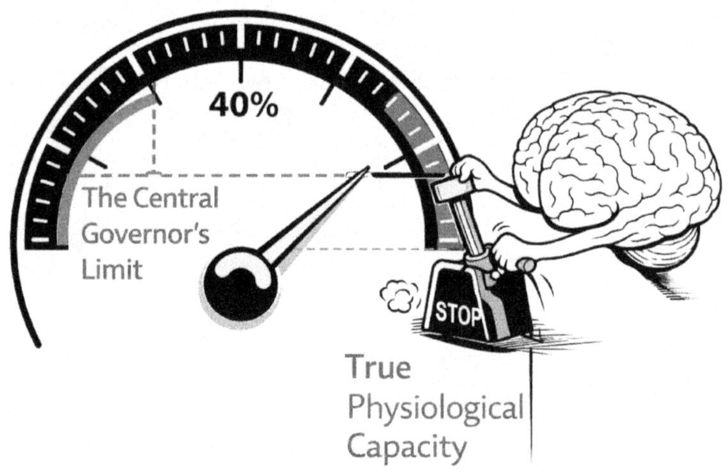

We live in the Age of Anesthesia.

From the moment you wake up to the moment you close your eyes, your entire existence is engineered to eliminate friction. You sleep on memory foam that contours to your spine. You wake up in a climate-controlled box set to 72 degrees. You walk on cushioned soles. You have infinite calories delivered to your door with a single tap. You have the sum of human knowledge and entertainment in your pocket to ensure you never experience a single second of boredom.

We have conquered the elements. We have conquered hunger. We have conquered physical toil.

And in doing so, we have created a catastrophic side effect: **Psychological Atrophy.**

Just as a muscle creates atrophy when it is placed in a cast, your willpower atrophy when it is placed in a cocoon of comfort. Biological systems operate on a "Use It or Lose It" principle. If you do not require your Prefrontal Cortex to override pain, discomfort, or frustration, the neural pathways responsible for that override begin to degrade.

This is why modern humans are so fragile. It is not a moral failing; it is an environmental consequence. We have removed the very stimuli—cold, heat, hunger, physical strain—that evolution used to forge the human spirit.

In **Chapter 1**, we fueled the engine. Now, in **Chapter 2**, we are going to take that engine off-road.

We are going to discuss the science of **Hormesis** and the neurology of the **Anterior Mid-Cingulate Cortex (aMCC)**. We are going to introduce the practice of **Intentional Discomfort**. You are going to learn how to "micro-dose" misery to callous your mind, ensuring that when life inevitably throws real suffering your way, you remain unbreakable.

The Neuroscience of "Doing What You Hate"

For decades, scientists searched for the "seat" of willpower in the brain. Was it in the frontal lobe? Was it a chemical balance?

Recent research has pinpointed a specific brain structure that acts as the hub of tenacity: the **Anterior Mid-Cingulate Cortex (aMCC)**.

This structure is fascinating because of its plasticity. Studies on "Super-Agers" (elderly people who maintain the cognitive sharpness of 25-year-olds) show that they possess an unusually thick and robust aMCC. Conversely, in people who suffer from obesity or depression, this structure is often shriveled and thin.

Here is the critical discovery: **The aMCC only grows when you engage in behavior that you do not want to do.**

If you love running and you go for a run, your aMCC does not grow. You are enjoying yourself. There is no friction. If you hate running, and it is raining, and you are tired, and you go for a run anyway... **the aMCC activates and grows.**

This structure is literally the "Grind Muscle." It connects the autonomic systems (heart rate, breathing) with the executive systems (planning, logic). When you force yourself to endure discomfort for the sake of a long-term goal, you are physically building the bridge between your animal body and your logical mind.

This is the biological argument for **Intentional Discomfort**. We are not seeking pain for the sake of masochism. We are seeking pain because it is the only signal that stimulates the growth of the aMCC. If your life is entirely comfortable, you are physiologically incapable of building grit.

The Theory of Hormesis: The Dose Makes the Poison

To practice intentional discomfort safely, we must understand the biological principle of **Hormesis**.

Hormesis is the phenomenon where a beneficial effect results from exposure to low doses of an agent that is otherwise toxic or lethal when given at higher doses.

- **Exercise** is hormetic stress: You tear muscle fibers (damage) to signal regrowth (strength).

- **Vaccines** are hormetic stress: You introduce a deactivated virus (threat) to signal immune response (resilience).

- **Callouses** are hormetic stress: You apply friction to the skin (damage) to signal the skin to thicken (protection).

Most people live in a state of "Chronic Comfort" (Under-dosing stress), which leads to fragility. Others live in a state of "Chronic Trauma" (Over-dosing stress), which leads to burnout and PTSD.

The goal of this chapter is to find the **"Hormetic Zone."** We want to inject short, sharp shocks of controlled discomfort into your daily routine. These shocks must be intense enough to trigger the "I want to quit" response in the brain, but short enough to be recoverable.

We are going to explore four primary vectors of Intentional Discomfort: **Thermal, Metabolic, Cognitive, and Physical.**

There is no faster, more effective, or more accessible way to train willpower than **Cold Water Immersion**.

It requires no equipment, no gym membership, and no time. It only requires the courage to turn a handle.

The Mechanism of the "Flinch" Stand naked in your shower. The water is warm. Your hand is on the temperature dial. In your mind, you know you are about to turn it to cold. In that split second before you turn the handle, your Limbic System screams. It predicts the shock. It begs you to stop. It rationalizes: *"I'll do it tomorrow,"* or *"I don't need this today."*

This moment is **The Flinch.**

The Flinch is the physical manifestation of resistance. When you turn that handle *despite* the screaming in your head, you are executing a "Hostile Takeover" of your nervous system. You are training the Prefrontal Cortex to override the Amygdala.

The Neurochemical Cascade When the cold water hits your skin, you experience a "Cold Shock Response." You gasp. Your heart rate spikes. Simultaneously, your brain releases a massive flood of **Norepinephrine** (focus and agitation) and **Dopamine**. Studies show that cold immersion can increase dopamine levels by 250%, and unlike drugs, this elevation lasts for hours.

You are effectively using pain to create a state of hyper-focus.

The Protocol: The Daily Reset

1. **The Tail-End Shower:** Start with your normal warm shower. Wash, shave, relax.

2. **The Transition:** Grab the handle. Observe the hesitation. Do not negotiate with it. Turn it all the way to cold.

3. **The Duration:** Stay under the water for **30 to 60 seconds**.

4. **The Control:** Your body will want to hyperventilate. This is the panic response. Your goal is to force your breathing to slow down. Long inhale, slow exhale.

When you step out of that shower, you have started your day with a victory. You have proven to your biology that *you* are in charge, not the temperature of the room.

Hunger is the most primal signal in the animal kingdom. For billions of years, hunger meant "move or die."

In the modern world, we treat hunger as a medical emergency. If we feel the slightest grumble in our stomach at 10:00 AM, we rush for a snack bar. We are terrified of the sensation of emptiness.

This constant feeding has made us metabolically flexible (we can only burn sugar) and psychologically weak (we cannot function without immediate satiety).

The Ghrelin Wave Hunger is not a linear sensation that gets worse until you starve. Hunger comes in **waves** driven by the hormone **Ghrelin**. Ghrelin spikes at your habitual meal times. If you usually eat at 8:00 AM, Ghrelin will spike at 7:55 AM. If you ignore it, *levels will drop naturally* within 60 minutes.

Most people never ride the wave. They crash into it.

The Protocol: The 16-Hour Fast We are not fasting for weight loss; we are fasting for **Grit**.

1. **The Window:** Stop eating at 8:00 PM. Do not eat again until 12:00 PM the next day.

2. **The Friction:** Around 9:00 AM, you will feel the urge. Your brain will say, *"I can't focus,"* or *"I'm getting a headache."* (Note: If you are hydrated and salted as per Chapter 1, you are not physically compromised; you are just uncomfortable).

3. **The Reframing:** When the hunger pang hits, visualize it as **"The Burn."** Just like the burn in a bicep curl signals muscle growth, the gnawing in your stomach signals willpower growth. You are teaching your brain that it can survive—and thrive—in a state of deprivation.

By the time you break your fast at noon, you will have completed four hours of deep work while your animal brain was screaming for food. That is elite training.

We have discussed physical and metabolic discomfort. Now we must address the most pervasive weakness of the modern mind: **The inability to endure boredom.**

We have become "Dopamine Junkies." If we have to wait in an elevator for 15 seconds, we pull out our phones. If we are driving, we need a podcast. If we are eating, we need Netflix. We have lost the ability to simply *be* with our own thoughts.

This intolerance for boredom is fatal to "Deep Work." Deep work is often boring. It is difficult. It is slow. If your brain is trained to expect constant entertainment, it will rebel the moment the work gets hard.

The Protocol: The "Wall Stare" This exercise sounds ridiculous, but it is excruciatingly difficult for the modern brain.

1. **Set a Timer:** 15 minutes.
2. **The Environment:** Sit in a chair facing a blank wall. No phone, no music, no notebook, no meditation mantra.
3. **The Task:** Do nothing. Keep your eyes open. Sit there.
4. **The Agitation:** Within 3 minutes, your brain will start to itch. You will remember an email you need to send. You will feel an urge to scratch your nose. You will wonder if the timer is broken.

This agitation is **Dopamine Withdrawal**. Your brain is throwing a tantrum because it is not being fed stimuli.

Sit through the tantrum.

By forcing yourself to endure 15 minutes of "high-friction boredom," you are lowering your dopamine threshold. You are resetting your brain's sensitivity. When you finish this session and turn to your work, the work will seem stimulating by comparison. You are training your "Patience Muscle."

Protocol 4: Physical Exertion and the "Central Governor"

Endurance sports are the crucible of mental toughness.

When you are running, rowing, or rucking, and you feel like you "can't go another step," you are almost always lying to yourself.

Physiologists have developed the **Central Governor Theory**. It states that the brain induces the sensation of fatigue *long before* the muscle is actually depleted. It is a safety buffer. Your brain shuts you down at 40% capacity to ensure you save energy for a hypothetical lion attack.

Most people stop when the Governor whispers. The elite stop only when the muscle fails.

The Protocol: The "One More" Rep You do not need to run a marathon to train this. You can do it in the gym or on the living room floor.

1. **The Failure Point:** Pick an exercise (Pushups, Plank, Wall Sit). Go until you physically want to stop. That is your "Governor's Line."

2. **The Buffer Zone:** Once you hit that line, your goal is to stay there for **10 more seconds** or do **2 more reps**.

3. **The Dissociation:** During those final seconds, the pain will be loud. Do not fight it. Observe it.

    o   *Amateur Strategy:* "This hurts, I need to stop."

    o   *Pro Strategy:* "This is just a sensation of heat and tension. It is data. It is not damage."

Every time you push past the Governor's first warning, you move the line. You are recalibrating your brain's definition of "impossible."

The "Suck" Bucket: Micro-Dosing Misery

You cannot do all of these every day. That leads to burnout. Instead, you need to gamify your discomfort.

Imagine a bucket labeled **"The Suck."** Your goal is to put one drop in the bucket every single day.

- **Monday:** Cold Shower (Thermal).
- **Tuesday:** Skip Breakfast (Metabolic).
- **Wednesday:** No Music during workout (Cognitive/Boredom).
- **Thursday:** Maximum duration Plank (Physical).
- **Friday:** Walk in the rain without an umbrella (Environmental).

This is **"Opportunistic Toughness."** When it starts raining, most people run for cover. You should walk. When the elevator is broken, most people complain. You should take the stairs.

When you view these inconveniences as "Reps for your Willpower," you stop being a victim of your environment and start using the environment as your gym.

The Danger Zone: Managing the Recovery Debt

A warning is necessary here.

In our enthusiasm to build grit, it is easy to cross the line into masochism or injury. Remember the principle of Hormesis: the dose makes the poison.

If you combine sleep deprivation (from Chapter 1 failure) with a 24-hour fast and a 10-mile run in the cold, you are not building grit. You are building a cortisol spike that will crash your immune system.

The "Stress Budget" Rule: You have one bucket of energy for *all* stressors—work stress, relationship stress, gym stress, and discomfort training.

- If work stress is 10/10, your discomfort training should be 2/10 (Maintenance).
- If life is calm and work is steady, crank your discomfort training to 8/10 (Growth).

Do not add artificial stress when life is already crushing you. That is not discipline; that is stupidity. Use Intentional Discomfort to simulate stress during peace times, so you are ready for war times.

The Identity Shift: From Comfort-Seeker to Friction-Seeker

The ultimate goal of Chapter 2 is not to make you a person who enjoys cold showers. The goal is to shift your identity.

Most people approach life asking: *"What is the easiest way to do this?"* You are learning to ask: *"Where is the resistance?"*

When you practice intentional discomfort, you start to develop a strange relationship with difficulty. You stop fearing it. You realize that the "Flinch" is a compass.

If you are afraid to make a sales call, that fear is a signal: **Do it.** If you are dreading a difficult conversation, that dread is a signal: **Do it.** If you are hesitating to jump into the cold water, that hesitation is a signal: **Jump.**

You begin to trust that the friction is not a wall, but a door. The things that scare you, the things that are uncomfortable, the things that are hard—these are the only things that contain the nutrients your aMCC needs to grow.

The "Cookie Jar" Concept

David Goggins, the ultra-endurance athlete, speaks of the **"Cookie Jar."**

Every time you survive a cold shower, every time you fast through the hunger, every time you hold the plank for 10 extra seconds, you are putting a "Cookie" in the jar.

Six months from now, when you are in a genuine crisis—when your business is failing, or you lose a loved one, or you are physically exhausted—you reach into the jar. You remind yourself: *"I am the person who stands in the freezing cold. I am the person who stares at the wall. I am the person who doesn't quit when it hurts. I can handle this."*

You are building a reservoir of self-respect.

Comfort cannot give you self-respect. Comfort can only give you pleasure. Self-respect is earned only through the overcome of resistance.

Summary: The Calloused Mind

We have now fueled the brain (Chapter 1) and we have hardened the mind (Chapter 2). You are no longer chemically fragile or psychologically soft.

But there is a trap waiting for you.

You can have the strongest will in the world, but if you have to use it *all day long* to fight off thousands of tiny temptations, you will eventually lose. Even the strongest muscle fails if it is under constant tension.

We need a strategy to protect this newfound strength. We need to learn how to fight temptation without actually fighting.

Chapter 2 Checklist

1. **The Thermal Audit:** Tomorrow morning, take the cold shower. 30 seconds. No negotiation.
2. **The Hunger Test:** Pick one day this week to delay your first meal by 4 hours. Observe the Ghrelin wave.

3. **The Boring 15:** Schedule 15 minutes of "Wall Staring" to reset your dopamine baseline.

4. **The Identity Mantra:** When you feel discomfort, tell yourself: *"This is just weakness leaving the body."*

CHAPTER 3

USE IMPLEMENTATION INTENTIONS TO FIGHT TEMPTATION

Homeostasis

You have fueled the engine of your biology in Chapter 1. You have calloused the "grind muscle" of your mind through intentional discomfort in Chapter 2. By now, you possess more raw willpower than 95% of the population. You are capable of enduring the cold, the hunger, and the grind.

But here is the sobering reality: **Willpower, no matter how hardened, is a finite resource.**

If you rely on raw "white-knuckle" discipline to get through every hour of your day, you are essentially engaging in a war of attrition with your own environment. Every time you walk past a vending machine and say "no," you spend a unit of mental energy. Every time you feel the vibration of a notification and choose not to look, you spend a unit. Every time you have to decide whether or not to go to the gym, you spend a unit.

Eventually, the bucket runs dry. This is when the elite fall. They don't fall because they are "weak"; they fall because they were inefficient. They spent their mental gold on trivial skirmishes, leaving them bankrupt when the real battle arrived.

In Chapter 3, we move from **Brute Force** to **Strategic Automation**. We are going to introduce the most scientifically validated tool in the history of behavioral psychology: **Implementation Intentions**.

You are about to learn how to pre-program your brain with "If-Then" scripts that bypass the need for willpower entirely. We are moving the decision from the *moment of temptation* (where you are weak) to the *moment of planning* (where you are strong).

The "If-Then" Logic: Outsourcing Your Discipline

The concept of Implementation Intentions was pioneered by psychologist Peter Gollwitzer in the late 1990s. His research focused on a simple but profound gap: the **Intention-Behavior Gap**.

We all have "Goal Intentions."

- *"I intend to lose weight."*
- *"I intend to be more productive."*
- *"I intend to stay calm during meetings."*

Goal Intentions are weak because they are abstract. They reside in the high-level, slow-processing areas of the Prefrontal Cortex. When a temptation hits—like a warm plate of cookies or a snarky comment from a colleague—the Limbic System reacts in milliseconds. By the time your "Goal Intention" wakes up and tries to argue, the cookie is already in your mouth.

Implementation Intentions change the architecture of the choice. They take the form of a simple algorithm:

"IF [Situation X] occurs, THEN I will perform [Behavior Y]."

By linkng a specific situational cue to a specific response, you are effectively "pre-deciding." When Situation X happens, the brain doesn't ask, *"Should I do this?"* It simply executes the script. You have moved the behavior from the effortful System 2 (Decision Making) to the effortless System 1 (Automatic Response).

The Neuroscience of the "Neural Tripwire"

Why does this simple linguistic shift work so well? It comes down to **Perceptual Readiness**.

When you form an Implementation Intention, you are sensitizing your brain to a specific cue. You are creating a "Neural Tripwire." The brain begins to scan the environment for the "If" condition.

For example, if your plan is: *"If the waiter asks if I want dessert, then I will immediately order a peppermint tea,"* your brain is now on high alert for the specific phrase "would you like dessert?" The moment those words are uttered, the brain's "If" detector fires, and the "Then" response is triggered with almost no conscious effort.

In fMRI studies, participants using Implementation Intentions show significantly less activity in the Prefrontal Cortex during the execution of a task than those relying on willpower. This means they are getting the same result while **conserving mental energy**.

This is the secret of the "Natural" high-performer. They aren't constantly fighting themselves; they are simply running highly efficient, pre-programmed scripts.

The Five Pillars of a Robust Script

Most people fail with "If-Then" plans because they are too vague. A weak script is just a Goal Intention in disguise. To be effective, your Implementation Intention must follow the **V.I.S.O.R.** framework:

1. V - Visualizable (The Cue) The "If" must be a concrete, unmistakable sensory event.

- *Weak:* "If I feel stressed..." (Stress is internal and blurry).
- *Strong:* "If I feel my heart rate increase and my palms get sweaty..." (These are physical, undeniable cues).

2. I - Immediate (The Timing) The "Then" must follow the "If" without a gap. The goal is to create a seamless chain. If there is a delay, the Limbic System will fill the gap with a rationalization.

3. S - Specific (The Action) You must know exactly what you are going to do.

- *Weak*: "...then I will do something healthy."
- *Strong*: "...then I will drink 16 ounces of cold water."

4. O - Obstacle-Based (The Defensive Script) Implementation Intentions are most powerful when used to navigate "High-Risk Situations." You must identify the specific obstacles that usually derail you and build scripts specifically for them.

5. R - Rehearsed (The Neural Path) A script only becomes automatic through repetition. You must mentally rehearse the "If-Then" sequence until the visualization feels as real as the memory.

Advanced Strategy 1: The "If-Then" Shield for Social Pressure

Social pressure is the "Willpower Killer." Even the most disciplined individuals often fold when they are in a group. This is due to our evolutionary need for social belonging; the brain perceives social rejection as a survival threat.

When a friend says, *"Come on, just have one drink,"* or *"Stay out for one more hour,"* your brain undergoes a "Social Amygdala Hijack." You don't want to be the "boring" one.

The Scripting Solution: You must pre-program your social "No."

- **"If** someone offers me a second drink, **then** I will say, 'No thanks, I've got a big morning tomorrow,' and immediately ask them a question about their work."

Notice the second part of the "Then." You aren't just saying no; you are **redirecting the energy**. By asking a question, you shift the spotlight away from your refusal and back onto the other person. This lowers the social tension and protects your "mask" while maintaining your discipline.

Advanced Strategy 2: Managing the "What-The-Hell Effect"

One of the most dangerous psychological patterns is the **"What-The-Hell Effect"** (formally known as Counter-Regulatory Eating/Behavior).

This happens when you have a small slip-up—you eat one cookie, or you miss one workout—and your brain says, *"Well, I've already ruined the day, so I might as well eat the whole box/skip the whole week."* This is a binary thinking trap.

You need an Implementation Intention designed specifically for **Recovery**.

- **"If** I miss my morning workout, **then** I will perform 20 air-squats before lunch to keep the identity alive."
- **"If** I eat something off-plan, **then** I will immediately log it in my tracker and drink a glass of water, ending the cycle there."

These are "Damage Control" scripts. They prevent a single mistake from turning into a systemic collapse.

Advanced Strategy 3: The "Focus-Guard" for Deep Work

In Book 2, we talked about environmental design to reduce distractions. But in Book 3, we acknowledge that digital distractions are often internal. You are working, and suddenly, you feel a "twitch" to check the news or social media.

This twitch is a Limbic surge. If you fight it with willpower, you've already lost the "Flow" state.

The Script:

- **"If** I feel the urge to open a new browser tab, **then** I will close my eyes, take two deep breaths, and tell myself 'Not now,' then return to the current task."

This script acknowledges the impulse without judging it, provides a physical "Pattern Interrupter" (the breaths), and gives a clear command. It acts as a "Focus-Guard" that keeps you in the Deep Work zone for 40% longer on average, according to productivity studies.

Mental Contrasting: The WOOP Method

Implementation Intentions are powerful, but they are even more effective when combined with a technique called **Mental Contrasting**.

Developed by Dr. Gabriele Oettingen, this is the **WOOP** process:

1. **W - Wish:** What is the goal? (e.g., "I want to finish this report by 5 PM").
2. **O - Outcome:** What is the best possible result? (e.g., "I feel accomplished and can enjoy my evening").

3. **O - Obstacle:** What is the *internal* obstacle that will stop you? (e.g., "The fear that the report isn't good enough, leading to procrastination").

4. **P - Plan:** This is your Implementation Intention. ("**If** I feel the urge to procrastinate due to perfectionism, **then** I will tell myself 'B-minus work is the goal for now' and type for 5 minutes straight.")

Most people only do the first two steps (Wish and Outcome). This is "Positive Fantasizing," which actually **reduces** willpower because the brain feels like it has already achieved the goal. By focusing on the **Obstacle**, you create the "Cognitive Tension" necessary to trigger the Plan.

The "Identity Anchor" Script

The ultimate use of Implementation Intentions is to reinforce the **Identity Shifts** we discussed in Book 2. Your scripts should not just be about "doing" things; they should be about "being" the person you want to become.

- "**If** I see a flight of stairs, **then** I will take them, because I am an athlete."

- "**If** I am about to speak to a stranger, **then** I will make eye contact and smile, because I am a leader."

These scripts turn every mundane moment of your day into a "Vote" for your new identity. You are no longer "deciding" to be disciplined; you are simply acting in accordance with the laws of your nature.

The "Urge Surfing" Technique

Sometimes, a temptation is so strong that a simple "If-Then" script feels insufficient. This often happens with addictions or deeply ingrained habits (smoking, sugar, social media).

In these moments, we use the **"If-Then" for Urge Surfing.** The "Urge" is like a wave in the ocean. It starts small, builds to a peak of intensity, and then—invariably—it breaks and recedes. Most people try to build a wall against the wave (willpower), and the wave eventually knocks them over.

The Script:

- **"If** I feel a 10/10 urge to [temptation], **then** I will set a timer for 10 minutes and 'Surf the Urge.'"

During those 10 minutes, you don't fight the feeling. You observe it. You look at it with clinical curiosity. *"Where do I feel this urge? Is it in my chest? My throat? How intense is it right now?"* By the time the timer goes off, the neurochemical spike has almost always subsided. You didn't "beat" the temptation; you outlasted it.

The Maintenance Audit: When Scripts Decay

Just like physical habits (Book 2), Implementation Intentions can suffer from "Semantic Satiation"—where the words lose their meaning through over-repetition, and the brain stops responding.

Every Sunday, you must perform a **Script Audit**:

1. **Which scripts worked this week?** (Keep these).
2. **Which scripts did I ignore?** (These were either too vague or the "If" was too hard to detect. Re-write them).
3. **What new obstacles appeared this week?** (Write a new script for these).

You are a programmer, and your brain is the hardware. You must constantly update your code to handle the new "bugs" that life introduces.

The Paradox of Choice and the Rule of Three

A final warning: Do not try to script your entire life at once.

If you have 50 different "If-Then" plans, you will suffer from "Script Overload." Your brain won't be able to remember which "Then" goes with which "If."

Start with the **Rule of Three**. Identify the three most persistent temptations or obstacles in your current life.

1. The one that ruins your **Morning**.
2. The one that ruins your **Work**.
3. The one that ruins your **Evening**.

Master these three. Once they are truly automated—once the "Then" happens without you even thinking about it—only then can you move on to the next set of scripts.

Summary: The Architect of the Automatic

In Chapter 1, you learned that you are a biological machine. In Chapter 2, you learned that the machine can be hardened. In Chapter 3, you have learned that the machine can be **Programmed**.

Willpower is the battery, but Implementation Intentions are the circuitry. By pre-deciding your responses to the world, you preserve your "Mental Gold" for the things that truly matter: creativity, connection, and high-level strategy.

You are no longer a victim of temptation. You are the architect of your own reactions.

Chapter 3 Checklist

1. **Identify Your "Big Three":** What are the three obstacles that cost you the most willpower each day?

2. **Write Your V.I.S.O.R. Scripts:** Craft one "If-Then" plan for each of those obstacles.

3. **The Social Pre-Load:** Write one script for a social situation you have coming up this week.

4. **Mental Rehearsal:** Spend 5 minutes tonight visualizing yourself encountering the "If" and immediately executing the "Then."

CHAPTER 4

REDUCE DECISION FATIGUE THROUGH DAILY SYSTEMS

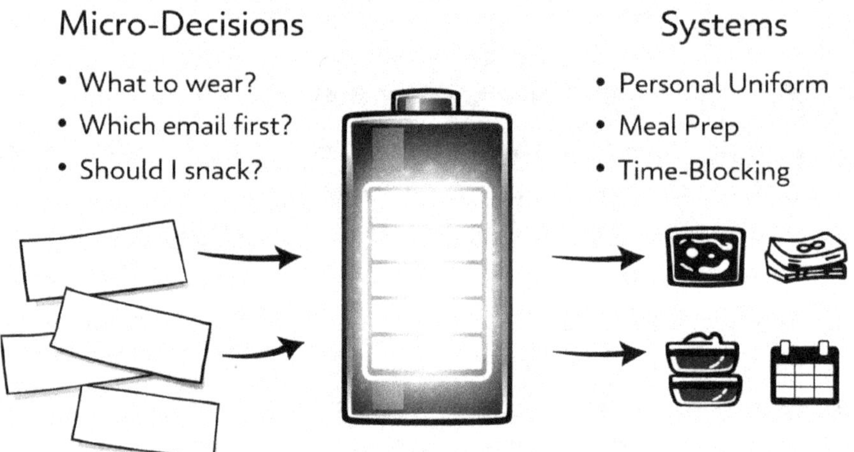

In the previous chapters, we focused on the internal engine. We fueled your biology, calloused your mind against discomfort, and programmed your neural responses with "If-Then" logic. You are now a high-performance vessel. But even the most advanced nuclear submarine will eventually run out of power if it is forced to navigate a sea filled with millions of tiny, unnecessary obstacles.

In Chapter 4, we shift our focus to the **Operational Environment**.

We are going to address the "Silent Killer" of high-performance: **Decision Fatigue**. You may have the strongest Prefrontal Cortex in the world, but if you are using it to decide what brand of toothpaste to buy, what shirt matches your trousers, or which email to answer first, you are committing "Cognitive Malpractice."

By the time you reach your most important work—your "Lead Domino"—you have already spent thousands of units of willpower on trivialities. You are essentially trying to win a marathon while carrying a backpack full of pebbles.

This chapter is about **Systemic Minimalism**. We are going to build a "Choice-Minimal Life" that preserves your mental gold for the 5% of decisions that actually determine your destiny. We will move from the "Mental" to the "Industrial," applying systems engineering to your daily routine.

The Science of the "Willpower Tax"

To understand why systems are mandatory, we must look at the math of the mind. As we discussed in the introduction to Book 3, the average modern human makes approximately **35,000 decisions every single day**.

Each of these decisions, no matter how small, requires a "Withdrawal" from your Prefrontal Cortex. Neuroscientists refer to this as the **Willpower Tax**.

A fascinating study conducted at the University of Minnesota looked at the effects of making choices on subsequent self-control. One group of participants was asked to make a series of choices between consumer products (e.g., "Do you prefer this pen or that candle?"), while the other group simply rated the products without choosing.

Afterward, both groups were given a classic test of self-control: holding their hand in ice-cold water. The group that had made the choices—even though the choices were trivial and fun—quit the cold-water task significantly faster than the group that had not.

The conclusion was undeniable: **Choosing is draining.** It doesn't matter if the choice is "Which stock should I buy?" or "Which socks should I wear?" The metabolic cost is roughly the same. If you start your morning by making 50 small decisions before you even leave the house, you have already "taxed" your brain to the point where your creative output is compromised.

The goal of this chapter is to reduce your 35,000 decisions down to 500. We are going to "Auto-Pay" your Willpower Tax so you never have to think about it again.

The Architecture of the "Default"

In systems theory, there is a concept called **The Power of the Default.**

Human beings are "Cognitive Misers." We almost always choose the path of least resistance. If a computer comes with a pre-set background, 90% of people never change it. If an organ donation program is "Opt-Out" (meaning you are a donor by default unless you check a box), the participation rate is nearly 100%. If it is "Opt-In," the rate drops to 15%.

High-performers do not rely on choices; they rely on Defaults.

They don't "choose" to exercise; it is their morning default. They don't "choose" what to eat for lunch; they have a default meal. They don't "choose" their priorities; they have a default system for ranking tasks.

We are going to apply this "Default Logic" to four key areas of your life: **The Wardrobe, The Kitchen, The Inbox, and The Schedule.**

Protocol 1: The Uniform (The Zuckerberg Strategy)

One of the most visible examples of decision fatigue reduction is the "Personal Uniform." Steve Jobs wore the black turtleneck and jeans. Mark Zuckerberg wears the grey t-shirt. Barack Obama wore only blue or grey suits.

When asked why, Obama said: *"I'm trying to pare down decisions. I don't want to make decisions about what I'm eating or wearing. Because I have too many other decisions to make."*

Every morning, you have a finite amount of "Creative Bandwidth." Using that bandwidth to coordinate colors is a waste of your genius.

The System: The Modular Wardrobe

1. **Standardization:** Choose a "base color" (e.g., black, navy, or charcoal).

2. **Compatibility:** Ensure that every shirt you own works with every pair of trousers you own.

3. **The "Pre-Flight" Layout:** Never decide what to wear *in* the morning. The "Night-Before Rule" is law. By laying your clothes out the night before, you move the decision to a time when your

"Governor" is already winding down, preserving your morning "Peak" for deep work.

Protocol 2: The Nutritional Algorithm

Food is perhaps the single greatest source of decision fatigue. We think about food, we crave food, we choose food, and we negotiate with food hundreds of times a day.

- *"Should I have eggs or cereal?"*
- *"Should I go to the deli or the salad bar?"*
- *"I've been good today, maybe I deserve a treat?"*

This internal negotiation is a massive drain on your Prefrontal Cortex.

The System: The "Same-Same" Breakfast and Lunch To eliminate food fatigue, you must adopt the **Rule of Consistency**.

1. **Automated Breakfast:** Choose one high-protein, brain-fueling breakfast (as discussed in Chapter 1) and eat it every single morning for 30 days. No variation. No choice.
2. **The "Power Lunch" Template:** Create a "Template" for your workday lunch. (e.g., "Protein + Green + Healthy Fat").
3. **The "Menu-Free" Kitchen:** Use a rotating 7-day meal plan for dinners. Tuesday is Taco night. Wednesday is Salmon night.

By removing the "What's for dinner?" question, you eliminate the 5:00 PM willpower collapse that leads to fast-food binges. You aren't "dieting"; you are **Systematizing.**

Protocol 3: The Inbox Zero Fallacy vs. The Batching Reality

In the digital age, the "Inbox" is a casino. Every time you open your email or Slack, you are pulling the lever of a slot machine. You don't know if you'll find a rewarding compliment, a stressful crisis, or a mountain of junk.

The constant checking of notifications is a form of **Reactive Decision Making.** Each time a message pops up, you have to decide: *Do I answer this? Do I delete it? Do I archive it?*

This "Micro-Decision" cycle creates a state of **Continuous Partial Attention**, which is the enemy of the Hardened Mind.

The System: The Batching Protocol

1. **The "Twice-Daily" Rule:** Disable all notifications. Check your email only at 11:00 AM (after your morning Peak) and 4:00 PM.

2. **The "Two-Minute" Filter:** If an email requires a decision that takes less than two minutes, do it immediately. If not, it moves to a "Task List."

3. **The "Communication Vacuum":** Never check your phone in the first hour of the day. This is the hour where your "Executive Governor" is most powerful. Do not hand the keys of your brain to other people's priorities before you have set your own.

Protocol 4: The Time-Blocked Architecture

The most common cause of decision fatigue is the "Blank Calendar." When you wake up with a list of tasks but no specific time to do them, you have to "choose" what to do next every time you finish a task.

This "What's next?" moment is a friction point where procrastination thrives.

The System: Time-Blocking Instead of a "To-Do List," use a **"To-Do Schedule."** 1. **Fixed Appointments with Yourself:** Block out 9:00 AM to 11:00 AM for your "Lead Domino." During this time, the decision has already been made. You are not "deciding" to work; you are executing a scheduled event. 2. **The Buffer Block:** Schedule a 30-minute "Chaos Block" in the afternoon to handle the unexpected decisions that life inevitably throws at you. 3. **Shutdown Ritual:** End your day by creating the schedule for the *next* day.

The "One-Space-One-Use" Rule (Contextual Priming)

We discussed "Contextual Contamination" in Book 2, but in Book 3, we look at it through the lens of **Cognitive Load.**

If you use your bed for sleeping, watching TV, eating, and answering emails, your brain has to "decide" which mode to be in every time you lie down. This creates a state of **Neural Conflict.**

The System: Environmental Specialization

1. **The Deep Work Sanctuary:** Have one specific chair or desk where you *only* do high-level work. No social media. No snacks.

2. **The Rest Zone:** The bedroom is for sleep and intimacy. No screens.

3. **The Transition Trigger:** Use a specific "Cue" (like a specific lamp or a certain playlist) that signals to your brain: "The decision-making phase is over; the execution phase has begun."

By specializing your environment, you use **Associative Memory** to automate your mental state, saving your willpower for the work itself.

The "Rule of Three" (Reducing Priority Fatigue)

Most people fail because they try to prioritize 20 things. Priority, by definition, is singular. When you have multiple "Top Priorities," you are forcing your brain into a state of **Analysis Paralysis**.

The System: The Rule of Three

1. Each night, identify the **Three Outcomes** that would make the next day a success.

2. Rank them 1, 2, and 3.

3. You are not allowed to think about #2 until #1 is complete.

This eliminates the "Which one should I work on?" fatigue. You have a linear path. You have removed the "Choice" and replaced it with a **Sequence**.

Automation: The Willpower Lever

In the 21st century, we have tools that the Stoics could only dream of. Every task you "outsource" to an algorithm is a gift to your future self.

The System: Digital Delegation

1. **Bill Pay:** Auto-pay every recurring expense.

2. **Subscriptions:** Use "Subscribe & Save" for household staples (toilet paper, soap, vitamins).

3. **The "Second Brain":** Use a digital tool (like Notion, Evernote, or a physical notebook) to store all information. Do not use your brain for storage; use it for **Processing**.

When you know that your bills are paid and your pantry is stocked, you remove a layer of "Background Anxiety" that slowly siphons off your mental energy.

We must address a psychological trap: **The Maximizer vs. The Satisficer.**

- **The Maximizer** tries to make the "Optimal" choice. They spend hours researching the best laptop, the best flight, or the best protein powder.

- **The Satisficer** looks for a "Good Enough" choice that meets their criteria. Once they find it, they stop looking and commit.

Research by Barry Schwartz (*The Paradox of Choice*) shows that Maximizers are consistently more stressed, more prone to regret, and suffer from significantly higher decision fatigue.

The System: The "Good Enough" Rule For any decision that will not matter in one year (what to eat, what book to read, what brand of towels to buy), give yourself a **60-second timer.** If you can't decide in 60 seconds, pick the first option that meets your basic needs.

You are trading "The Best" for **"The Available Bandwidth."** In the long run, the bandwidth is worth infinitely more than the "perfect" choice of towels.

Dealing with "Decision Leakage"

Even with perfect systems, life will try to drag you back into the chaos. This is **Decision Leakage**—when other people's lack of systems becomes your problem.

- The "Quick Question" from a colleague.

- The "Emergency" text from a family member.

- The "Urgent" request for a meeting.

The System: The Firewall

1. **Office Hours:** Tell your team: *"I am unavailable for quick questions between 9 and 11, but I am wide open at 1:00 PM."*

2. **The "No" Default:** If an invitation is not a "Hell Yes," it is a "No." This is the ultimate willpower-saving script.

3. **The Email Delay:** Never answer an email immediately unless it is a true fire. By waiting, you train others that you are not a "Reactive Resource."

The "Shutdown Ritual": Resetting the Battery

The final system in this chapter is the most important for your long-term sanity. To prevent Decision Fatigue from compounding day after day, you must have a clear **Termination Point**.

If you leave your "Work Brain" on all evening, you are constantly making micro-decisions about work while you should be resting. This is why people wake up "tired" even after 8 hours of sleep; their brain never truly stopped processing.

The System: The Shutdown Ritual

1. **The Progress Review:** Check off your "Rule of Three" tasks.

2. **The Brain Dump:** Write down everything you are worried about for tomorrow. Get it out of your biological RAM and onto paper.

3. **The Verbal Cue:** Say out loud: *"Shutdown Complete."* This ritual tells your Prefrontal Cortex that it is officially "Off-Duty." It allows the Glymphatic System (from Chapter 1) to do its work effectively because you have lowered your cortisol levels.

Summary: The Freedom of the System

There is a common misconception that "Systems" and "Defaults" make life boring or robotic. People say, *"I want to be spontaneous!"*

The truth is the exact opposite. **Discipline equals freedom.** By systematizing the mundane—your clothes, your food, your schedule, and your chores—you liberate your mind to be spontaneous where it matters. You aren't wasting your soul on "What should I have for lunch?" You are saving it for "How can I change the world?"

A Hardened Mind is not one that makes *better* trivial decisions; it is one that refuses to make them at all.

Chapter 4 Checklist

1. **Wardrobe Audit:** Set out your clothes tonight. Move toward a modular "Uniform."

2. **Nutritional Default:** Pick your "Standard" breakfast and lunch for the next 7 days.

3. **The Rule of Three:** Before you go to sleep tonight, write down your 3 outcomes for tomorrow.

4. **Batch the Digital:** Turn off your notifications. Set your two check-in times for tomorrow.

CHAPTER 5

APPLY COGNITIVE REFRAMING TO HIGH-STRESS SITUATIONS

You have reached the final tactical frontier of Book 3.

By this point, you have optimized your biological fuel (Chapter 1), calloused your mind through intentional discomfort (Chapter 2), automated your responses with "If-Then" scripts (Chapter 3), and minimized decision fatigue through systems (Chapter 4). You are, by all traditional measures, a master of self-control.

But there is one final test.

It is the moment when the system breaks. It is the high-stakes presentation where the projector fails, the family emergency that interrupts your deep work, the financial crisis that threatens your security, or the physical exhaustion that hits during a critical mission. In these moments, your heart begins to race, your palms sweat, and your "Executive Governor"—your Prefrontal Cortex—threatens to go offline in favor of a "Fight or Flight" response.

This is the "Limbic Hijack." It is the moment when all your training is put to the fire.

Chapter 5 is about **Neuro-Chemical Mastery**. You are going to learn how to keep your cool when the world is burning. We are moving beyond "managing" stress and into **Cognitive Reframing**—the art of literally changing the biological impact of stress on your body by changing the narrative in your mind.

You are about to learn how to transition from a **Threat Appraisal** to a **Challenge Appraisal**, effectively turning cortisol into fuel.

The Biology of the Stress Response

To reframe stress, you must first understand what it actually is. Stress is not an "emotion"; it is an **Autonomic Arousal**.

When your brain perceives a threat—whether it is a literal lion or a figurative "angry email from the boss"—it activates the **Sympathetic Nervous System**. This triggers a cascade of physiological changes designed to help you survive:

1. **The Adrenal Surge:** Your body releases adrenaline and norepinephrine to increase heart rate and blood flow to muscles.

2. **The Cortisol Release:** Your body releases cortisol to mobilize glucose for quick energy.

3. **The Blood Divert:** Blood is diverted away from "non-essential" systems (like digestion and the Prefrontal Cortex) and toward the limbs.

4. **The Cognitive Narrowing:** Your focus narrows. You lose the ability to think creatively or see the big picture. You become hyper-focused on the immediate threat.

In a high-stress situation, your self-control fails because your brain has literally "starved" the Prefrontal Cortex of blood and oxygen to prepare for a physical fight. You become impulsive, reactive, and short-tempered.

The Master's Secret: The physiological signals of "Anxiety" (pounding heart, fast breathing, sweating) are almost identical to the signals of "Excitement" or "Readiness." The only difference is the label your brain attaches to them.

Threat Appraisal vs. Challenge Appraisal

The core of Cognitive Reframing lies in the **Transactional Model of Stress and Coping**, developed by Dr. Richard Lazarus. He discovered that the body's reaction to a stressor depends entirely on two "Appraisals":

1. **Primary Appraisal:** "Is this situation a threat to my well-being?"
2. **Secondary Appraisal:** "Do I have the resources to handle this?"

If you decide the situation is a threat and you lack the resources, you enter a **Threat State**. In this state, your blood vessels constrict (vasoconstriction), your heart efficiency drops, and your brain remains in a state of fear.

However, if you decide the situation is a **Challenge** and you believe you have the resources (even if it will be difficult), you enter a **Challenge State**. In this state, your blood vessels dilate (vasodilation), allowing more oxygen to reach the brain. Your heart pumps more efficiently. You release higher levels of **DHEAS**—a neurosteroid that buffers the negative effects of cortisol and actually helps the brain grow from the experience.

In a Challenge State, you aren't "calm." You are **Aroused**. But because you have reframed the arousal as "Readiness," your Prefrontal Cortex stays online. You maintain your self-control. You maintain your grit.

Protocol 1: The "Arousal Appraisal" Reframe

The next time you feel the physical symptoms of stress—the "butterflies" in your stomach or the pounding in your chest—do not try to "calm down."

Trying to calm down when you are highly aroused is a biological mismatch. It's like trying to slam a car into reverse while going 100 mph. Instead, use the **Arousal Reframe**.

The Script: Tell yourself, out loud if possible: **"My body is getting ready for battle. This heart rate is pumping oxygen to my brain so I can**

think faster. These sweaty palms are helping me grip the situation. I am not anxious; I am prepared."

In a famous Harvard study, participants who were told to "reappraise their arousal as a functional tool" performed significantly better on public speaking and math tests than those who were told to "ignore the stress" or "try to relax." They didn't just feel better; their cardiovascular profile shifted from a Threat State to a Challenge State.

Protocol 2: Tactical Breathing (The Parasympathetic Reset)

While the mental reframe is powerful, sometimes the physical "engine" is revving too high for logic to take hold. In these moments, we use the only part of the Autonomic Nervous System that we can control consciously: **The Breath**.

Your breathing is a two-way street. Stress makes you breathe shallowly and quickly; breathing shallowly and quickly makes you stressed. By hacking the breath, you send a direct signal to the **Vagus Nerve** to activate the **Parasympathetic Nervous System** (the "Rest and Digest" system).

The "Box Breathing" Technique (Navy SEAL Standard):

1. **Inhale** through the nose for 4 seconds.
2. **Hold** for 4 seconds (keeping the lungs full).
3. **Exhale** through the mouth for 4 seconds (like breathing through a straw).
4. **Hold** for 4 seconds (keeping the lungs empty).

The "Hold" phases are the most important. They increase the concentration of carbon dioxide in the blood, which triggers the "Vagal Tone" and slows the heart rate. This provides a "Micro-Reset" for your Prefrontal Cortex, allowing you to re-engage your self-control.

Protocol 3: The "Third-Person" Perspective (Self-Distancing)

When we are in high-stress situations, we are "submerged" in our own emotions. We use "I" language: *I am failing," "I can't handle this," "I am so stressed."* This "First-Person" perspective keeps the Amygdala in the driver's seat.

Psychologist Ethan Kross has shown that **Self-Distancing**—referring to yourself in the third person—creates a "Psychological Buffer." It allows you to look at your situation as if you were a coach or a consultant rather than a victim.

The Technique: Instead of saying, *"I need to get it together,"* say, **"[Your Name], you have been here before. You know exactly what to do. Focus on the next step."**

This simple linguistic shift activates the brain's "social cognition" networks, which are located in the Prefrontal Cortex. By talking to yourself like a friend, you literally force your brain to move out of the "Panic Zone" and back into the "Executive Zone."

Protocol 4: The "Stoic Decatastrophizing" (Premeditatio Malorum)

Stress often comes from the "Fear of the Unknown." We allow our brains to create vague, terrifying fantasies of failure. This vagueness drains willpower because the brain is trying to "defend" against everything at once.

We use the Stoic practice of **Premeditatio Malorum** (The Premeditation of Evils) to turn the "Vague Threat" into a "Specific Problem."

The Exercise:

1. **Define the Worst Case:** What specifically happens if this goes wrong? (e.g., "I lose the client").

2. **Assess the Reality:** Would I survive? (e.g., "Yes, I would still have my health, my family, and my skills").

3. **Develop the Contingency:** "If that happens, what is the first move I will make?"

Once you have a plan for the "Worst Case," the Amygdala stops screaming. You have "tamed" the monster by looking it in the eye. This frees up your mental energy to focus on the **Best Case**.

Protocol 5: Selective Information Diet (The Stress Firewall)

In high-stress seasons, your Prefrontal Cortex is already under heavy load. You cannot afford "Cognitive Leakage."

During a crisis, most people increase their consumption of news, social media, and "checking." They are looking for certainty. But in the digital age, more information usually equals more "Neural Noise" and more stress.

The Firewall Rule: When you are in a "High-Stress Execution" phase (e.g., a launch, a deadline, a personal crisis), implement a **Total Information Blackout** on anything that does not directly contribute to the solution.

- No news.
- No social media.
- No "opinion" checking.

Protect your "Mental Bandwidth" with the same ferocity you protect your bank account. You need every milligram of glucose for the task at hand.

Protocol 6: The "Process vs. Outcome" Pivot

Stress is almost always focused on the **Outcome**—a future event that you do not fully control. Willpower thrives on the **Process**—the immediate action that you *do* control.

When you feel overwhelmed, your brain is "time-traveling" to a future failure. You must pull it back to the present moment.

The "Shrink the Horizon" Technique: In Special Forces "Hell Week," candidates don't think about Friday. They don't even think about lunchtime. They think about **"The next 200 yards."** If you are in a high-stress work situation, do not think about the final result. Ask yourself: **"What is the single most important action I can take in the next 15 minutes?"** By shrinking the time horizon, you make the task "Moneageable" for your Prefrontal Cortex. Every small 15-minute win releases a hit of dopamine, which acts as an antagonist to cortisol and restores your sense of agency.

Reframing Fatigue: The "Second Wind"

In Chapter 2, we talked about the Central Governor—the brain's tendency to shut you down when you still have 60% left in the tank. In high-stress situations, this "Fatigue Signal" hits early and hard.

The Reframe: When you feel the overwhelming urge to quit or "zone out" during a stress event, reframe that fatigue as **"The Gateway."** Tell yourself: *"This feeling of exhaustion is just the Central Governor trying to protect me. This is the moment where the real training begins. If I push through this 'Wall,' I will find the 'Second Wind.'"*

The "Second Wind" is a real physiological event. It occurs when the body switches from burning glycogen to burning fat/ketones, and the brain releases endorphins to mask the pain. But you can only reach the "Second Wind" if you refuse to accept the "First Fatigue."

The "Post-Traumatic Growth" Mindset

Finally, we must reframe the **Aftermath** of stress.

Most people view stress as "Damage." They think, *"This is taking years off my life."* This "Stress is Debilitating" mindset is a self-fulfilling prophecy. Studies by Dr. Alia Crum show that people who believe stress is harmful suffer more cardiovascular damage than those who believe **"Stress is Enhancing."**

The Reframe: Every high-stress situation you survive is a **"Neural Stress Test."** You are not being "damaged"; you are being **"Tempered."** Like steel being plunged into ice water, the intensity of the moment is what gives you your edge.

After the stress event is over, do not just "recover." Perform an **After-Action Review (AAR):**

1. **What did I learn about my "Flinch" point?**
2. **How did my reframing scripts work?**
3. **How am I stronger now than I was yesterday?**

By finding the "Gain" in the "Pain," you ensure that your willpower muscle grows proportionally to the stress you endured.

Summary: The Invincible Fortress

The Hardened Mind is not one that avoids stress. It is one that **Transmutes** it.

You now have the tools to:

1. Change your **Biology** through breathing.
2. Change your **Narrative** through Arousal Reappraisal.
3. Change your **Perspective** through Self-Distancing.

4. Change your **Focus** through Process-Pivoting.

You are no longer a victim of your Autonomic Nervous System. You are the Commander. When the pressure rises, you don't rise to the occasion; you sink to the level of your training. And your training is now elite.

Chapter 5 Checklist

1. **Identify Your Stress Cues:** What are your "Physical Early Warning Signs"? (Fast heart, tight jaw, etc.)

2. **Practice the Arousal Reframe:** Next time you feel "anxious," say: *"I am excited and ready for battle."*

3. **Box Breathing Drill:** Practice 4 rounds of box breathing tonight before bed to "prime" the Vagal response.

4. **The Third-Person Audit:** During your next difficult task, talk to yourself using your own name.

CONCLUSION

LIVE WITH DISCIPLINE AS A DEFAULT

You have navigated the rigorous terrain of **Book 3: Grow Willpower and Self-Control**. By now, the tactical components should be familiar to you: the biological fueling of the Prefrontal Cortex, the hardening of the Anterior Mid-Cingulate Cortex through intentional discomfort, the algorithmic precision of Implementation Intentions, the industrial efficiency of systemic minimalism, and the psychological alchemy of cognitive reframing.

However, as we stand at the threshold of the final chapter, we must confront the ultimate objective. This book was not merely a collection of "productivity hacks" or a manual for "trying harder." It was an architectural blueprint for a fundamental shift in your existence. The goal is to move beyond the exhausting cycle of "exerting" willpower and into a state where your highest potential is your automatic setting.

We are here to master the art of living with **Discipline as a Default.**

In the world of software engineering, a "default" is the pre-selected option adopted by a computer program when no alternative is specified by the user. If you do not consciously choose a font, the program chooses one for you. If you do not set a notification sound, the system plays the standard one.

Most people live their lives with "Default Settings" that were programmed by their ancestors (survival instincts), their environment (consumer culture), or their weaknesses (instant gratification). Their default is to hit snooze. Their default is to avoid the cold. Their default is to react with anger under stress.

To live with the **Hardened Mind**, you must perform a hostile takeover of your own operating system. You must overwrite those lazy, primal defaults with high-performance protocols.

When discipline becomes your default, you stop "negotiating" with yourself. Negotiation is the primary leak in the bucket of willpower. The moment you ask, *"Do I really need to go to the gym today?"* or *"Can I just check my phone for a second?"* you have opened a trial in the courtroom of your mind. Even if you "win" the argument and do the right thing, the very act of arguing has consumed a measurable amount of glucose and mental energy.

A person with **Discipline as a Default** has settled the court cases in advance. The verdict is already in. The gym is happening. The phone is off. The task is being attacked. This is the only way to achieve true freedom—by automating the non-negotiables so your conscious mind can focus on creation.

Revisiting the Five Pillars of the Default Architecture

To ensure these systems stick, we must synthesize the lessons of the previous chapters into a singular daily flow. A default lifestyle is built on five structural pillars that reinforce one another.

Pillar 1: Biological Stewardship (The Hardware)

You cannot run a 2026 operating system on 1990s hardware. As we discussed in **Chapter 1**, your Prefrontal Cortex is a metabolic hog. If you allow your blood sugar to crash or your brain to swim in the toxic byproducts of sleep deprivation, your "Default Setting" will automatically revert to your most primitive, impulsive self.

Living with discipline as a default means your "Default Meal" is protein-rich and low-glycemic. Your "Default Night" includes a digital sunset that allows the glymphatic system to sanitize your neural pathways. You treat your brain chemistry with the same reverence a professional athlete treats their hamstrings.

Pillar 2: The aMCC and the "Friction Habit"

In **Chapter 2**, we learned that the **Anterior Mid-Cingulate Cortex** is the physical seat of tenacity. It only grows when we do things we find difficult. Therefore, to make discipline your default, you must make **friction** your default.

Most people spend their lives trying to make things easier. They want the shorter line, the warmer room, the softer chair. By doing so, they are inadvertently "thinning" their aMCC. To maintain a Hardened Mind, you must intentionally choose the "High-Friction Path" multiple times a day.

- Your default is the stairs, not the elevator.
- Your default is the cold finish to the shower.
- Your default is the difficult conversation, not the passive-aggressive text.

When you consistently choose friction, your brain stops perceiving discomfort as a "crisis" and begins to perceive it as "data." You become a person who is comfortable being uncomfortable.

Pillar 3: Algorithmic Automation (The If-Then Scripts)

Willpower fails because it is slow. Temptation is fast. In **Chapter 3**, we used **Implementation Intentions** to close that speed gap.

Living with discipline as a default means you have a library of "If-Then" scripts for every high-risk situation in your life. You have pre-decided that *If* someone offers you a drink you don't want, *Then* you use your pre-written refusal. You have pre-decided that *If* you feel the urge to procrastinate, *Then* you set a five-minute timer.

You are moving the behavior from the "Executive Governor" to the "Basal Ganglia"—the part of the brain responsible for habits and patterns. You are effectively "outsourcing" your discipline to your subconscious.

Pillar 4: Environmental Engineering (The Path of Least Resistance)

As explored in **Chapter 4**, the environment always wins in a war against raw will. If you have to "decide" to be productive while your phone is buzzing next to your hand, you are taxing your brain unnecessarily.

The **Default Lifestyle** uses "Choice Architecture" to make the right thing easy and the wrong thing hard.

- Your default workspace has no distractions.
- Your default kitchen has no processed sugar.
- Your default morning routine is laid out the night before.

You aren't "being disciplined"; you are simply following the path of least resistance that you strategically engineered for yourself.

Pillar 5: Cognitive Transmutation (The Challenge State)

Finally, from **Chapter 5**, we know that stress is inevitable. A default discipline means your **automatic reaction to pressure** is a "Challenge Appraisal."

Instead of the default "I am overwhelmed," your new default is "My body is priming me for a high-stakes event." You use **Tactical Breathing** to stay in the "Hormetic Zone" where stress makes you sharper rather than duller. You have trained your nervous system to stay online when others are shutting down.

The Danger of Moral Licensing: The Silent Saboteur

As you finish this book, you face a psychological trap called **Moral Licensing**.

This occurs when your brain feels it has "earned" a reward for doing something virtuous. Because you spent hours reading and reflecting on discipline, your brain might say, *"I've been so good at learning about willpower, I can afford to be lazy this weekend."*

This is the exact opposite of **Discipline as a Default**. Moral Licensing treats discipline like a bank account—you put "good" in so you can take "bad" out. But in the architecture of the Hardened Mind, discipline is not a currency; it is a **structural integrity**. If you take a brick out of the foundation of a building as a "reward" for the building being so tall, the whole structure eventually collapses.

To stay in the "Default Zone," you must view every act of discipline not as a sacrifice that requires a reward, but as a **vote for your future identity**. Every cold shower is a vote. Every ignored notification is a vote. Every protein-rich meal is a vote. You are not "buying" a donut with your workout; you are building a person who no longer wants the donut.

The 1% Shift and the Power of Compounding

You do not become "Disciplined as a Default" overnight. It is a process of **Neural Compounding**.

If you improve your default settings by just 1% each day, you aren't just 365% better at the end of the year—you are exponentially transformed.

- **Week 1:** You fix the "Wake-up Default." You no longer hit snooze.
- **Month 1:** You fix the "Morning Default." You now take the cold shower and eat the high-protein breakfast without thinking.
- **Month 6:** You have fixed the "Work Default." Deep work is now your standard operating procedure.
- **Year 1:** You look back and realize that your "hardest" days a year ago are now your "easy" days today.

Your "Floor" has been raised. The things that used to require 10/10 willpower now require 2/10. This is the ultimate goal of Book 3: to raise your "Baseline Performance" so high that even your "bad days" are better than most people's "best days."

The "Inner Citadel": Your Final Fortress

The Stoic philosopher Marcus Aurelius wrote about the **Inner Citadel**—a place of absolute self-regulation that nothing external can touch.

When you live with **Discipline as a Default**, you are living from within that citadel.

- If the economy crashes, your default is to find opportunity, not to panic.
- If a relationship ends, your default is to maintain your self-care, not to spiral.

- If you experience a physical injury, your default is to focus on the recovery you *can* control.

You are no longer a "Reactive Organism." You are a **Proactive Architect**. You have moved from being a victim of your biology to being the commander of it.

The Call to Action: The Permanent Protocol

As you close this book, I want you to define your **"Default Day."** Don't write what you *hope* to do. Write what you commit to doing even when you are at your absolute worst—when you are tired, grumpy, and unmotivated.

- What is the "Default Wake-up Time"?
- What is the "Default First Action"?
- What is the "Default Workspace Setting"?
- What is the "Default Response to Stress"?

Once you define these, **hold the line.** Do not negotiate. Do not listen to the "Governor" when he tells you to slow down. Do not accept the "Moral Licensing" bribe.

You have the fuel. You have the grit. You have the scripts. You have the systems. You have the reframes.

The architecture is complete. Now, live within it.

REFLECTION QUESTIONS
TEST YOUR SELF-CONTROL THRESHOLDS

Information is the raw material of change, but **reflection** is the forge. You have spent the last five chapters absorbing the biological, psychological, and systemic protocols of the Hardened Mind. You understand the "why" and the "how." Now, we must address the "where"—as in, where do these principles meet the reality of your specific life?

Self-control is not a global attribute; it is a localized skill. You may have the willpower of a monk when it comes to your morning workout, but the self-control of a toddler when it comes to late-night digital scrolling. To reach the state of **Discipline as a Default**, you must perform a forensic audit of your current thresholds.

The following reflection exercises are designed to be uncomfortable. They are intended to poke at the soft spots in your resolve and expose the rationalizations you use to avoid friction. Treat this chapter as a "Stress Test" for your psyche.

The first pillar of Book 3 was the acknowledgment that you are a biological machine. If the hardware is compromised, the software of "willpower" cannot run. This section forces you to reconcile your daily habits with your executive performance.

1.1 The Glucose-Impulse Correlation

Think back to your last significant "lapse" in self-control. Perhaps you snapped at a colleague, abandoned a difficult project halfway through, or succumbed to a craving you had sworn off.

- **The Question:** What was the state of your blood sugar in the two hours leading up to that lapse? Had you consumed a high-glucose "spike" (sugar/processed carbs) followed by a crash, or had you gone too long without stable fuel?

- **The Deep Dive:** Most people blame their "character" for their failures, but often it is simply a metabolic deficit. How would that situation have played out differently if you had anchored your brain with stable, long-burning fuel (protein/healthy fats) 90 minutes prior?

1.2 The Glymphatic Sanitization Review

The Prefrontal Cortex (PFC) is the first area of the brain to "dim" when toxic metabolic waste accumulates due to poor sleep.

- **The Question:** On a scale of 1 to 10, how much harder do you have to "push" yourself to stay focused on a day following five hours of sleep versus a day following eight hours?

- **The Integration:** If your "default" is to sacrifice sleep for productivity, you are effectively taking out a high-interest loan on your willpower. You get an extra two hours of work tonight at the cost of a 40% reduction in executive function tomorrow. Is that a trade you are willing to continue making?

1.3 Hydration and the "Fog" Threshold

- **The Question:** Can you identify the exact time of day when your "mental fog" sets in? Cross-reference that time with your water intake. Are you using caffeine to "mask" the symptoms of a dehydrated brain?

- **The Challenge:** For the next 48 hours, commit to drinking 16 ounces of water before every coffee or meal. Note the shift in your "threshold" for frustration.

In Chapter 2, we learned about the **Anterior Mid-Cingulate Cortex (aMCC)**. It is the "grind muscle." If you are not choosing the path of most resistance, this muscle is atrophying.

2.1 The "Flinch" Identification

Everyone has a "Flinch Point"—the exact millisecond your brain says, *"No, not today,"* or *"This is too much."*

- **The Question:** Where does the "Flinch" live in your body? Is it a tightening in your chest? A sudden heaviness in your limbs? A specific thought like *"I'll just do it tomorrow"*?

- **The Practice:** Describe the last time you obeyed the Flinch. Now, describe the last time you **overrode** it. What was the physical sensation of the override? That sensation is the feeling of aMCC growth.

2.2 The Comfort Creep Audit

Modern life is designed to eliminate friction. This makes us "physiologically illiterate."

- **The Question:** List three luxuries in your daily life that you have come to view as "necessities" (e.g., the thermostat always at 72°F, hot water, background entertainment while working).

- **The Discomfort Protocol:** Which of these are you willing to "Micro-Dose" with discomfort this week? Will you take a cold finish to your shower? Will you sit in a room that is slightly too cold or too hot without adjusting the air? Will you work in total silence?

2.3 The Central Governor's Wall

- **The Question:** When you are exercising or working on a grueling task, what are the "Early Warning Signals" your brain sends to gct you to stop?

- **The Threshold Test:** The next time you feel you are at "100% capacity," pause and acknowledge the Governor. Remind yourself that you are likely only at 40%. Can you commit to five more minutes or one more set? What does that "extra 5%" feel like in your mind?

Section 3: The Programming and Scripting Audit

Willpower is slow; algorithms are fast. This section tests your ability to outsource your discipline to pre-written "If-Then" scripts.

3.1 The "Willpower Leak" Map

We all have "High-Risk Situations" where our self-control historically fails.

- **The Question:** What are your top three willpower leaks? (e.g., social media at 9:00 PM, the office snack tray, the "one more episode" trap).

- **The Scripting Exercise:** Apply the **V.I.S.O.R.** framework (Visible, Immediate, Specific, Obstacle-based, Rehearsed) to one of these leaks.

    - *If [The Situation Happens], then I will [The Specific Action].*

    - Write it down. Rehearse it mentally five times. Does having a "script" make the temptation feel less powerful?

3.2 The "What-The-Hell" Recovery Test

Most people don't fail because of one mistake; they fail because of the **"What-The-Hell Effect"**—the spiral that follows the mistake.

- **The Question:** After you slip up (miss a workout, eat off-plan), what is the "Secondary Script" you run? Is it a script of shame ("I'm a failure, I might as well give up") or a script of recovery ("I made a mistake, I am resetting now")?

- **The Default Reset:** Draft a "10-Minute Recovery Protocol." *If I slip up, then I will [take 3 breaths/drink water/log the error] and immediately return to the plan.*

The most disciplined people are those who have engineered their lives so that willpower is rarely required.

4.1 The Decision Fatigue Inventory

- **The Question:** How many choices are you making before 10:00 AM that have zero impact on your long-term goals? (e.g., What to wear, what to eat, which route to drive, which news article to click).

- **The Industrialization Plan:** Which of these can you "industrialize" this week? Can you set a uniform? Can you meal-prep? Can you set a "Default Route" and a "No-News" morning rule?

4.2 The Environmental Friction Test

- **The Question:** Look at your workspace. How much "effort" (in seconds) does it take to get distracted? (e.g., If your phone is on the desk, it takes 0.5 seconds). Now, how much effort does it take to do the right thing? (e.g., If your gym bag is in the car, it takes 5 minutes to go get it).

- **The Flip:** How can you add 20 seconds of friction to your bad habits and remove 20 seconds of friction from your good ones?

4.3 The Rule of Three vs. The Infinite List

- **The Question:** Do you end your day feeling "busy but unproductive"? This is often a symptom of "Priority Fatigue."

- **The Audit:** For the next three days, identify your **Lead Domino**—the one task that makes everything else easier. If you only did that one thing, would the day be a success? Why are you allowing other "Shallow Work" to crowd out this one priority?

This is the final test: how you handle the pressure when the systems fail.

5.1 The Arousal Labeling Exercise

- **The Question:** The last time you felt "anxious," what were the physical symptoms? (e.g., racing heart, shallow breath).

- **The Reframe:** If you had labeled those exact same symptoms as "Excitement" or "Readiness," how would your performance have changed?

- **The Drill:** The next time you feel the "Stress Spike," say out loud: *"My body is giving me the energy I need to crush this."* Observe how the "Threat" turns into a "Challenge."

5.2 The Third-Person Distance Test

- **The Question:** When you are self-critical, do you use "I" language? (*"I'm so stupid," "I can't do this"*).

- **The Shift:** Try describing your current struggle in the third person. (*"John is feeling overwhelmed because he has three deadlines. John knows that if he focuses on the first one, he will be fine."*)

- **The Reflection:** Does this "Psychological Buffer" make the problem feel more solvable? Why?

5.3 The "Shrink the Horizon" Strategy

- **The Question:** When you feel like quitting, is it because you are looking at the "Mountain" (the next 6 months) instead of the "Stepping Stone" (the next 15 minutes)?

- **The Practice:** Can you identify a current project that feels overwhelming? What is the "15-Minute Slice" of that project? If you ignore the rest and only commit to those 15 minutes, does your resistance decrease?

Section 6: Integration—Living with Discipline as a Default

To conclude this reflection, we must look at the "Identity Shift."

- **The Final Question:** If you were to live the next 365 days with **Discipline as your Default setting**, who would you become? Describe that person in detail—their energy levels, their bank account, their relationships, and their sense of self-respect.

- **The Commitment:** What is the one "Default Setting" change you are making **today** to ensure that version of you becomes a reality?

BOOK FOUR
STAY FOCUSED IN A WORLD OF DISTRACTION

INTRODUCTION
PROTECT YOUR MOST VALUABLE RESOURCE

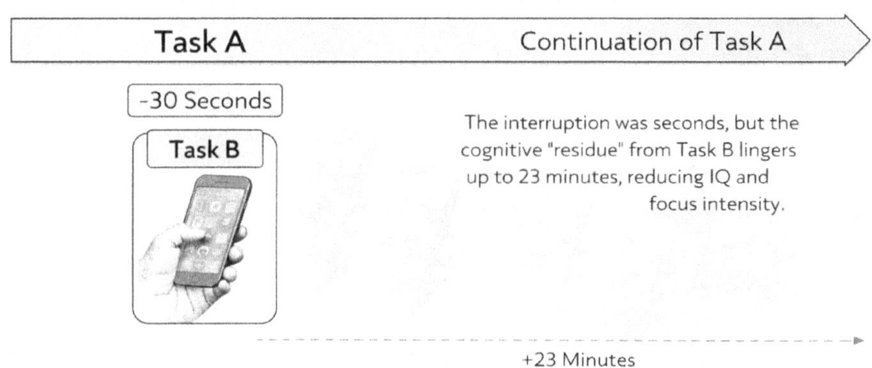

We have spent the previous three books of this series building the "Hardened Mind." We have optimized your biological hardware, installed the software of high-performance habits, and calloused your willpower against the friction of life. But as we enter Book 4, we must confront a cold, modern reality: You can have the strongest engine in the world, but if you cannot keep your hands on the steering wheel, you will never reach your destination.

In the 21st century, **attention is your most valuable resource.** It is more precious than money, more influential than talent, and more finite than time itself. Time is merely the container of your life, but attention is the content. How you allocate your focus determines the quality of your work, the depth of your relationships, and the very structure of your brain.

Yet, we live in an era of "The Attention Economy," where your focus is a commodity to be mined, harvested, and sold to the highest bidder.

You are currently navigating a world designed by the most brilliant engineers and psychologists on the planet, armed with billions of dollars in venture capital, all working toward a single goal: **breaking your concentration.**

This introduction is your call to arms. We are going to define the stakes of the war for your focus and establish why protecting this resource is the ultimate "meta-skill" of the modern age.

The Cognitive Crisis: Why Focus is Failing

To protect a resource, you must first understand why it is under threat. We are currently living through a biological mismatch of epic proportions. Our brains evolved in an environment of **information scarcity**, where a novel stimulus (a rustle in the grass, a new berry bush) usually signified a survival opportunity or threat. Consequently, our brains developed a "Novelty Bias"—a hit of dopamine whenever we encounter something new.

In the ancestral environment, this was an advantage. In the modern environment, this is a vulnerability that has been weaponized against us. Every notification, every "Breaking News" banner, and every infinite scroll is a "Supernormal Stimulus" designed to hijack that primitive dopamine circuit.

The result is a state that researchers call **"Continuous Partial Attention."** We are rarely fully present in one task; instead, we are constantly scanning the horizon for the next hit of digital novelty. This is not just a productivity problem; it is a neurological one. When you train your brain to respond to every ping, you are physically weakening the neural pathways of the Prefrontal Cortex (the seat of focus) and strengthening the pathways of the Limbic System (the seat of impulsivity).

The "Attention Residue" Trap

The most common lie we tell ourselves is: *"I'll just quickly check this one message, then I'll get back to work."* We believe that attention works like a light switch—that we can flip it from one task to another with zero cost.

Neuroscience tells a different story. When you switch from "Task A" (writing a report) to "Task B" (checking a Slack message), your attention does not follow you immediately. A significant portion of your cognitive resources stays stuck on the previous task. This is known as **Attention Residue.**

Even if the interruption lasts only 30 seconds, the "residue" can linger for twenty minutes or more. If you check your phone every ten minutes, you are effectively working with only a fraction of your brain's capacity at any given time. You are operating in a state of **Cognitive Dilution.** You are essentially trying to win a grandmaster chess match while someone is throwing pebbles at your head.

In this book, we are going to learn how to eliminate residue and work with **Singular Intensity.**

The Economic Value of the Deep Mind

Why does this matter? Because the economy is changing in a way that favors the focused. In the industrial age, the primary driver of value was physical labor or adherence to a process. In the information age, the primary driver of value is **Complex Problem Solving and Creative Synthesis.**

As automation and Artificial Intelligence take over routine tasks, the only skills that remain uniquely valuable are those that require **Deep Work.** Deep work is the ability to focus without distraction on a cognitively demanding task. It is the only way to master a difficult craft or produce elite-level results.

Most people are moving in the opposite direction. They are becoming "Human Routers," spending their days processing emails and messages without ever producing anything of lasting value. This creates a massive market opportunity for you. If you can cultivate the ability to focus for three to four hours a day on a single hard problem, you will possess a skill that is becoming increasingly rare at exactly the same time it is becoming increasingly valuable. **Focus is the new IQ.**

The Biology of the "Focus Shield"

In the following chapters, we will build what I call the **Focus Shield.** This is a multi-layered defense system that protects your Prefrontal Cortex from the chaos of the modern world. We will address four distinct layers of your experience:

1. **The Environmental Layer:** Your physical workspace is either an ally or an enemy. We will learn how to "Contextually Prime" your room so that your brain enters a flow state the moment you sit down.

2. **The Systemic Layer:** We will implement "Deep Work Sessions"—structured blocks of time that are defended with the same ferocity as a military perimeter.

3. **The Digital Layer:** We will reclaim your devices. Your smartphone will stop being a master and start being a tool. We will implement protocols for "Digital Boundaries" that force the world to wait on your terms.

4. **The Internal Layer:** We will address the "Monkey Mind." Through mindfulness and attention training, we will learn how to notice a distracting thought and let it pass without being hijacked by it.

The Psychological Price of Distraction

Beyond productivity and economics, there is a profound human cost to a life of distraction. **Attention is the lens through which you experience your life.** If your lens is cracked and scattered, your life will feel chaotic and shallow.

There is a direct correlation between fragmented attention and increased levels of anxiety and stress. When the "Bottom-Up" system of the brain is constantly scanning for pings, your body remains in a state of low-grade "Fight or Flight." Cortisol levels remain elevated. You feel a persistent sense of "hurry sickness," even when there is no actual emergency.

By reclaiming your focus, you are reclaiming your **presence**. You are regaining the ability to have a deep conversation without checking your watch. You are regaining the ability to read a book for an hour without looking for a screen. You are regaining the ability to experience **Flow**—that magical state where the self vanishes, time dilates, and you are fully immersed in the joy of the craft.

The war for your attention is not a fair fight. You are up against algorithms that know your psychology better than you do. But you have something they don't: **The ability to choose.**

In Book 4, we are going to stop being "users" and start being "architects." We are going to stop reacting to the world and start imposing our will upon it. This book is not about "time management." It is about **Cognitive Sovereignty.** It is about taking back the keys to your own mind.

You have built the engine in Books 1, 2, and 3. Now, it's time to point it in a single direction and push the throttle forward.

The Anatomy of Attention: Top-Down vs. Bottom-Up

To protect your focus, you must understand the two ways your brain processes the world. Think of your attention as a high-powered spotlight.

1. Top-Down Attention (The Executive Spotlight): This is controlled by the Prefrontal Cortex. It is voluntary, goal-directed, and conscious. When you decide to read this book, you are using Top-Down attention. It is powerful, but it is metabolically expensive. It burns glucose quickly and is prone to fatigue. This is the system we want to protect.

2. Bottom-Up Attention (The Stimulus Alarm): This is controlled by the sensory cortex and the amygdala. It is involuntary, automatic, and ancient. If a fire alarm goes off or someone shouts your name, your Bottom-Up system takes over. It is designed for survival.

The problem is that the modern digital world is designed to trigger your **Bottom-Up** system constantly. A red notification dot on an app is a "Bottom-Up" trigger. It signals a potential social reward or threat, and your primitive brain cannot ignore it. Every time a "Bottom-Up" trigger pulls your spotlight away, you lose focus.

In Book 4, we are going to learn how to "mute" the Bottom-Up triggers so your Top-Down spotlight can do the work it was meant to do.

We must address the myth of multitasking. As we will explore in Chapter 4, the human brain cannot multitask; it can only **task-switch.** When you believe you are multitasking, you are actually jumping back and forth between tasks with incredible speed. Each jump incurs a **Switch Cost.** Your brain has to "load" the rules and context for the new task while "unloading" the old ones. This process creates a massive amount of "Cognitive Friction."

A study by the University of London found that workers who were constantly distracted by emails and phone calls saw a **10-point drop in their IQ.** That is more than the IQ drop seen after smoking marijuana or losing a full night's sleep. Distraction literally makes you dumber. It prevents you from seeing connections, thinking deeply, and producing original work.

Protecting your focus is not just a way to work faster; it is a way to work **better**. It is the only way to ensure that you are bringing your highest intelligence to the problems that matter most.

Building the Fortress of Focus

As we conclude this introduction, I want you to view your mind as a **sanctuary.** You would not allow a stranger to walk into your home, sit at your dinner table, and start screaming for your attention. Yet, most of us allow digital strangers to do exactly that every single day. We give away our most valuable resource to people who do not have our best interests at heart.

In the chapters to come, we will build the walls of your sanctuary.

- We will start with the **Physical Workspace**, turning your desk into a shrine of concentration.

- We will move to **Deep Work**, learning the ritual of the 90-minute "Sprints."

- We will tackle **Digital Boundaries**, silencing the noise of the world.

- We will master **Single-Tasking**, returning to the power of the "One."

- And we will finish with **Mindfulness**, repairing the damage done by years of distraction.

You have the biology of a high-performer. You have the habits of an achiever. You have the willpower of a leader. Now, it is time to give yourself the gift of **Focus.**

The modern world is a storm of noise. This book is your anchor. Let's begin.

CHAPTER 1

CREATE A DISTRACTION-FREE PHYSICAL WORKSPACE

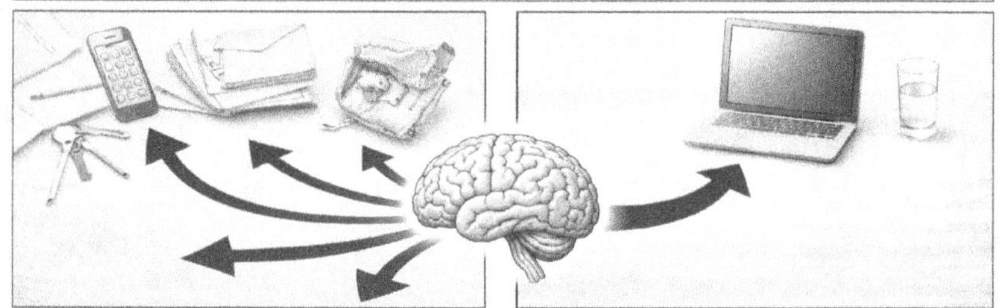

The internal architecture of the Hardened Mind is a masterpiece of biology and willpower, but even the most disciplined mind is subject to the laws of its surroundings. In the previous three books, we treated the brain as an isolated system—optimizing its fuel, its habits, and its grit. But focus is not a localized event that happens exclusively inside your skull. Focus is a **transaction** between your neural circuitry and the physical environment in which it operates.

One of the most common mistakes high-performers make is attempting to use raw, brute-force willpower to overcome a chaotic environment. They sit at a cluttered desk, in a loud room, with a smartphone buzzing within their peripheral vision, and they wonder why they feel "unmotivated" or "mentally fatigued." The truth is that they are not unmotivated; they are **contextually overstimulated.** Your brain is an incredibly sophisticated pattern-recognition engine. It is constantly scanning your physical surroundings for cues on how to behave. If you are in a space where you habitually eat, sleep, or consume passive entertainment, your brain will engage in a constant, invisible struggle to activate the neural circuits required for deep, analytical work. This struggle consumes the very glucose and willpower we worked so hard to preserve in Book 3.

To stay focused in a world of distraction, you must move from being a victim of your surroundings to being the **Architect of your Workspace.** This chapter is about engineering a physical "Sanctuary of Focus" that makes concentration the path of least resistance.

The Science of Environmental Priming

The fundamental principle of this chapter is **Environmental Priming.** This is a psychological phenomenon where exposure to a specific context or stimulus influences your subsequent behavior without your conscious awareness.

When you enter a church, a library, or a high-end surgical suite, your behavior shifts almost instantly. You lower your voice, your posture straightens, or you prepare for extreme cognitive effort. You do not have to "will" yourself to act this way; the environment does the heavy lifting for you. Your goal is to create that same "Sacred Space" effect for your professional and creative output.

Your workspace should send a singular, unmistakable signal to your brain: **"We are here to produce, not consume."**

To achieve this, we must systematically address the three "Environmental Leaks" that drain your focus: **Visual Friction, Auditory Interference**, and **Associative Contamination.**

Phase 1: Eliminating Visual Friction

Your visual field is the primary input for your "Bottom-Up" attention system. Evolutionarily, we are wired to scan for movement and change in our surroundings. In a modern office, this means that if your eyes see a pile of unpaid bills, a messy stack of papers, or even a television remote, your brain automatically begins processing those items.

This creates **Cognitive Load**—the mental effort used in the working memory. Even if you aren't consciously thinking about the mess, your brain is utilizing oxygen and glucose to "ignore" it. This is energy that should be going toward your "Lead Domino" tasks.

1.1 The "Clear Desk" Protocol

Research from Princeton University's Neuroscience Institute found that when multiple visual stimuli compete for your attention, it results in a significant decrease in performance and a measurable increase in cortisol (stress). To fix this, we implement the **Clear Desk Protocol**:

- **The Surface Rule:** At the start of a deep work session, the only items on your desk should be the tools required for that specific task. If you are writing, you need a computer (or paper), a pen, and water. Anything else—even a different book or a stray stapler—is a visual "anchor" pulling you back into shallow thought.

- **The Peripheral Sweep:** Anything within your 180-degree field of vision that triggers a "To-Do" thought must be removed. This includes sticky notes of other tasks, books you aren't currently reading, and especially physical mail. These items represent "unclosed loops" in your mind.

- **The Cable Cleanse:** Tangled, visible wires are perceived by the human brain as "Complexity" and "Chaos." Use cable management sleeves or clips to hide the mess. A clean visual line on your desk facilitates a clean line of logic in your work.

1.2 The "Digital Device" Exile

The single greatest source of visual friction in human history is the smartphone. Even if the phone is turned off and face down, its presence on the desk significantly reduces cognitive capacity. A landmark study titled *"Brain Drain"* from the University of Chicago proved that the mere proximity of a smartphone occupies limited-capacity cognitive resources, leaving less for the task at hand.

The researchers found that participants with their phones in another room significantly outperformed those with phones on their desks—

even though the phones were silent.

The Mandatory Rule: During focus hours, the phone does not live on the desk. It does not live in your pocket. It lives in another room, or at the very least, inside a closed drawer in a different part of the office. If you can see it, you are losing IQ points.

Phase 2: Mastering the Auditory Environment

Sound is the fastest way to trigger the "Bottom-Up" alarm system. Human beings are biologically wired to pay attention to sudden changes in sound and, most critically, to **human speech.** We cannot help but try to decipher the meaning of words we hear, which hijacks the "Phonological Loop" in our working memory.

2.1 The Problem with "Productive" Noise

Many people believe they work better with the TV on or with lyric-heavy music. The science says otherwise. The **Irrelevant Sound Effect** demonstrates that performance on complex tasks is significantly impaired when background speech is present. Your brain's language processing centers are forced to share bandwidth with your analytical centers.

2.2 The Acoustic Shield

To create an auditory sanctuary, you have two primary tools:

1. **Passive Noise Cancellation:** High-quality, over-ear noise-canceling headphones. These act as a physical signal to the world (and your own subconscious) that you are "offline."

2. **Sound Masking:** If you require sound to focus, use "White Noise," "Pink Noise," or "Brown Noise." Unlike music, these are constant frequencies that help drown out erratic background sounds (like a slamming door or a distant siren) without requiring any cognitive processing.

The Rule: For tasks requiring high-level synthesis (writing, coding, strategizing), silence is the gold standard. For repetitive or administrative tasks, use "Functional Music"—no lyrics, steady tempo, minimal melody.

One of the greatest killers of focus in the era of remote work is the "Multipurpose Room." If you work on your couch, your brain associates that physical location with relaxation and entertainment. If you work in bed, your brain associates that space with sleep and intimacy. This is called **Associative Contamination.**

3.1 The "One Space, One Use" Rule

The most successful focused individuals create a **Dedicated Work Anchor.** This is a specific location where *only* deep work happens.

- If you are at this desk, you do not check social media.
- If you are at this desk, you do not eat.
- If you are at this desk, you do not take casual phone calls.

If you find your focus slipping and you feel the irresistible urge to browse the web, **physically stand up and move to a different chair.** By doing this, you keep the "Deep Work" space chemically and psychologically "pure." Over time, the mere act of sitting in that specific chair will act as a neurological trigger, instantly lowering your resistance to concentration.

3.2 The Ritual of the "Workspace Shutdown"

Just as we learned in Book 3 about the "Shutdown Ritual" for willpower, you need a physical ritual to close the "Focus Loop." At the end of your work day, clear your desk back to the "Clear Desk Protocol" state.

1. **Closing the Day:** It signals to your brain that the "Output" phase is over, allowing your Prefrontal Cortex to enter recovery mode.

2. **Priming Tomorrow:** It ensures that tomorrow morning, your environment is already "Primed" for focus. You remove the friction of having to clean before you can work.

Phase 4: Ergonomics and Biology as Focus Anchors

Finally, we must address the physical comfort of the body. Focus is a delicate state; pain or discomfort are "Alarm" signals that will always take priority over deep work. If your neck is straining or your lower back is aching, your brain will divert attention away from your work to process those somatic signals.

- **The Eye-Level Rule:** Your screen should be positioned so that your eyes hit the top third of the monitor. Looking down for hours creates "Tech Neck," which reduces blood flow to the brain and increases cortisol.

- **The 90-90-90 Rule:** 90-degree angle at the elbows, 90 degrees at the hips, and 90 degrees at the knees. This alignment minimizes physical stress on the muscular-skeletal system.

- **Lighting and Alertness:** Natural light is the most effective "Focus Fuel." It regulates your circadian rhythm and keeps your cortisol-to-melatonin ratio in the "Alert" zone. If you work in a dark room, your brain will struggle to maintain the "Top-Down" attention spotlight.

Phase 5: Sensory Minimalism and Olfactory Cues

While visual and auditory distractions are the primary focus-killers, a truly distraction-free workspace accounts for the other senses as well.

5.1 Tactile Focus

Your chair and desk surface should not be sources of sensory distraction. If your chair is itchy, or your desk is sticky, or the temperature is too hot/cold, your "Bottom-Up" system will fire. The goal is "Sensory Neutrality." You want to be so comfortable that you forget you have a body. This allows for total immersion in the "World of the Task."

5.2 The Olfactory Anchor

The sense of smell is the only sense that bypasses the thalamus and goes directly to the brain's emotional and memory centers (the amygdala and hippocampus). You can use this to your advantage by using **Scent Priming.**

- Choose a specific essential oil or candle (e.g., Peppermint or Rosemary, both linked to alertness).

- Use this scent *only* when you are doing Deep Work.

- Over time, the scent itself will trigger a "Focus State" via classical conditioning.

If you work in an office or a shared home, your distractions aren't just objects—they are people.

6.1 The "Closed Door" Policy

A closed door is a physical manifestation of a boundary. If you don't have a door, you must create a visual "Do Not Disturb" signal. Whether it is a specific light, a flag, or simply wearing your noise-canceling headphones, you must train those around you that the signal means "I am in a Deep Work Session."

6.2 The "Office Hours" Concept

Distractions often happen because people don't know when you *are* available. By setting "Office Hours"—specific times when your door is open and your phone is on—you reduce the frequency of "quick questions" during your focus blocks. You are teaching others to respect your focus by respecting it yourself.

The Fortress of Focus: Implementation Checklist

To implement Chapter 1, you must view your workspace as a military perimeter. You are defending the "Executive Governor" of your brain from the "Sensory Alarms" of the world.

Immediate Action Items:

1. **The 2-Minute Sweep:** Every morning, before you touch your computer, remove every item from your desk that isn't essential for your current project.

2. **The Out-of-Sight Rule:** Place your phone in a separate room or a timed lockbox.

3. **The Auditory Anchor:** Choose one "Focus Track" (Brown noise or non-lyrical music) that you listen to *only* during deep work.

4. **The Lighting Audit:** Position your desk near a window or invest in high-CRI (Color Rendering Index) lighting that mimics the solar spectrum.

Your environment is the "silent partner" in your success. If you fight your environment, you will eventually lose. If you engineer your environment, your environment will fight for you.

You have built the biological hardware; now, you have built the **Physical Cradle** for your focus. We are now ready to move from the space you work in to the **process** of the work itself.

CHAPTER 2

USE DEEP WORK SESSIONS TO FINISH HARD TASKS

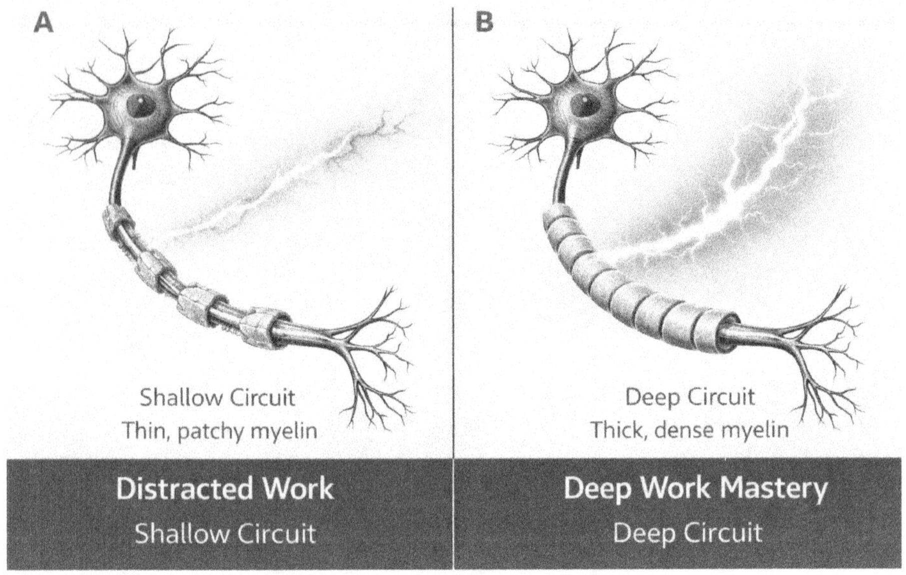

In the previous chapter, we built the **Physical Cradle** for your concentration. You have cleared the visual debris, silenced the auditory alarms, and anchored your workspace to a singular purpose. But a sanctuary is only as good as the rituals performed within it. You can have the most perfectly engineered desk in the world, but if you do not know how to engage your brain in the high-intensity act of production, your workspace is merely a museum of potential.

This chapter is about the transition from **passive focus** to **active execution**. We are going to master the high-performance protocol known as the **Deep Work Session**.

Deep work is a term coined by professor Cal Newport, defined as professional activities performed in a state of distraction-free concentration that push your cognitive capabilities to their limit. These efforts create new value, improve your skill, and are hard to replicate. In a world of "Continuous Partial Attention," the ability to perform deep work is becoming the gold standard of professional value. It is the only way to tackle "Hard Tasks"—those projects that require complex synthesis, original thought, or the mastery of difficult new skills.

The Neurobiology of the Deep Work State

To execute a Deep Work Session, you must understand what is happening inside your brain when you shift from "Shallow" to "Deep." When you focus intensely on a specific skill or problem, you are triggering a process called **Myelination.**

Myelin is a fatty tissue that wraps around the axons of your neurons, acting as insulation for the electrical signals. The more you fire a specific circuit in a state of intense concentration, the more myelin is layered onto those neurons. This makes the signal faster, crisper, and more efficient.

Deep Work is essentially a "Myelin Factory." Conversely, when you work in a distracted state—checking your phone every ten minutes—you are firing too many disparate circuits. You never stay on one circuit long enough to trigger significant myelination. This is why "Shallow Work" leads to stagnation, while "Deep Work" leads to mastery.

Furthermore, deep work allows you to reach the **Flow State**, a concept pioneered by Mihaly Csikszentmihalyi. In Flow, the brain undergoes "Transient Hypofrontality"—the part of your brain responsible for self-consciousness and the sense of time temporarily slows down, allowing the creative and analytical centers to communicate with unprecedented speed.

The Neuro-Economic Reality of Depth

Before we dive into the specific mechanics of the session, we must address the "why" through a lens of cognitive survival. In the modern economy, we are seeing a Great Bifurcation. On one side, there is a growing class of "Shallow Workers"—individuals who spend their days in a state of frenetic superficiality, responding to pings, attending redundant meetings, and shifting between minor tasks. On the other side is a shrinking, elite class of "Deep Workers"—those who can consolidate their cognitive energy to produce original, complex, and high-value output.

As Artificial Intelligence and automation begin to handle the "Shallow" (the routine, the predictable, the administrative), the market value of "Depth" is skyrocketing. If you cannot focus, you are replaceable. If you can focus, you are a master. Deep work is the only process through which you can achieve **Extreme Productivity**, which is the ability to produce in a few hours what takes others a week to accomplish.

The Biological Mechanics of "The Click"

The most difficult part of any Deep Work Session is the first twenty minutes. This is the period of **Cognitive Friction**. Your brain, currently habituated to the high-dopamine "ping" of digital life, will physically resist the quiet intensity of focus. This resistance is often felt as a mild form of anxiety, boredom, or an itch to "just check one thing."

During this initial phase, your Prefrontal Cortex is working to clear the **Attention Residue** from your previous activities. If you were just scrolling through emails, fragments of those emails are still occupying your working memory. "The Click" is the moment when that residue is finally cleared, and your neural pathways align toward the singular task at hand. Once you achieve "The Click," the effort required to stay focused drops significantly, and you enter the "Flow Window."

The Four Depth Philosophies: Choosing Your Mode

Not everyone can integrate deep work into their life in the same way. Depending on your career and lifestyle, you must choose a "Depth Philosophy" that serves as the framework for your sessions.

1. The Monastic Philosophy

This is the most extreme version. You eliminate or radically minimize shallow obligations. You essentially go "off-grid" for weeks or months at a time to focus on a single monumental output. This is the path of the novelist finishing a manuscript or the researcher on a sabbatical.

2. The Bimodal Philosophy

You divide your life into clearly defined stretches of deep and shallow work. For example, you might spend four days a week in "Monastic" focus and three days handling all meetings and administrative tasks.

3. The Rhythmic Philosophy

This is the most effective for the modern high-performer. You create a regular "rhythm" by scheduling deep work sessions at the same time every day. This removes the need for willpower; deep work becomes a habit.

4. The Journalistic Philosophy

You fit deep work into your schedule whenever you can find a pocket of time. This is only recommended for those who have already "Hardened" their focus through months of practice, as the "Switch Cost" is high.

The Tactical Execution of a 90-Minute Sprint

The human brain generally operates on **Ultradian Rhythms**—cycles of high-frequency brain activity followed by periods of lower frequency. Research suggests that the optimal window for peak concentration is roughly **90 minutes**.

Minutes 0–15: The Ritual of Entry

- **The Intentional Lock-In:** Explicitly state your goal. "In this session, I will solve the logic error in the core API."
- **The Physical Anchor:** Use a specific sensory cue—a specific playlist (no lyrics) or a specific scent. This tells the brain: *The ritual has begun.*
- **The Digital Firewall:** Ensure all "Bottom-Up" triggers are silenced. Put your phone in the "Exile Zone" (another room).

Minutes 15–75: The Deep Dive

- **The Boredom Barrier:** When you hit a difficult patch, **do not move.** This is the "Point of Growth." The urge to switch tabs is the urge to avoid the discomfort of neural rewiring. Sit with the frustration.

- **The "No-Negotiation" Rule:** If you feel the urge to get a snack, evaluate it. Is it a physical need or a "Distraction Proxy"? Usually, it is a Distraction Proxy. Tell yourself you can go in ten minutes. Often, the urge vanishes once you re-engage.

Minutes 75–90: The Taper and Shutdown

- **The Progress Capture:** As cognitive fatigue sets in, do not just stop. Write a "bridge to tomorrow." Note exactly where you left off and what the first step is for the next session. This prevents "Attention Residue" from haunting your recovery time.

- **The Success Metric:** Record the session. Did you stay focused the whole time? If not, what was the "Leak"?

Active Recovery: The "Analog" Requirement

The biggest mistake people make is finishing a Deep Work Session and immediately rewarding themselves by checking their phone. This is like finishing a marathon and smoking a cigarette to "relax."

After intense "Top-Down" focus, your Prefrontal Cortex is metabolically exhausted. To recover, you must engage the **Default Mode Network (DMN)**. This is the part of the brain that activates when you are not focused on a specific task. The DMN is responsible for "Incubation"—the process where the subconscious mind makes creative connections between the data points you just processed.

The Rule of Recovery: Recovery must be **Analog and Low-Stimulus.**

- Walk without headphones.
- Perform a rhythmic, manual task (making coffee, washing a dish).
- Stare out a window for five minutes.

If you jump immediately to a screen, you are subjecting your brain to a new flood of "Bottom-Up" stimuli. You are preventing the DMN from doing its work, and you are starting the "Attention Residue" cycle all over again.

Overcoming the "Depth Resistance"

The greatest obstacle to Deep Work is the **Boredom Barrier**. We have become so habituated to the high-dopamine "ping" of digital life that silence and focus feel physically painful. This is "Cognitive Withdrawal."

To overcome this, you must stop treating boredom as a problem to be solved and start treating it as **Training**.

- **Practice "Productive Meditation":** When walking or driving, choose a specific professional problem and focus only on that. When your mind wanders, gently pull it back.

- **Embrace the Stall:** When you hit a hard part of your task during a session, do not switch tabs. Sit with the frustration. The moment of frustration is the moment of growth.

Scheduling Depth: The Time-Block Method

If you do not schedule your deep work sessions, they will not happen. "Shallow Work" (emails, meetings, slack) is like a gas; it will expand to fill every corner of your day unless it is compressed into specific containers.

The Strategy: Fixed-Schedule Productivity.

1. **Identify your "Peak Focus Window":** For most people, this is 2–4 hours after waking. This is when your circadian rhythm naturally supports high-level executive function.

2. **Block the Time:** Mark these hours as "Deep Work" on your calendar. This is a non-negotiable appointment with yourself.

3. **The Shutdown Ritual:** At the end of your day, look at the next day's schedule. Knowing *when* you will do your deep work removes the "Decision Fatigue" of trying to find time in the moment.

The Metric of Success: The Deep Work Ratio

To improve your focus, you must measure it. Every day, track how many hours you spent in a state of true, undistracted "Depth."

- **The Goal for Beginners:** 1 Hour of Deep Work per day.

- **The Goal for Elites:** 3–4 Hours of Deep Work per day.

Note: It is biologically impossible for a human to perform true Deep Work for more than 4–5 hours a day. If you think you are doing eight hours of deep work, you are likely doing "Semi-Deep" work. Focus on **Intensity**, not just Duration.

Why go through this trouble? Why not just work "hard" in a normal way? The answer lies in the **Myelin Sheath**. When you perform Deep Work, you are forcing specific neural circuits to fire repeatedly without interruption. This signals the glial cells to wrap those axons in myelin—a fatty insulation that increases the speed and strength of the electrical signal.

The more you work in "Depth," the more "Hard Tasks" become "Easy Tasks." Masters in any field (musicians, grandmasters, elite coders) are not just "smarter" than you; they have more myelinated circuits in their specialized domains.

Implementation: Your First Deep Work Sprint

To start today, choose one "Hard Task" you have been avoiding.

1. Clear your desk.
2. Exile your phone.
3. Set a timer for 90 minutes.
4. Commit to staying in the chair, even if you are just staring at a blank screen.

You are not just finishing a task; you are rewiring your brain. You are building the myelin that will make you an elite performer. You have the workspace (Chapter 1); now you have the **Ritual of Depth**. Next, we must address the "Digital Sirens" that will try to pull you out of these sessions. We move to the boundaries of the digital world.

CHAPTER 3

SET BOUNDARIES WITH DIGITAL NOTIFICATIONS

You have built the physical sanctuary. You have mastered the ritual of the 90-minute sprint. But as you sit at your perfectly ergonomic desk, deep within your rhythmic session, a silent predator is waiting in your pocket. A small, haptic vibration or a red numeric badge on your screen is all it takes to shatter the myelin-building process you have painstakingly initiated.

In the previous chapters, we addressed the "Visible" distractions. Now, we must confront the **Digital Sirens**.

In the modern world, your digital devices are not neutral tools. They are "Persuasive Technologies," designed by thousands of the world's most talented engineers to exploit your evolutionary vulnerabilities. To stay focused in 2026, you cannot rely on "common sense" usage. You must implement a radical, defensive architecture that treats every notification as a hostile intrusion into your cognitive sovereignty.

To effectively build boundaries, one must first recognize that the modern digital landscape is an environment of **high-stakes psychological warfare**. Your smartphone is not just a communication device; it is a "Slot Machine" that you carry in your pocket. The designers of these interfaces utilize a principle from behavioral psychology known as **Variable Ratio Reinforcement**.

This is the same mechanism that keeps a gambler pulling the lever on a slot machine. You don't get a "reward" (a meaningful email, a positive comment, a fascinating piece of news) every time you check your phone, but you get one *occasionally* and *unpredictably*. This uncertainty triggers a much higher release of dopamine than a predictable reward ever could. Your brain becomes addicted to the "possibility" of a hit.

When you allow notifications to remain active, you are allowing billion-dollar corporations to run experiments on your dopamine receptors. Living without digital boundaries is the equivalent of trying to stay sober while sitting in a bar with a shot glass taped to your hand. To protect your focus, you must dismantle the machine.

The Neurobiology of the Notification: The Orientation Response

Why is it so hard to ignore a buzzing phone? The answer lies in the **Orientation Response**. This is an ancient reflex designed to shift your focus toward any sudden change in your environment—a flash of light, a sharp sound, or a vibration. In the ancestral environment, this reflex saved your life. In the digital environment, it is the primary tool used to hijack your Prefrontal Cortex.

When your phone vibrates, your brain undergoes a **Dopamine Loop**:

1. **The Cue:** The vibration or the ping.
2. **The Craving:** The uncertainty of the message (Who is it? Is it a like?).
3. **The Action:** You check the phone.
4. **The Reward:** A small hit of dopamine from the novelty of the information.

The problem is the **Interference Effect**. Even if you don't check the phone, the mere awareness of a notification creates "Background

Processing." Your brain is now using metabolic energy to decide *not* to check it. This is a silent drain on your willpower that makes "The Click" of deep focus impossible to maintain. This phenomenon, known as **Attention Residue**, ensures that even after a five-second glance at a text, your brain remains partially tethered to that digital interaction for up to twenty minutes.

The first step in digital boundary engineering is a total "cleansing" of your devices. Most people operate on a "blacklist" mentality—they only turn off notifications that are actively annoying. To be an elite performer, you must move to a **"Whitelist" mentality**: All notifications are guilty until proven innocent.

1.1 The Whitelist Protocol

Open your system settings right now and navigate to the notification center. Your goal is to reach a state where **95% of your apps have zero permission to alert you.**

- **Social Media:** Instagram, TikTok, LinkedIn, and Facebook should never have notification permissions. These apps are designed for consumption, not production.

- **News and Media:** These apps are the primary sources of "Bottom-Up" anxiety. Turn them off. If the world is ending, you will hear about it through other channels.

- **Email:** Email is an asynchronous tool. It was never intended to be an instant messenger. By having email notifications on, you are allowing anyone in the world to interrupt your thoughts at their convenience.

1.2 The Death of the "Red Badge"

The red numeric circles on app icons are designed to trigger a sense of "Unclosed Loops" in the brain. They create a psychological tension known as the **Zeigarnik Effect**—the tendency to remember uncompleted tasks more than completed ones. Your brain will fixate on that little red "1" until you click it. **Turn off all "Badge App Icons."** You should only know there is a message when you *choose* to open the app, not when the app chooses to scream at you.

Once the pings are silenced, you must solve the problem of "Compulsive Checking." Just because the phone doesn't beep doesn't mean you won't reach for it out of habit. We must shift from **Reactive Communication** to **Proactive Batching.**

2.1 The Communication Reservoir

Imagine your incoming messages as a river. If you try to drink from the river as it flows, you will drown. Instead, you must build a "Reservoir."

- **The Protocol:** Set two or three "Communication Windows" per day (e.g., 11:00 AM and 4:00 PM).

- **The Benefit:** When you batch 50 emails into one 30-minute block, you take advantage of "Task Momentum." You can process them five times faster than if you responded to each one individually throughout the day.

2.2 The "Airplane Mode" Standard

During your 90-minute Deep Work Sessions, your phone should not just be on silent; it should be in **Airplane Mode** or a "Focus Mode" that only allows "Emergency Contacts" (spouse, child's school) to break through. Airplane mode ensures that even if the "Bottom-Up" alarm fires, there is no digital fuel to feed it.

Phase 3: The Architecture of the Home Screen (Choice Architecture)

Your phone's home screen is a piece of "Choice Architecture." If the first thing you see when you unlock your phone is a dopamine-rich app, that is where you will go. We use **Friction Engineering** to protect our focus.

3.1 The "Slot Machine" Exile

Move every social media, news, and entertainment app off your primary home screen and into a folder on the third or fourth page.

- Your primary home screen should only contain **Utility Tools**: Calendar, Maps, Notes, Camera, and Calculator.

- By adding "Swipe Friction," you force your Prefrontal Cortex to intervene before you fall into a mindless scroll. This small hurdle provides the "Pause" necessary for executive control to override impulsive habits.

3.2 Grayscale Mode: The "Boring" Phone

Color is a powerful emotional trigger. The vibrant reds, blues, and yellows of app icons are carefully chosen to be "Visually Delicious."

- **The Hack:** Set your phone to **Grayscale Mode**. When the world of the screen is grey, the dopamine hit of the "Reward" is significantly diminished. Your brain stops seeing the phone as a toy and starts seeing it as a tool. Neuroscience shows that removing color significantly reduces the "Arousal" levels triggered by smartphone use.

Phase 4: Setting External Boundaries (The Social Contract)

One of the biggest fears people have when setting digital boundaries is the fear of being perceived as unresponsive or missing a critical update. This is a form of **Social Anxiety** that fuels the distraction economy.

4.1 Training Your Environment

You are the one who trains people on how to treat your time. If you always respond to emails within three minutes, you are telling the world that your time is not valuable.

- **The Expectations Re-Set:** Tell your team or family: *"I'm moving to a deep-work schedule to improve the quality of my output. I'll be checking messages at 11 AM and 4 PM. If it's a true emergency, please call."*

- **The Power of the Phone Call:** Real emergencies happen via a phone call. Digital distractions happen via text and DM. By pushing "Urgency" to the phone call, you filter out 99% of the noise.

4.2 The Professional Auto-Responder

During deep work, use status indicators or auto-responders. On Slack or Email, be explicit: *"In Deep Work until 1:00 PM. Focusing on [Project Name]."* This removes the anxiety of "leaving people hanging" because you have provided them with a clear "Expected Response Time."

Phase 5: Digital Hygiene and the "Sunset" (Protecting Recovery)

As we learned in Book 1, your brain needs "Down-Time" to process information and "Sanitize" neural waste. Blue light and the high-cortisol nature of late-night digital "checking" destroy this recovery.

5.1 The "1-Hour" Rule

Your digital boundaries must extend into your evening to protect your sleep architecture.

- **The Protocol:** 60 minutes before bed, all "interactive" screens (phones, tablets, laptops) are off.

- This allows your **Melatonin** to rise naturally and prevents "Attention Residue" from leaking into your sleep. Engaging in a low-stimulation activity like reading a physical book or meditating allows the brain to shift into the parasympathetic "Rest and Digest" state.

Phase 6: Defending the Desktop Environment

While the smartphone is the primary predator, your computer is often the "Trojan Horse." Notification banners on a laptop are even more disruptive because they happen while you are actively trying to produce work.

6.1 The "Full Screen" Mandate

Whenever you are in a Deep Work session, your work application must be in **Full Screen Mode**. This hides the "Menu Bar" and the "Dock," removing the visual temptation of other app icons or clock-watching.

6.2 Browser Hygiene

The browser is a portal to infinite distraction.

- **The "Tab Limit" Rule:** Never have more than five tabs open at once. Each open tab represents a potential "Task Switch" and a drain on your working memory.

- **Site Blockers:** Use software (like Freedom or Cold Turkey) to physically block access to distracting websites during your focus blocks. Don't rely on willpower when you can rely on code.

The Digital Sovereignty Checklist

To master Chapter 3, you must stop being a "User" and start being a "Commander."

1. **The Notification Purge:** Spend 15 minutes today disabling every non-human notification on all devices.

2. **The Grayscale Shift:** Turn your phone to Grayscale to "de-gamify" the experience.

3. **The Folder Exile:** Move addictive apps three swipes away from the home screen.

4. **The Batching Commitment:** Pick your two communication windows for tomorrow and put them in your calendar.

5. **The 1-Hour Sunset:** Commit to an analog hour before sleep tonight.

The world will not stop spinning because you didn't check your notifications for 90 minutes. In fact, you will find that the world begins to spin around **you** and the high-value work you are finally able to produce.

You have the workspace. You have the ritual. Now, you have the **Digital Firewall**. We are now ready to address the internal habit of the mind: **The Practice of Single-Tasking.**

CHAPTER 4

PRACTICE SINGLE-TASKING FOR HIGHER QUALITY OUTPUT

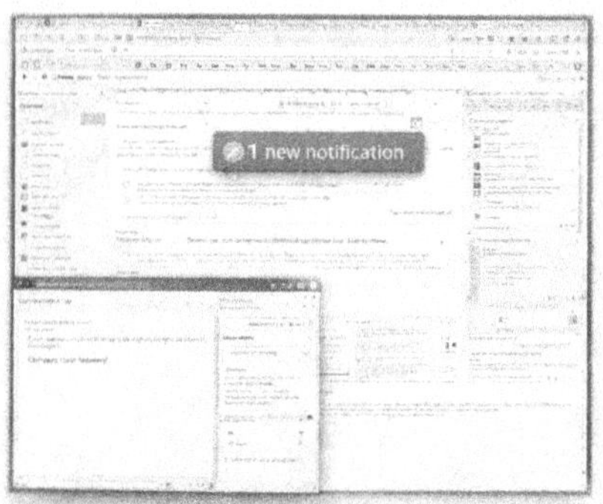

Productive Procrastination

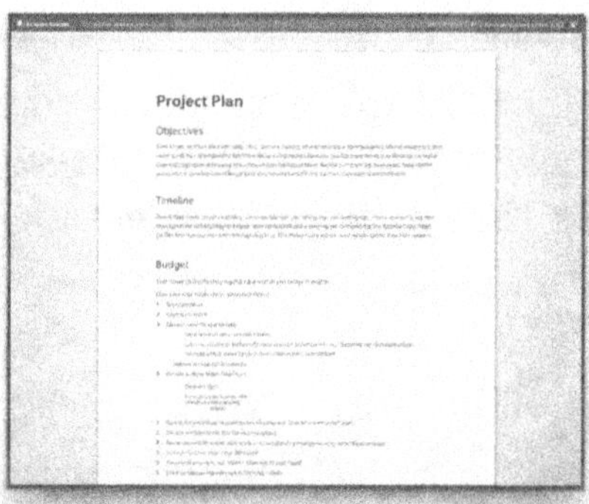

High-Precision Output

Tab Zero: Engineering your digital field of vision to enforce a singularity of intent.

We have meticulously engineered your external world. Your desk is a sanctuary of physical order; your digital devices have been stripped of their predatory power. But now, we must cross the final frontier: the internal habits of your conscious mind. You can sit in a silent room with a phone in "Airplane Mode," but if your mind is still attempting to perform the cognitive gymnastics of multitasking, you will remain trapped in a state of superficiality.

In this chapter, we confront the most pervasive and damaging lie of the modern corporate era: the myth of multitasking. We are going to dismantle the illusion that doing "many things at once" is a sign of efficiency. Instead, we will install the discipline of **Single-Tasking**—the practice of absolute, singular immersion in one objective until its completion or the conclusion of a session.

The Biological Fraud of Multitasking

To master single-tasking, you must first accept a physiological fact: **The human brain cannot multitask.** From a neurobiological standpoint, our executive function is a "serial processor," not a "parallel processor." When you believe you are multitasking—answering an email while listening to a conference call—you are actually engaging in **Rapid Task-Switching**. Your Prefrontal Cortex is frantically jumping back and forth between two different sets of rules, contexts, and goals.

This jumping comes at a staggering metabolic and cognitive price. Every time you switch your attention, your brain must perform a "load" and "unload" cycle. This creates **Executive Function Friction**.

Research conducted at Stanford University by Professor Clifford Nass revealed that self-identified "heavy multitaskers"—those who thought they were good at it—were actually worse at filtering out irrelevant information and were significantly slower at switching from one task to another compared to light multitaskers. By trying to do everything, they had trained their brains to be permanently distracted. They had physically thinned their capacity for concentration.

The neural architecture of the human brain simply does not allow for two cognitively demanding tasks to be processed simultaneously. We have a "bottleneck" in the posterior secondary prefrontal cortex. While you can perform a cognitive task (like writing) while doing a physical, automated task (like walking), you cannot perform two "Top-Down" tasks at once. You are not "multitasking"; you are simply degrading your performance in two directions at once.

The Switch Cost Effect: Losing Your "Deep" IQ

When you switch from Task A to Task B, you don't just lose the time it takes to move your eyes. You lose **Cognitive Momentum**. This is known as the **Switch Cost Effect**.

Studies have shown that task-switching can reduce your productive time by as much as **40%**. More alarmingly, as we noted in the introduction, the drop in functional intelligence during multitasking is equivalent to losing 10 IQ points. You are effectively choosing to do your most important work while in a state of cognitive impairment.

The Anatomy of a Switch:

1. **Goal Shifting:** You decide to do Task B instead of Task A.
2. **Rule Activation:** Your brain has to turn off the "rules" for Task A (e.g., the syntax of a coding language) and turn on the "rules" for Task B (e.g., the social nuances of an email).
3. **Attention Residue:** As discussed in earlier chapters, a ghost of Task A remains in your working memory, creating "noise" that prevents you from fully engaging with Task B.

Single-tasking is the only way to eliminate these costs. It allows you to enter **The Tunnel**—a state where the external world disappears and 100% of your available neurons are firing in service of a single problem.

The Psychology of "Productivity Porn"

If multitasking is so inefficient, why do we do it? Why does it *feel* so productive?

The answer is **Dopamine**. Every time you complete a small, trivial task (sending a two-word Slack, checking a notification, clearing an easy email), your brain releases a small burst of dopamine. This creates a "Reward Loop." Multitasking allows you to clear dozens of tiny, low-value items in a short period, sending you into a state of "False Achievement."

You feel busy, but you are not being productive. This is what I call **"Productive Procrastination."** You are using the "shallow" tasks to avoid the "Hard Task" that actually requires your full intelligence. Single-tasking is difficult because it forces you to forgo those easy dopamine hits in favor of the delayed, much larger reward of significant accomplishment.

To transition to single-tasking, you must become comfortable with the feeling of "not doing enough" in the short term. You must realize that one hour of deep, single-tasked focus is worth more than eight hours of fragmented "busyness."

To implement single-tasking, we return to the 90-minute sprint but add a strict **Singularity Constraint**.

1.1 The "Definition of One"

Before you begin your session, you must identify your **Singular Objective**.

- **Bad Goal:** "Work on the marketing project." (This allows for switching between tabs, research, and design).

- **Good Goal:** "Write 500 words for the landing page copy."

If you finish the goal before the 90 minutes are up, you do not "check email." You pick the *next* logical sub-task related to that specific project, or you end the session early and take an analog break.

1.2 The "Tab Zero" Rule

Your digital environment must reflect your singular intent. If you are writing a document, the only window open on your screen should be that document. Every other tab—even if it is "related" to work—is a latent distraction. If you need a reference, look at it, then close the tab immediately.

Phase 2: Mastering "The Waiting Room"

The most common reason we break our single-tasking discipline is the **"Quick Thought" Distraction**. While working on Task A, you suddenly remember you need to buy milk, or you have an idea for Task B.

2.1 The "Capture Sheet" (Analog Buffer)

Do not switch tasks to address the thought. Keep a physical piece of paper next to your keyboard. When a stray thought enters your mind, write it down in two words: *"Buy milk"* or *"Idea for B."* This "captures" the thought, signaling to your brain that it won't be forgotten. This clears the working memory and allows you to return to Task A within seconds. You process the "Capture Sheet" *only* after your session is over.

This technique utilizes the **Zeigarnik Effect** in your favor. By writing it down, you "close the loop" temporarily, satisfying the brain's need to hold onto the information.

Phase 3: The Slow-Work Movement

Single-tasking is part of a larger philosophy of **Slow Work**. In the modern world, "fast" is often a proxy for "shallow." To produce high-quality output, you must be willing to go slow.

- **Linear Thinking:** Deep problems are solved linearly. You follow a thread of logic from point A to point B to point C. If you multitask, you are constantly breaking the thread.

- **The Complexity Ceiling:** There is a level of complexity that simply cannot be reached without 60+ minutes of singular focus. If you never single-task, you will never solve the hardest problems in your field. You will be stuck in the "Shallow End" of the labor market.

When you commit to one thing, you allow your subconscious to begin making deeper connections. This is where original insight comes from. You cannot have an "Aha!" moment if you are constantly toggling between spreadsheets and Slack.

Phase 4: Training Your "Attention Muscle"

Single-tasking is a physical discipline. Just as you cannot walk into a gym and deadlift 500 pounds on day one, you cannot expect to single-task for four hours immediately.

4.1 The "Stare" Exercise

To strengthen your attention muscle, practice the **Focus Stare**. Set a timer for three minutes. Choose a small object (a pen, a leaf, a candle flame). Try to hold your entire conscious awareness on that object. When your mind wanders—and it will—gently pull it back. This is "Weightlifting for the Prefrontal Cortex."

4.2 The "No-Phone" Transitions

Most of us use "Gap Time" (waiting for an elevator, sitting in a taxi, standing in line) to multitask by checking our phones. This prevents the brain from ever being "at rest." **The Rule:** Practice "Being Nowhere." Use transitions to simply be present. This lowers your baseline "Dopamine Requirement," making it easier to single-task when you sit down to work.

Phase 5: The "Finished" vs. "Done" Distinction

In a single-tasking framework, we must change how we measure progress. We move away from the "To-Do List" mentality and toward the **"Completion mindset."**

When you multitask, you often end the day with five tasks that are "80% finished." In reality, an 80% finished task provides zero value. It cannot be shipped, it cannot be sold, and it cannot be used. It simply remains as "Attention Residue" in your mind, cluttering your focus for the next day.

Single-tasking demands that you take one task to 100% completion before moving the "spotlight" of your attention elsewhere. This creates a sense of **Cognitive Closure**, which reduces stress and improves sleep quality.

The Single-Tasking Manifesto

To succeed in Book 4, you must adopt the following creed:

1. **I will not open a second tab unless the first is closed.**
2. **I will not "check" anything during a deep work session.**
3. **I will treat every task-switch as a 10-point drop in my IQ.**
4. **I will value the Quality of one completed task over the Volume of ten started ones.**
5. **I will embrace the "boredom" of the singular path as the price of mastery.**

The modern world is a "Multitasking Trap." It wants you to be a shallow, reactive consumer of information. By choosing to single-task, you are performing a radical act of rebellion. You are choosing to use your brain as it was evolved to be used: as a high-precision instrument for the mastery of the world.

CHAPTER 5

USE MINDFULNESS TO RE-TRAIN YOUR FOCUS

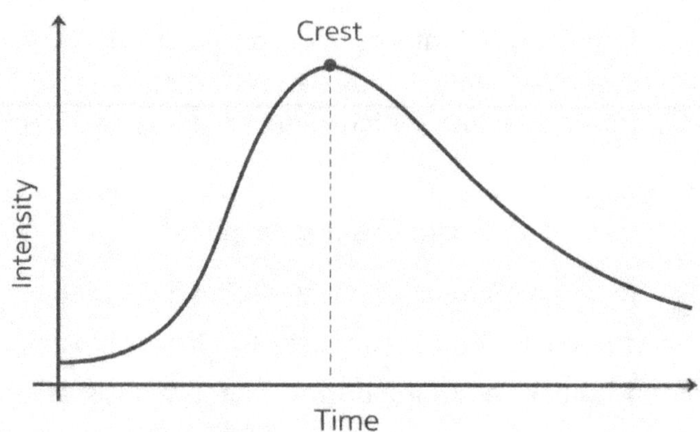

The 90-Second Window: Most neurological urges dissolve if observed but not fed.

We have arrived at the final pillar of the focus architecture.

In Chapter 1, you built the fortress—the physical environment that protects you. In Chapter 2, you learned the ritual of the 90-minute sprint. In Chapter 3, you erected the digital firewall to silence the external noise. In Chapter 4, you committed to the discipline of single-tasking.

But there is one variable we have not yet addressed: **The noise inside your own head.**

You can sit in a silent, white room with no internet connection, a perfect ergonomic chair, and a clear desk, and *still* fail to produce Deep Work. Why? Because your brain is a chaotic, chatter-filled machine. It is a time-traveling device that constantly pulls you into the regrets of the past or the anxieties of the future. It generates a stream of intrusive thoughts: *"Did I lock the door?" "What did that email mean?" "I'm hungry." "I'm bored."*

To become an elite performer, you cannot simply remove external distractions. You must upgrade the internal hardware. You must train the "Attention Muscle" itself.

This chapter is not about spirituality, incense, or chanting on a mountaintop. This chapter is about **Cognitive Weightlifting**. We are going to strip mindfulness of its mystical connotations and look at it through the lens of pure neurobiology. We will use mindfulness as a tactical tool to physically restructure the grey matter of your brain, enlarge your Anterior Cingulate Cortex, and give you the "Executive Control" necessary to command your focus at will.

The Neurobiology of the "Monkey Mind"

To understand why mindfulness is a non-negotiable skill for the Hardened Mind, we must first understand the default state of the human brain.

Neuroscientists have identified a specific network in the brain called the **Default Mode Network (DMN)**. This network activates whenever you are not focused on a specific task. It is the "daydreaming" circuit. Evolutionarily, the DMN was useful; it allowed our ancestors to simulate future scenarios, process social hierarchies, and consolidate memories.

However, in the modern world, an overactive DMN is the enemy of productivity. When the DMN is running hot, you are ruminating. You are worrying. You are essentially hallucinating problems that do not exist yet.

Opposed to the DMN is the **Task-Positive Network (TPN)**. This is the network that lights up when you are engaged in a demanding, external task—solving a math problem, writing code, or performing surgery.

Here is the critical biological rule: **The DMN and the TPN are anticorrelated.** When one is on, the other is off. You cannot be in a state of deep, analytical focus (TPN) and a state of neurotic daydreaming (DMN) at the same time.

Most people have a "weak" switch. They try to engage the TPN to do work, but their DMN keeps firing, interrupting their focus with stray thoughts. Mindfulness is the training protocol that strengthens the "Switch." It teaches you to notice when the DMN has hijacked your attention and gives you the neurological strength to shut it down and re-engage the TPN.

The Anatomy of a "Mental Rep"

The biggest misconception about mindfulness is that "success" means having a blank mind. This is false. The goal of mindfulness is not to stop thinking; the goal is to **stop being carried away by thinking.**

We must view mindfulness practice exactly like a gym workout. In the gym, you lift a weight (resistance), and you lower it. That is one repetition. In mindfulness, the "weight" is your distraction.

Here is the anatomy of a **Cognitive Bicep Curl**:

1. **The Anchor:** You place your attention on a specific target (usually the breath).

2. **The Wander:** Inevitably, your attention slips. You start thinking about lunch or an email. (This is not failure; this is the *resistance*).

3. **The Metacognition (The "Notice"):** You suddenly realize, *"I am not watching my breath; I am thinking about lunch."* This moment of awareness is the most critical part of the process. You have stepped out of the stream of thought and become the **Observer**.

4. **The Return:** You gently but firmly disengage from the thought and pull your attention back to the breath.

That is one rep.

If you sit for ten minutes and your mind wanders 100 times, and you bring it back 100 times, you have not failed. You have just completed 100 reps of "Attention Training." You have physically thickened the **Anterior Cingulate Cortex (ACC)**—the part of the brain responsible for conflict monitoring and cognitive control.

If you sit for ten minutes and your mind never wanders, you have done zero reps. You have just napped. We *want* the resistance. We *want* the struggle. That is where the growth happens.

This is the foundational exercise. It is the "Deadlift" of attention training. It builds raw holding power.

The Protocol:

1. **Posture:** Sit in a chair with your feet flat on the floor and your spine self-supporting (not leaning back). This signals alertness to the brain.

2. **The Target:** Direct your attention to the physical sensation of air moving in and out of your nostrils. Do not "think" about breathing. *Feel* the temperature change. *Feel* the friction of the air.

3. **The Count:** To help stabilize the mind, count each exhale. Inhale... Exhale (1). Inhale... Exhale (2). Count to 10, then start over at 1.

4. **The Reset:** When (not if) you lose count and realize you are thinking about your To-Do list, simply note it ("Thinking") and return to "1."

Dosage: Start with 10 minutes every morning. This is not a spiritual ritual; it is a pre-work warm-up. You are priming the TPN before you open your email.

Once you have built some stability with Focused Attention, you move to **Open Monitoring**. This is the "Situational Awareness" of the mind. Instead of focusing on one thing (the breath), you open your awareness to *everything*—sounds, sensations, and thoughts—without latching onto them.

The goal here is to develop **Metacognition**—thinking about thinking. You want to be able to see a distraction coming before it hits you.

The Visualization: Imagine you are sitting on the bank of a river. The river is your stream of thought.

- Most people are *in* the river, drowning in the current, swept away by every emotion.

- Open Monitoring trains you to sit on the *bank*, watching the debris (thoughts) float by. You see a thought: *"I am worried about the presentation."* You label it: *"Worrying."* And you watch it float downstream. You do not jump in the water to retrieve it.

Why this matters for Focus: When you are in a Deep Work session and a stressful thought arises, the untrained mind chases the thought, leading to a 20-minute spiral of anxiety. The trained mind notes the thought ("There is stress"), realizes it is just a neurological event, and lets it pass without breaking the flow state.

Protocol 3: Urge Surfing (The Anti-Addiction Tool)

In Chapter 3, we discussed the dopamine loops of digital distraction. Mindfulness provides the specific tactical counter-measure to the "Craving" phase of that loop. This technique is called **Urge Surfing**.

When you are working on a hard task and you feel the sudden, burning desire to check your phone or eat a snack, your brain is screaming for dopamine relief.

- **The Amateur** gives in immediately.
- **The Stoic** tries to fight it with willpower (which eventually runs out).
- **The Master** surfs the urge.

The Protocol:

1. **Acknowledge:** You feel the urge to check Instagram. Stop. Do not check it. Do not fight it.
2. **Locate:** Where do you feel this urge in your body? Is it a tightness in the chest? A buzzing in the head? A restlessness in the legs?
3. **Observe:** Watch the physical sensation. Treat it like a wave. It will rise in intensity, crest, and then break.
4. **Wait:** Research shows that most urges last less than 90 seconds if they are not fed. Watch the sensation shift and dissolve. Once it fades, return to work.

By "Surfing the Urge," you are breaking the conditioning between "Discomfort" and "Distraction." You are rewiring the basal ganglia to understand that boredom is not a lethal threat.

Protocol 4: Productive Meditation (Newport's Algorithm)

This is a concept adapted from Cal Newport, specifically designed for knowledge workers. It combines physical motion with intense cognitive focus. It is the ultimate test of your new single-tasking and mindfulness skills.

The Protocol:

1. **The Activity:** Go for a walk (or a run/swim). Your body must be moving, but the route must be familiar so you don't have to navigate.

2. **The Problem:** Choose *one* specific professional problem to solve. (e.g., "How do I structure the introduction of the report?").

3. **The Loop:** As you walk, think about the problem.

   o When you notice your mind wandering to your weekend plans, trigger the **"Notice and Return"** rep. Pull it back to the report.

   o When you notice your mind looping on the same useless thought ("I'm stuck, I'm stuck"), acknowledge the loop and push the focus to the *next step* of the logic.

Why this is Hard: This is incredibly difficult. Your brain will resist. It wants the walk to be "Shallow Time." By forcing it to be "Deep Time," you are engaging in high-intensity interval training for your focus. If you can hold a single complex problem in your mind for a 40-minute walk, sitting at a desk will feel easy by comparison.

The "Interstitial Reset" (Micro-Mindfulness)

You do not always have 20 minutes to meditate. But you always have 60 seconds. We can use mindfulness to eliminate **Attention Residue** between meetings or tasks.

Most people finish a Zoom call and immediately check their email. This carries the stress of the call into the inbox, and the stress of the inbox into the next project. This is "Cognitive Contamination."

The Protocol: Between Task A and Task B, insert a **60-Second Reset**.

1. Close your eyes.

2. Take three "Physiological Sighs." (A double inhale through the nose to fully inflate the alveoli, followed by a long, slow exhale through the mouth).
3. Visualize the previous task being "filed away."
4. Ask: *"What is the singular goal of the next task?"*
5. Open your eyes and begin.

This acts as a "Palate Cleanser" for the brain, ensuring that you enter every new context with a fresh supply of executive resources.

The Neuroscience of Structural Change: Cortical Thickening

Why commit to this? Because unlike willpower, which is a fleeting resource, mindfulness creates **Structural Change**.

A landmark study from Harvard University using MRI scans showed that after just eight weeks of mindfulness training, participants had measurable increases in grey matter density in the **Hippocampus** (learning and memory) and the **Temporo-Parietal Junction** (perspective taking).

More importantly, they saw a *decrease* in the size of the **Amygdala**—the brain's fear center. This means that a mindful brain is biologically less reactive to stress. When a deadline looms or a crisis hits, the untrained brain panics (amygdala hijack), shutting down the Prefrontal Cortex. The trained brain observes the stress, regulates the emotion, and keeps the Prefrontal Cortex online.

You are literally building a better brain. You are upgrading the processor speed and increasing the RAM.

Phase 5: Troubleshooting the Practice

As you begin this chapter's protocols, you will encounter resistance. Here are the common traps and how to reframe them.

The "I'm Bad at Meditation" Trap

"I tried to focus on my breath, but I thought about work the whole time. I'm bad at this." **Correction:** No. You had a heavy workout. If you went to the gym and the weights felt heavy, you wouldn't say, "I'm bad at lifting." You would say, "This is a good workout." The difficulty *is* the point. Every time you catch yourself thinking about work, that is a victory of awareness.

The "I Don't Have Time" Trap

"I am too busy to sit for 10 minutes." **Correction:** If you are too busy to spare 10 minutes for brain training, you are operating inefficiently. You are likely losing 90 minutes a day to "Switch Costs" and "Attention Residue." Investing 10 minutes to reclaim those 90 minutes is a simple ROI calculation.

The "It's Boring" Trap

"I get bored just sitting there." **Correction:** Boredom is the withdrawal symptom of dopamine addiction. When you feel bored, it means your brain is re-calibrating its dopamine receptors. "Boredom" is simply the sensation of the brain healing itself from the damage of the digital age. Embrace it.

Implementation: The Daily Focus Algorithm

To integrate Chapter 5 into your life, we layer it into the "Hardened Mind" daily routine.

- **Morning (Pre-Input):** 10 Minutes of **Focused Attention** (Protocol 1). Do this before you look at a screen. This sets the "Anchor" for the day.

- **During Deep Work:** Use **Urge Surfing** (Protocol 3) whenever the impulse to distract arises.

- **Transition Points:** Use the **Interstitial Reset** (60 seconds) between major blocks of work.

- **Afternoon Slump:** Instead of coffee, try a 10-minute **Open Monitoring** session (Protocol 2) to reset your situational awareness and clear the cognitive fatigue.

The Final Synthesis

We have now completed the external and internal architecture of focus.

1. **The Space:** A distraction-free sanctuary.
2. **The Time:** Rhythmic deep work sessions.
3. **The Boundary:** A ruthless digital firewall.
4. **The Action:** Single-tasking singularity.
5. **The Mind:** A trained, mindful instrument capable of metacognition.

You now possess the toolkit of the top 1% of performers. While the rest of the world is drowning in a sea of pings, notifications, and anxiety, you have built a boat. You have the ability to direct the beam of your attention like a laser.

In the Knowledge Economy, this ability is the ultimate leverage. Focus is the new IQ. Focus is the new currency. And you are now wealthy.

The journey of the "Hardened Mind" is not over. Focus is the engine, but we must now look at the *fuel*. In the next book, we will explore the biochemistry of energy—how to eat, sleep, and move to power this high-performance machine. But for now, your task is simple: **Sit down. Watch your breath. Build the muscle.**

CONCLUSION

KEEP YOUR FOCUS SHARP EVERY SINGLE DAY

You have reached the end of the manual. You have dismantled the physical chaos of your workspace, instituted the rhythmic discipline of the 90-minute sprint, erected a firewall against the digital siege, mastered the singularity of the single task, and trained the neural pathways of your own mind to resist the gravitational pull of distraction.

Technically, you now possess the complete architecture of the **Hardened Mind.**

However, there is a distinct difference between possessing a blueprint and living in the house. The greatest danger you face right now is the illusion of permanence. You might believe that because you have read this book and perhaps implemented a few of these strategies, you are now "fixed." You might believe that you have permanently ascended to a higher plane of cognitive existence where distraction can no longer touch you.

This is a dangerous lie.

Focus is not a diploma you hang on the wall. Focus is a **hygiene practice**. It is closer to dental care or physical fitness than it is to learning a fact. You do not brush your teeth once and declare yourself "dental-free" for the rest of your life. You do not lift weights for a month and expect to remain strong for a decade.

The forces of entropy are relentless. The algorithms designed to steal your attention are updating every single day, becoming smarter, faster, and more persuasive. The demands of the workplace will naturally drift toward chaos and urgency. Your own brain, seeking the path of least resistance, will constantly look for excuses to slide back into the warm, numbing bath of the Default Mode Network.

This conclusion is not a summary; it is a **Maintenance Protocol**. It is a guide to the "Long Game." We are going to explore how to protect your new cognitive infrastructure from the inevitable wear and tear of daily life. We will discuss how to handle the days when you fail, how to navigate a world that demands you be distracted, and how to turn these practices from a "productivity hack" into a permanent state of being.

The Law of Cognitive Entropy

In physics, the Second Law of Thermodynamics states that isolated systems spontaneously evolve towards thermodynamic equilibrium—the state with maximum entropy. In simpler terms: **Order naturally degrades into chaos.**

Your focus is a highly ordered system. Therefore, without constant energy input, your focus will naturally degrade.

- **Week 1:** You are zealous. Your phone is in the other room. You are crushing 90-minute sprints.

- **Week 4:** You leave your phone on the desk, "just in case." You start checking email during your deep work breaks.

- **Week 8:** You are back to "multitasking" during meetings and doom-scrolling in bed.

This is not a moral failure; it is physics. To combat Cognitive Entropy, you must stop viewing focus as a "decision" you make every day and start viewing it as an **Operating System** that runs automatically.

You cannot rely on willpower. Willpower is a battery; it drains. You must rely on **Systems and Identity**.

The Identity Shift: "I am a Deep Worker"

The strongest force in the human personality is the need to remain consistent with how we define ourselves. If you define yourself as "someone who is trying to be less distracted," you will fail. "Trying" implies a struggle against your true nature.

You must fundamentally shift your identity. You must look in the mirror and say, **"I am a Deep Worker."**

- A Deep Worker does not apologize for being offline; they protect their time as their most valuable asset.

- A Deep Worker does not feel "FOMO" (Fear Of Missing Out) regarding social media; they feel "JOMO" (Joy Of Missing Out) because they know the value of what they are creating.

- A Deep Worker views distraction not as "fun," but as "damage."

When you adopt this identity, the decisions become easy. You don't turn off notifications because you "have to"; you turn them off because *that is what people like you do.*

The Daily Maintenance Routine: A Chronological Guide

To keep your focus sharp every single day, you need a standard operating procedure. This is a template for a "High-Fidelity Day."

1. The Morning Prime (The Zero-Input Start)

The battle for your focus is won or lost in the first 30 minutes of the day.

- **The Trap:** Waking up and immediately checking your phone. This floods your brain with cortisol and external demands before you have even brushed your teeth. You are effectively handing the keys to your consciousness to the internet.

- **The Protocol:** The first hour of the day is "Output Only." No email. No news. No social media. You hydrate, you move your body, and you plan your day. You engage your Prefrontal Cortex on *your* terms before the world engages it on theirs.

2. The Daily Architecting

Before you open your inbox, you must define the "Win."

- **The Protocol:** Write down the **one to three** "Hard Tasks" that define a successful day. These are your Deep Work targets. Everything else is gravel. If you do not define the target, you will spend the day shooting at decoys.

3. The Deep Work Anchors

Schedule your deep work blocks. Do not "find" time for them; **make** time for them.

- **The Protocol:** If you are a morning person, lock in 9:00 AM to 11:00 AM. If you are a night owl, lock in 8:00 PM to 10:00 PM. Protect these hours with the ferocity of a bodyguard.

4. The Shutdown Ritual

Your brain needs a clear signal that "Work" is done and "Recovery" has begun. Without this, you carry "Attention Residue" into your evening, ruining your sleep and your relationships.

- **The Protocol:** Close all tabs. Review tomorrow's calendar. Say a phrase out loud (e.g., "System Shutdown"). And then, crucially, **stop working.**

Navigating the "Distracted World" (Social Defense)

One of the hardest parts of maintaining focus is that you are living in a world designed for shallow interaction. Your boss expects an instant reply. Your spouse wants to show you a TikTok. Your friends are in a group chat that buzzes every 30 seconds.

Being a Deep Worker can feel lonely. It can feel like you are swimming upstream. Here is how to navigate the social friction without becoming a hermit.

1. Managing the Boss (The "Results" Negotiation)

If you work in a culture of "Instant Responsiveness," you cannot simply disappear without explanation. You must frame your unavailability as a benefit to the company.

- **The Script:** *"I've noticed that when I check email constantly, my coding/writing speed drops. I'm going to try checking email only at 11 AM and 4 PM so I can get this project done faster and with fewer errors. If there is a true emergency, please call my cell."*

- **The Reality:** Most bosses do not care about how fast you reply; they care about the quality of your output. If you produce exceptional work, they will forgive your slow email response time. Competence is the ultimate leverage.

2. Managing the Home (The "Presence" Covenant)

Focus isn't just for work. It is for love. When you are with your family but looking at your phone, you are signaling: *"This device is more interesting than you."*

- **The Protocol:** Implement "Phone-Free Zones" in the house (e.g., the dinner table, the bedroom). When you are with people, practice the same single-tasking you use at work. Be fully present. The quality of your relationships will improve drastically.

What to Do When You Fall Off the Wagon

You will fail. You will have a day where you sleep poorly, wake up late, check Instagram immediately, and spend eight hours in a fog of reactive multitasking. You will eat sugar. You will skip your meditation.

This is inevitable. The difference between a Master and an Amateur is not that the Master never fails; it is that the Master has a **shorter recovery time**.

The "Day Two" Rule

The danger is not the bad day. The danger is the *spiral*. A bad day leads to guilt, which leads to "what the hell" thinking ("I already ruined the week, might as well give up"), which leads to a bad month.

- **The Rule:** Never let a slip turn into a slide. If you miss your deep work session today, it becomes the **number one priority** for tomorrow. You can miss one day. You must never miss two.

The "Micro-Correction"

When you catch yourself doom-scrolling, do not berate yourself. Shame is a poor fuel for focus. Instead, use the mindfulness skills from Chapter 5.

1. **Notice:** "I am distracted."
2. **Accept:** "My brain is seeking dopamine."
3. **Correct:** "I am closing this app and taking three deep breaths."

Treat your focus like a GPS. When you miss a turn, the GPS doesn't scream at you. It simply says, *"Recalculating."* Be your own GPS.

The Audit: The Weekly Review

To fight entropy, you need a feedback loop. You cannot improve what you do not measure. Once a week (Sunday evenings are ideal), sit down for 15 minutes and audit your performance.

The Focus Scorecard:

1. **Deep Hours:** How many hours of true Deep Work did I log this week?
2. **The Leaks:** What was the primary source of distraction? (Was it slack? Was it fatigue? Was it the news?)
3. **The Adjustment:** What is *one* thing I will change next week to plug that leak?

This simple act of reflection keeps the system tight. It prevents a small bad habit from calcifying into a permanent lifestyle.

The Deep Life: Beyond Productivity

Throughout this book, we have framed focus largely in terms of productivity—getting more done, finishing hard tasks, earning more money. These are valid motivations. But if you view focus only as a tool for capitalism, you are missing the profound beauty of the "Hardened Mind."

Focus is the gateway to **Richness of Experience**.

Think about the best moments of your life. Maybe it was watching a sunset, playing a sport, having a deep conversation, or creating something with your hands. Were you checking your phone? Were you multitasking? No. You were entirely, singular, rapturously present.

The "Shallow Life" is a life of skimming. You skim articles. You skim relationships. You skim nature. You are everywhere, and therefore you are nowhere.

The "Deep Life" is a life of texture. When you train your mind to focus, you unlock the ability to truly *taste* your food, truly *hear* music, and truly *understand* another person. You reclaim the vividness of childhood.

By hardening your mind against the noise, you are not closing yourself off from the world. You are opening yourself up to the parts of the world that actually matter. You are trading the cheap dopamine of the screen for the slow, deep serotonin of connection and mastery.

The Competitive Advantage of the Future

We are entering a new economic era. The Industrial Revolution leveraged physical strength. The Information Revolution leveraged connectivity. The AI Revolution will leverage **Human Depth**.

Artificial Intelligence can already write average emails. It can summarize data. It can write basic code. It can handle the "Shallow Work" faster and cheaper than you ever could. If your job consists of moving information from one tab to another, you are in danger.

But AI cannot (yet) perform Deep Work. It cannot synthesize disparate ideas into a paradigm-shifting strategy. It cannot navigate complex, emotional human negotiations with empathy. It cannot produce art that speaks to the human soul.

These things require deep, sustained, human attention.

As the world becomes more distracted, the ability to focus is becoming the rarest and most valuable commodity in the marketplace. By mastering the skills in this book, you are doing more than just "getting organized." You are future-proofing your career. You are becoming an elite cognitive athlete in a world of couch potatoes.

While your peers are drowning in the noise, you will be the one building the boat.

The Final Charge

The concepts in this book are simple, but they are not easy. The world will try to break you. The apps on your phone employ the smartest psychologists in the world, and they wake up every morning with one goal: to steal your time.

- They want your outrage.
- They want your anxiety.
- They want your clicks.

Do not give it to them.

Your attention is your life. It is the only currency you truly possess. How you spend your attention is how you spend your life.

Do not spend it on things that make you angry, hollow, or anxious. Spend it on your craft. Spend it on your loved ones. Spend it on your own evolution.

You have the tools.

- **Clear the desk.**
- **Block the time.**
- **Silence the phone.**
- **One task.**
- **Breathe.**

The path of the Hardened Mind is a path of resistance. It is the uphill road. But the view from the top is clarity. The view is freedom.

REFLECTION QUESTIONS

IDENTIFY YOUR PRIMARY FOCUS KILLERS

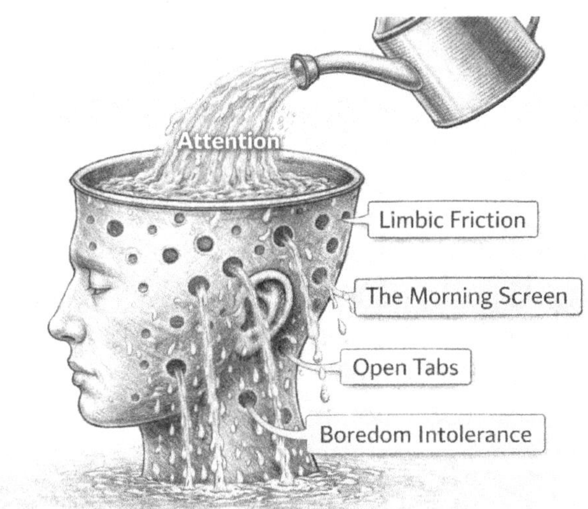

Identifying the Leaks: You cannot increase the "flow" of focus until you plug the structural holes in your habits.

An Audit of the Hardened Mind

You have read the theory. You have seen the protocols. Now, we must turn the spotlight inward.

It is easy to read a book about focus and nod in agreement. It is infinitely harder to look at your own daily behaviors and admit that you are an addict. It is painful to acknowledge that the reason you are not elite is not because you lack talent, but because you lack the discipline to sit in a chair and do the work.

This section is not a quiz. It is a forensic audit. In the corporate world, when a company is bleeding money, they bring in auditors to find the leak. Right now, you are bleeding cognitive potential. You are hemorrhaging attention.

We are going to go through the five pillars of the book—Environment, Deep Work, Digital Boundaries, Single-Tasking, and Mindfulness—and we are going to interrogate your habits.

233

Do not rush through this. Do not answer these questions in your head. The brain is a master of rationalization; it will lie to you to protect your ego. It will say, *"I only check email a lot because my job requires it,"* or *"I need a messy desk to be creative."*

Write your answers down. When you write, you objectify your thoughts. You make them external and undeniable. Grab a physical notebook and a pen. We are going to find the leaks.

Part 1: The Environmental Interrogation (The Physical Cradle)

In Chapter 1, we established that the brain is an energy-conserving machine that processes every photon of visual data entering your eyes. Your environment is either a cradle for focus or a cage of distraction.

1. The Peripheral Vision Audit Sit in your primary work chair. Look directly at your monitor. Without moving your head, allow your awareness to expand to your peripheral vision. List every single object that you can see that is **not** immediately necessary for the task you are currently performing.

- *The Context:* Every object in your field of vision represents an "Attention Tax." A stack of unpaid bills creates low-level anxiety. A half-read book creates a sense of guilt. A coffee mug from yesterday creates a sense of disorder.

- *The Deep Dive:*
    - How many of these objects are "Open Loops"—tasks you haven't finished?

    - How many are "Identity Conflicts"—hobbies or interests that have nothing to do with your work?

    - If you were to sweep your arm across the desk and knock everything onto the floor except your computer and notebook, would you feel panicked or relieved? (If the answer is "relieved," your environment is suffocating you).

- *The Action:* Remove 5 items from your desk right now. Not tomorrow. Now.

2. The Auditory Defense Check Close your eyes in your workspace for 60 seconds. Listen. Really listen. What is the soundscape of your productivity?

- *The Context:* The brain's auditory cortex never sleeps. It evolved to hear predators snapping twigs. Erratic, intermittent noise (conversations, traffic, notifications) triggers a low-level "alert" response, flooding your system with cortisol.
- *The Deep Dive:*
  - Can you hear human speech? (The brain is hardwired to process language; you cannot ignore it).
  - Are you relying on "Willpower" to ignore the noise? (Willpower is a finite resource. If you use it to ignore noise, you have none left for your work).
  - Do you own noise-canceling headphones? If yes, why aren't they on your head?
- *The Action:* If your environment scores below a 7/10 for silence, you must commit to a "Sound Masking" protocol (White Noise or Headphones) immediately.

3. The Ergonomic Pain Threshold Recall your last Deep Work session that lasted longer than an hour. At what point did your body start to speak to you?

- *The Context:* Physical discomfort is a massive cognitive drain. Proprioception (the sense of body position) will override higher thought if the body is in pain. You cannot think deeply if your lower back is screaming.
- *The Deep Dive:*
  - Do you end your day with neck strain or eye fatigue?
  - Is your monitor actually at eye level, or are you looking down (creating "Tech Neck")?
  - Is your chair supporting your spine, or are you collapsing into it?
- *The Reality Check:* Most people prioritize the aesthetics of their workspace over the biology of their workspace. An ugly chair that allows you to focus for 4 hours is infinitely superior to a beautiful chair that breaks your back in 40 minutes.

In Chapter 2, we discussed the 90-minute sprint and the neurobiology of myelination. Now, we must assess your ability to execute.

4. The "Fake Work" Ratio Look at your output for the last five workdays. Categorize your hours into two buckets: **Deep Work** (Creating new value, high concentration) and **Shallow Work** (Logistics, meetings, email, slack).

- *The Context:* The Pareto Principle applies here. 20% of your work produces 80% of your results. Usually, that 20% is Deep Work. However, most people spend 90% of their time on Shallow Work because it is easier and less scary.

- *The Deep Dive:*

    o What is your actual ratio? (Be honest. Is it 10/90? 20/80?).

    o If you continued working at this specific ratio for the next five years, would you achieve your highest career ambitions? Or would you simply be a "responsive employee"?

    o What is the one "Hard Task" you have been avoiding for a month by doing "Easy Tasks"?

- *The Reality Check:* Being "Busy" is often a form of laziness—lazy thinking and indiscriminate action.

5. The Friction Point Analysis (The "Wall") Think about the last time you sat down to do something difficult (e.g., writing a report, coding a complex feature). At what minute mark did you feel the first urge to stop, check your phone, or get a snack?

- *The Context:* This is the "Limbic Friction." Your brain wants to conserve energy. It screams at you to stop. This is the moment where "The Click" happens—if you push through.

- *The Deep Dive:*

    o Did you succumb to the urge?

    o What was the specific *emotion* you felt right before the urge? Was it boredom? Was it "Imposter Syndrome" (fear that you can't do the task)? Was it confusion (lack of clarity)?

- o Do you interpret this friction as a sign that "something is wrong," or do you recognize it as the necessary metabolic cost of engaging the Prefrontal Cortex?

6. The Calendar Integrity Test Open your calendar for the past week. Can a stranger look at your calendar and immediately identify your most important priority?

- *The Context*: If your calendar is a solid block of meetings, you are not in control of your time; you are a victim of other people's priorities. Deep Work must be defended on the calendar like a doctor's appointment.

- *The Deep Dive:*
    - o Do you schedule Deep Work blocks, or do you just hope to find time "in the cracks"? (Hope is not a strategy).
    - o When someone asks for a meeting during your Deep Work time, do you protect the time, or do you cave immediately?
    - o Do you have a "Shutdown Ritual" marked on the calendar, or does your work just bleed into your evening until you fall asleep?

Part 3: The Digital Sovereignty Audit (The Firewall)

In Chapter 3, we declared war on the Notification Economy. Now we check your defenses.

7. The "Pavlovian Dog" Check Unlock your phone. Go to Settings > Screen Time > Pickups. How many times did you pick up your phone yesterday?

- *The Context*: The average user picks up their phone 58 to 150 times a day. If you are awake for 16 hours, that is a distraction every 10 minutes. You are not working; you are being interrupted.

- *The Deep Dive:*
    - o Divide your total pickups by your waking hours. What is your "Interruption Rate"?
    - o How many of those pickups were *intentional* (you needed a specific tool) versus *reactive* (you saw a light or felt a buzz)?

- o Do you feel a "Phantom Vibration" in your pocket when your phone isn't there? (This is a sign of hyper-sensitized dopamine pathways).

8. The Morning Cortisol Injection What is the very first thing your eyes process when you wake up in the morning?

- *The Context*: If the answer is "My Smartphone," you have lost the day before it began. You are flooding your brain with "Bottom-Up" stimuli (other people's demands, bad news, comparison) before your "Top-Down" control systems (executive planning) are online.

- *The Deep Dive*:
    - o Do you sleep with your phone in the bedroom? Why? (Buy an alarm clock).
    - o What is the lie you tell yourself to justify this? ("I need to see if there's an emergency"). Has there ever actually been an emergency at 6:30 AM via email?
    - o How would your anxiety levels change if you didn't look at a screen for the first 60 minutes of the day?

9. The "Just Checking" Loop Which app is your digital pacifier?

- *The Context*: We all have one app we open unconsciously to soothe anxiety or boredom. It might be Instagram, Twitter, LinkedIn, or even Email. This is your "Slot Machine."

- *The Deep Dive*:
    - o When you are waiting for a microwave, an elevator, or a file to download, where does your thumb go?
    - o Are you willing to delete this specific app from your phone for 7 days?
    - o If the thought of deleting it causes physical anxiety, you must admit that you have a dependency. It is not a tool; it is a drug.

In Chapter 4, we learned that multitasking drops your IQ by 10 points. Are you protecting your intelligence?

10. The Browser Tab Confessional When you are in the middle of a work session, how many tabs are typically open in your browser?

- *The Context*: Browser tabs are "Visual Noise." Each tab represents a potential task switch. They sit in your peripheral vision, begging to be clicked. They are a constant drain on working memory.

- *The Deep Dive:*

    o Do you use tabs as a "To-Do List"? (This is a disastrous strategy. It forces you to re-process the decision of "what to do with this" every time you look at the tab).

    o Do you have the discipline to close a tab once you are done with it?

    o Can you commit to the "One Window" rule—only having the application you are currently using visible on the screen?

11. The "Second Screen" Syndrome Do you watch TV or use a tablet while you are supposed to be working or relaxing?

- *The Context*: "Dual Screening" is the ultimate training ground for distraction. It trains the brain that "one stream of information is not enough." It creates a high threshold for stimulation that makes deep, slow work feel impossibly boring.

- *The Deep Dive:*

    o Can you watch a movie without looking at your phone?

    o Can you sit in a meeting without checking your email "on the side"?

    o Do you realize that when you dual-screen, you are retaining almost zero information from either source?

12. The Switch Cost Calculation Think of the last time you tried to "quickly" answer an email in the middle of a project.

- *The Context:* It takes an average of 23 minutes and 15 seconds to get back to full focus after an interruption.
- *The Deep Dive:*
    - Do you delude yourself into thinking you are a "good multitasker"? (Science says the people who think they are good at it are actually the worst at it).
    - Are you willing to set an auto-responder that says, "I check email twice a day," or are you addicted to the dopamine hit of being "responsive"?

Part 5: The Mindset Mastery (The Internal State)

In Chapter 5, we addressed the noise inside your head. This is the final frontier.

13. The Boredom Tolerance Test This is the most critical question in the book. Can you be bored?

- *The Context:* Boredom is not a defect; it is a filter. Great ideas only arrive after you have waded through the sludge of boredom. If you numb the boredom with a phone, you numb the brilliance that comes after it.
- *The Deep Dive:*
    - When you have 3 minutes of downtime, do you panic?
    - Can you sit in a chair for 10 minutes and just... think?
    - Do you consume content (podcasts, music) constantly because you are afraid of the silence in your own head? What are you trying to drown out?

14. The "Inner Critic" Awareness When you lose focus (and you will), what is the tone of voice you use with yourself?

- *The Context:* Shame is a poor fuel for focus. If you berate yourself ("I'm so lazy," "I'm broken"), you trigger a stress response. Stress kills the Prefrontal Cortex. It becomes a self-fulfilling prophecy.
- *The Deep Dive:*
    - Do you view a moment of distraction as a "failure of character" or a "lapse in the system"?

- o Can you apply the "Mindfulness Rep" (Notice -> Return) without judgment?
  - o Do you understand that the goal is not "Perfect Focus" but "Quick Recovery"?

15. The Ultimate "Why" Why are you doing this?

- *The Context*: Mastering the Hardened Mind is painful. It requires sacrifice. It requires being the "weird" one who doesn't reply to texts instantly. If your motivation is weak, you will quit.

- *The Deep Dive*:
  - o Do you want to focus just to "get more done" (Productivity Porn)? Or do you want to focus because you have a Masterpiece inside you that requires it?
  - o Who loses if you remain distracted? (Your family? Your future self? The world?).
  - o Write down your "Deep Life Mission Statement." *I am building a Hardened Mind so that I can...*

The Final Audit Calculation

Look at your answers.

If you were honest, you likely found that your environment is cluttered, your calendar is porous, your phone is a master over you, and your mind is terrified of boredom.

Good.

Diagnosis is the first step of the cure. You now have a list of targets. You know exactly where the leaks are. You know that the problem isn't that you are "stupid" or "lazy." The problem is that you have been operating without a manual in a world designed to break you.

You now have the manual. You have identified the killers. Now, you pick up the weapon of Focus, and you systematically eliminate them.

One by one. Day by day. Rep by rep.

The audit is complete. Now, go do the work.

BOOK FIVE

REACH YOUR GOALS WITH PRECISION

INTRODUCTION

FROM VAGUE DREAMS TO CONCRETE RESULTS

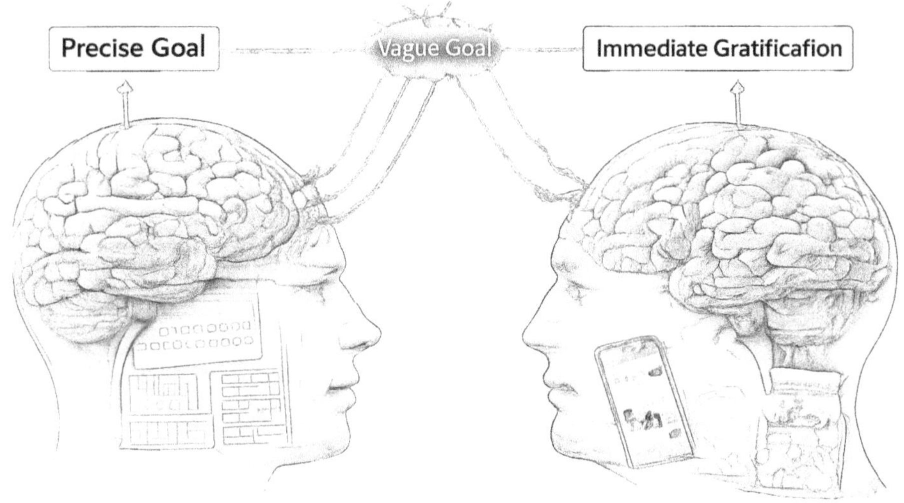

You have mastered your environment. You have reclaimed your attention from the digital sirens. You have built a mind capable of deep, singular focus. But focus, in its rawest form, is merely an engine. Without a steering wheel and a destination, a high-powered engine simply burns fuel in an empty parking lot, generating heat and noise but achieving no displacement.

We enter Book 5 to address the most common tragedy of the high-performer: **The Efficient Failure.**

This is the individual who works 12 hours a day, executes flawless 90-minute sprints, and maintains a pristine digital firewall, yet wakes up three years later to realize they have moved a thousand miles in the wrong direction—or worse, haven't moved at all. They have been "busy," but they have not been *effective*. They have focused on the "how" while neglecting the "where." They have perfected the art of climbing the ladder, only to realize the ladder is leaning against the wrong wall.

In the hyper-competitive landscape of 2026, the world no longer rewards raw effort; it rewards **precision**. We live in an era of infinite paths, where the greatest risk is not failing to work hard, but failing to choose the right target. In a world of AI-driven automation and global competition, "working hard" is the baseline—it is the table stakes. The winners are those who can apply that hard work to a specific, high-leverage point with mathematical accuracy.

This book is about **Goal Architecture**. We are moving away from the soft, comforting world of "New Year's Resolutions" and "Vague Intentions" and entering the hard, uncompromising world of **Precision Engineering**. We are going to treat your life's ambitions with the same clinical rigor that a NASA engineer applies to a moon landing or a heart surgeon applies to a bypass.

The Pathology of the "Vague Dream"

Most people fail to reach their goals because they never actually set any. They set "Wishes." A wish is a goal without a skeleton. It is a cloud of desire that lacks the structural integrity to withstand the pressures of reality.

Consider the standard lexicon of the unhardened mind:

- **The Wish:** "I want to be successful."
- **The Wish:** "I want to get in shape."
- **The Wish:** "I want to grow my business."

The human brain is an incredible problem-solving machine—it is a "servo-mechanism" designed to bridge the gap between a current state and a target state. However, like any advanced computer, it requires specific parameters to function. If you feed a computer vague instructions, you get an error message. If you feed your brain a vague goal, you get **procrastination**.

A vague goal is like a low-resolution map; it gives you the general direction of north, but it doesn't tell you about the cliffs, the rivers, or the specific coordinates of the treasure. When the destination is blurry, the brain's internal GPS cannot calculate a route. Consequently, the brain defaults to the "Standard State": conservation of energy.

When a goal is vague, the **Prefrontal Cortex (PFC)**—the seat of executive function and planning—cannot calculate the "Energy-to-Reward" ratio. If the brain doesn't know exactly what the prize is, it refuses to authorize the metabolic expenditure required to win it. This is why you feel "unmotivated." You aren't lazy; you are just poorly defined. Precision is the only antidote to this neurological paralysis.

The Physics of Progress: Velocity vs. Speed

In physics, there is a vital distinction between speed and velocity that perfectly mirrors the difference between "busyness" and "results."

- **Speed** is a scalar quantity; it measures how fast you are moving. It doesn't care about direction. If you run in a perfect circle at 20 miles per hour, your speed is high, but your displacement—your actual progress away from your starting point—is zero.

- **Velocity** is a vector quantity; it measures how fast you are moving *in a specific direction.*

Most "productivity" advice focuses on speed—how to do things faster, how to squeeze more tasks into a day, how to "hustle" harder. This is a recipe for burnout and circular motion. This book focuses on **Velocity**. We are going to ensure that every ounce of energy you expend—every 90-minute sprint you execute—results in a measurable displacement toward your ultimate objective.

In the Hardened Mind framework, we do not care about how many hours you worked today. We care about the **Delta**: the measurable change between where you started at 8:00 AM and where you stood at 5:00 PM. If your Delta is zero, your speed was irrelevant.

The Biological Cost of Ambiguity

Ambiguity is not just a strategic error; it is a biological toxin. When your goals are unclear, your brain remains in a state of **Cognitive Dissonance**. You know you should be doing "something," but you aren't sure exactly what "it" is. This creates a "leaky" cognitive system where energy is wasted on constant re-evaluation.

This uncertainty triggers the **Amygdala**, the brain's ancient threat-detection center. To your primitive brain, a lack of clarity is synonymous with a lack of safety. If the path ahead is foggy, there could be a predator in the mist. This results in a constant, low-level release of **Cortisol**, the stress hormone.

High cortisol levels have a devastating effect on the Hardened Mind:

1. **PFC Inhibition:** It physically "shuts down" the Prefrontal Cortex, making it harder to think logically or plan long-term.

2. **Dopamine Depletion:** It makes it harder for your brain to feel the "reward" of small wins.

3. **Tunnel Vision:** It forces you into a "reactive" state where you only focus on the immediate, noisy problems (shallow work) rather than the important, quiet problems (deep work).

By defining your goals with precision, you provide your brain with a "Neural Reward Map." When you define a specific, measurable milestone, you give the brain a target for **Dopamine** release. Dopamine is not just about pleasure; it is the molecule of *motivation* and *persistence*.

When you achieve a sub-goal that you have clearly defined, your brain receives a "Reward Signal." This signal reinforces the behavior, making it easier to start again tomorrow. Precision allows you to turn your journey into a series of predictable dopamine hits, making "the grind" not only tolerable but biologically addictive.

The Three Pillars of Goal Architecture

To transition from vague dreams to concrete results, we will build your strategy upon three foundational pillars that will be explored in depth throughout this book:

1. The Metric of Truth (Measurability)

If a goal cannot be measured, it does not exist in the physical world; it exists only in your imagination. We are moving beyond "feelings" of progress. In Book 5, we will learn to define success so clearly that a stranger—or even an AI auditor—looking at your data could tell you, without a shadow of a doubt, whether you succeeded or failed today. We will develop "Binary Goals": either the box is checked, or it isn't. There is no "I kind of did it."

2. Temporal Inverse Mapping (Backward Planning)

Most people plan from the present forward. They look at where they are today and ask, "What should I do next?" This is a mistake. The present is cluttered with your current limitations, your current fears, and your current environment.

Precision thinkers plan from the **Future Backward**. We start at the finish line—the fully realized result—and we walk backward in time, asking what had to happen *just before* that. We continue this process until we reach the very first step you need to take tomorrow morning at 8:00 AM. This removes the guesswork and creates a "Path of Least Resistance."

3. The Accountability Scaffold (Social Pressure)

Focus is an internal battle, but success is an external reality. We often fail ourselves because we are the easiest people to lie to. We make excuses to ourselves that we would never make to a respected peer.

We will implement systems of "Social Pressure" and "Peer Review" that make it harder to quit than it is to continue. We will use the human "Status Drive" to pull you through the "Dip"—that middle period of a project where the novelty has worn off and only the work remains.

The Shift from "Outcome" to "Process"

A major theme of this book is the **Decoupling of Results**. This sounds counter-intuitive in a book about goals, but it is the secret to the Hardened Mind.

If you focus only on the final outcome (e.g., "I want to earn $1 million"), you are focusing on something you cannot entirely control. Markets change. Luck plays a role. Competition intervenes. This creates anxiety.

Instead, we use precision to identify the **Lead Actions**—the specific behaviors that, if performed with 100% consistency, make the result a mathematical probability.

- You don't "aim" for the million dollars.
- You "aim" for the 50 sales calls per day.
- You "aim" for the 2,000 words of code written per session.

When you define your goals with this level of precision, you shift your focus from the "Ghost" (the future result) to the "Machine" (your daily actions). You become obsessed with the quality of the machine. If the machine is precise, the results take care of themselves.

The High Stakes of 2026: Why Now?

We are living through a transition period in human history. The "Knowledge Work" era is being superseded by the "Insight and Execution" era. Information is no longer a competitive advantage; everyone has access to the same data via Large Language Models and instant connectivity.

The new competitive advantage is the ability to **Synthesize and Execute**.

If you have a vague goal, you will be outperformed by an algorithm or a more precise competitor within months. However, if you can define an objective with such precision that you can direct your "Hardened Focus" (developed in Book 4) toward it with laser-like accuracy, you become a "Super-Producer."

A Super-Producer can achieve in six months what a "vague worker" achieves in six years. This isn't hyperbole; it is the result of eliminating the "Friction of Indecision." When you know exactly what to do, you don't waste 4 hours "getting started." You simply engage.

What to Expect in Book 5

Over the next five chapters, we are going to transform you from a dreamer into an architect. We are going to take the raw power of your focused mind and give it a blueprint for world-class execution.

- **Chapter 1: Define Your Objectives with Measurable Criteria.** We will move beyond the basic SMART goal framework into "Aggressive Metrics." We will learn how to turn a dream into a number.

- **Chapter 2: Map Your Path with Backward Planning.** We will master the "Inverse Map." You will learn how to deconstruct a 12-month mission into 365 daily "Tactical Missions."

- **Chapter 3: Stay Accountable Using Peer Review Systems.** We will explore the "External Brain." You will learn how to build a board of advisors and peer groups that won't let you settle for mediocrity.

- **Chapter 4: Pivot Your Strategy Without Losing Your Focus.** Rigidity is the enemy of progress. We will learn the "Scientific Method" of goal pursuit—how to look at data, realize a tactic isn't working, and change the *how* without ever losing sight of the *what*.

- **Chapter 5: Measure What Matters to Ensure Daily Gains.** We will build your "Dashboard." You will learn the difference between "Lag Measures" and "Lead Measures" and how to track the small wins that lead to massive victories.

The "Hardened Mind" is no longer just a defensive tool to keep distractions away. It is now an offensive weapon. You have the engine. You have the fuel. Now, let's draw the map.

Results are not an accident; they are a mathematical certainty of precise planning and disciplined execution. It is time to stop wishing. It is time to start building.

CHAPTER 1

DEFINE YOUR OBJECTIVES WITH MEASURABLE CRITERIA

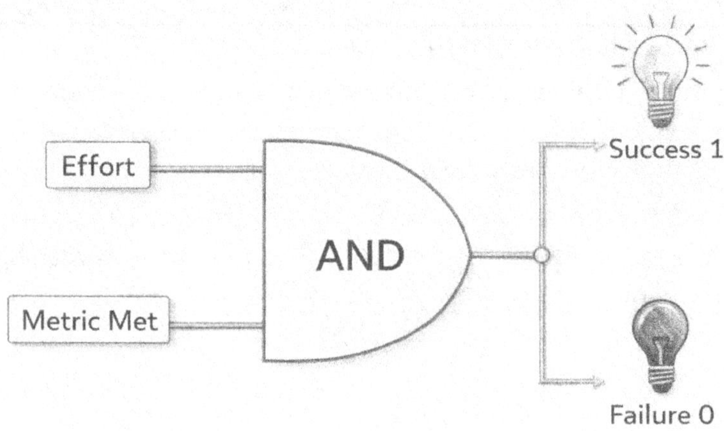

In the previous book, we focused on the "Hardened Mind" as a fortress—a defensive structure designed to repel the siege of digital distraction. Now, we begin the offensive. But an army that marches without a clear target is just a group of people taking a walk. In the realm of high-performance execution, your target must be defined with such clinical accuracy that there is zero room for interpretation.

Most failure is not a failure of effort; it is a **failure of definition**. We often hide behind vague language because vagueness is safe. If you say, "I want to be a better writer," you can never truly fail, because "better" is a subjective, moving target. Vagueness is the shield of the ego.

In this chapter, we are going to strip away that shield. We are going to move beyond the traditional "SMART" goals and move into the world of **Aggressive Metrics** and **Binary Outcomes**. We are going to learn how to translate a visceral desire into a mathematical objective.

The Subjectivity Trap: Why "Better" is the Enemy

The greatest enemy of a Hardened Mind is the word "better." When we use subjective adjectives to define our goals, we are inadvertently inviting our "Limbic System" to sit at the negotiation table.

Consider the internal dialogue of someone whose goal is to "be more productive." At 4:00 PM on a Tuesday, when fatigue sets in, the Limbic System—which seeks immediate comfort—begins to negotiate. It says, *"You've answered ten emails today. That's more than yesterday. You've been 'more productive.' It's okay to stop now."* Because the goal was never defined, the brain chooses the path of least resistance.

A Hardened Goal has no loopholes. It is **Binary**. It operates on the **Binary Standard**: At the end of the day, could a computer—devoid of emotion, nuance, or the ability to make excuses—determine if the mark was hit? If the answer is "it depends," your criteria are structurally compromised.

The Neurochemistry of the Binary Switch

The human brain is a biological machine driven by chemical incentives. To master your goals, you must understand the **Nucleus Accumbens** and its relationship with **Dopamine**. In a state of vagueness, your reward system is essentially paralyzed. If you don't know exactly when you've "won," your brain cannot release the dopamine required to reinforce the behavior.

Dopamine is the "molecule of more." It is the fuel of anticipation. When you define a goal with binary precision (e.g., "Write 1,000 words"), you create a neural toggle. The moment you hit word 1,000, the toggle flips from 0 to 1. This flip triggers a dopaminergic surge that tells the brain, *"This effort was worth it. Do it again tomorrow."* Without this switch, you are operating in a dopamine desert, which leads to "The Burnout of the Undefined"—the feeling of working hard but getting nowhere.

To define your criteria with precision, you must separate what you *want* from what you *do*. In the framework of Goal Architecture, we divide metrics into two categories: **Lag Measures** and **Lead Measures**.

1. The Lag Measure (The Destination)

A Lag Measure is the ultimate result you are chasing. It is called a "Lag" because by the time you receive the data, the event has already passed. It is history.

- *Example:* $100,000 in revenue, 180 lbs of body weight, a finished book manuscript.

2. The Lead Measure (The Lever)

A Lead Measure is the specific, predictive behavior that causes the Lag Measure to move. Unlike the Lag Measure, the Lead Measure is within your 100% control *right now*.

- *Example:* Making 20 sales calls, maintaining a 500-calorie deficit, writing for 90 minutes.

The Rule of Precision: Most people obsess over the Lag and ignore the Lead. The Hardened Mind does the opposite. You define the Lag with absolute clarity, and then you turn 100% of your focus to the Lead Measures. If you move the lever, the weight must move. It is a matter of physics, not luck.

To achieve a 4,000-word depth on this subject, we must look at the specific psychological resistance to precision. Why do we avoid it? Because precision creates **Accountability**. When a goal is vague, you can't fail. When a goal is a number, you can be wrong. The Hardened Mind embraces the possibility of being wrong as the only path to being right.

The "Granularity Scale"

Precision is not a one-time event; it is a nested hierarchy. A truly precise objective exists at three levels:

1. **Macro-Metric (The Year):** The ultimate Lag Measure.
2. **Meso-Metric (The Month):** The milestone that proves the trajectory is correct.

3. **Micro-Metric (The Day):** The Lead Measure that you can execute in a single focus block.

If you cannot trace a line from your daily Micro-Metric to your yearly Macro-Metric, your goal is a "Floating Objective"—it lacks the grounding required to withstand the gravity of daily life.

Thresholding: The Goldilocks Zone of Execution

To prevent "Metric Drift," where you do the work but lose the quality, you must establish **Thresholding**. High performers often fall into the trap of "Manic Execution," where they overwork one day and crash the next. Thresholding creates a stable platform for long-term power.

1. **The Floor (The "Non-Negotiable"):** The absolute minimum viable effort to keep the streak alive. Even on your worst day—when you have the flu, when your car breaks down, when the world seems to be ending—you do the Floor. (e.g., "Write 200 words").

2. **The Ceiling (The "Over-Training" Guard):** The point of diminishing returns. High performers often burn out by doing too much in one day. The Ceiling protects your focus for tomorrow. (e.g., "Stop at 2,000 words").

By operating within this zone, you build a sustainable rhythm. You avoid the "Hero-to-Zero" cycle. Precision is not just about the target; it is about the **Tolerance** of the system.

Parkinson's Law and the Neurobiology of the Deadline

Precision in criteria is meaningless without precision in **Time**. **Parkinson's Law** states that "work expands so as to fill the time available for its completion."

If you give yourself a month to finish a task, your brain will subconsciously reduce its focus intensity to match a 30-day burn. However, when you set a precise, aggressive deadline, the brain activates the **Anterior Cingulate Cortex (ACC)**. This region of the brain scans for errors and conflict, while simultaneously triggering the release of **Norepinephrine**. This chemical cocktail sharpens your physiological arousal, narrowing your visual and mental field until only the task remains.

The "Bright Line" Rule and the Elimination of Choice

Psychologically, precision allows for the creation of **"Bright Line" Rules**. These are standards that leave no room for interpretation.

- **Fuzzy Rule:** "I'll get some deep work done in the morning."
- **Bright Line Rule:** "I will be at my desk, phone in the drawer, at 8:00 AM sharp."

The Bright Line rule removes **Decision Fatigue**. When the criteria are precise, you don't have to "decide" to work. You have already made the decision during the planning phase. This preserves your **Executive Function** for the actual problem-solving of your task, rather than wasting it on the meta-work of getting started.

Applying Precision to "Soft" Goals

A common objection is that "soft" goals—like "being a better spouse" or "improving creativity"—cannot be measured. This is a fallacy. While the *outcome* is an emotion or an abstract state, the *inputs* are always physical actions.

- **To be a "Present Parent":** Metric = 30 minutes of "Device-Free Time" with the children per day.
- **To be "More Creative":** Metric = Producing 5 "Bad Ideas" every morning before 9:00 AM.

By putting a number on the behavior, you provide the structure in which the emotion can flourish. You cannot "force" a feeling, but you can "force" the conditions that create it.

The Anatomy of an Aggressive Metric (The ARID Framework)

To move beyond the basic SMART goals, we use the **ARID** framework.

- **Absolute:** There is no "more" or "less." Use integers.
- **Result-Oriented:** We don't measure "trying"; we measure "done."
- **Influenceable:** If you can't control it directly, it's a Lag Measure. Find the Lead Measure.
- **Deadline-Driven:** If it doesn't have a date, it's a dream, not a goal.

The "Success Definition" Document

To solidify this, you must create a physical document for every major objective. It acts as a contract between your present self and your future self. It must answer the question: *"At 11:59 PM on the deadline day, exactly what evidence will exist to prove success?"*

The Daily Metric Audit: The Feedback Loop

Finally, you must implement the **5-Minute Evening Audit**. At the end of every day, you look at your Lead Measures.

1. **Binary Check:** Did I hit the number? (1 or 0).

2. **Friction Analysis:** If no, what specific environmental or internal factor caused the failure?

3. **Adjustment:** What is the one change for tomorrow to ensure a 1?

This audit turns your life into a laboratory. You stop taking failure personally and start taking it clinically. You are an engineer optimizing a machine.

Conclusion: The Freedom of the Constraint

There is a profound paradox in precision: **Constraints create freedom.** The individual with vague goals is never truly at rest; they are haunted by the "Ghost of Unfinished Work." They always feel they *should* be doing more because they don't know where "enough" is.

The Hardened Mind, equipped with precise criteria, knows exactly when the day is won. When the metrics are met, the work is done. This allows for total presence in your rest and absolute intensity in your work. You are no longer a leaf in the wind; you are a navigator with a set of coordinates.

CHAPTER 2

MAP YOUR PATH WITH BACKWARD PLANNING

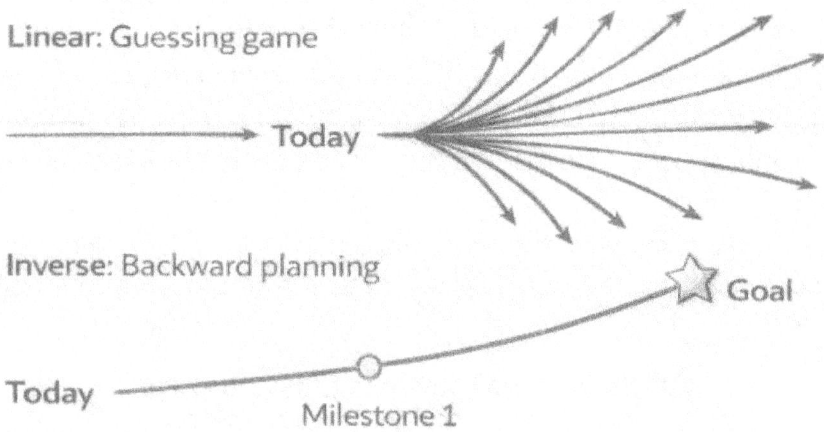

You have defined your target. You have stripped away the subjective fog of "getting better" and replaced it with the cold, hard logic of measurable criteria. You now have a destination. But a destination without a route is merely a source of anxiety. This is where most ambitious individuals stall: they stand at the base of a mountain, looking at the peak, and feel paralyzed by the sheer verticality of the climb.

Standard planning is **Linear Planning**. You look at where you are today and ask, "What should I do next?" While this feels intuitive, it is strategically flawed. Linear planning is constrained by your current environment, your current resources, and—most dangerously—your current fears. When you plan forward, you are essentially guessing your way toward a goal, often taking unnecessary detours or getting bogged down in "preparatory" tasks that don't actually move the needle.

In this chapter, we introduce **Backward Planning**, also known as **Inverse Mapping**. This is the strategic discipline of starting at the finish line and working your way back to the present moment. It is the secret of military commanders, master architects, and elite project managers. By reversing the chronological flow of your planning, you eliminate the "Friction of the Unknown" and create a path that is not just possible, but inevitable.

The Neurobiology of the Inverse Map

Why does backward planning feel so much more effective than forward planning? The answer lies in the **Prospective Memory** and the way the brain simulates the future.

When you plan forward, your brain views the goal as a distant, abstract concept. This triggers the **Default Mode Network (DMN)**, which often leads to daydreaming rather than action. However, when you start at the goal and work backward, you are engaging in a process called **Future Simulation**. You are forced to imagine the goal as already achieved. This shifts the brain from a "Possibility" mindset to an "Operational" mindset.

Research from the University of Iowa and the University of Pennsylvania suggests that people who plan backward experience higher levels of motivation and lower levels of stress. This is because backward planning creates a clear "Causal Chain." When you see exactly what had to happen *just before* you succeeded, the goal loses its mystical quality. It becomes a series of logistical steps. You aren't "hoping" to win; you are simply following a recipe.

Phase 1: The "Success Hindsight" Exercise

To begin backward planning, you must perform a mental time-travel exercise. Sit in a quiet space—ideally your "Focus Cradle" from Book 4— and transport yourself to the date of your deadline.

Imagine it is 11:59 PM on your deadline day. You have achieved your ARID criteria. The **Artifact of Proof** is in your hand.

1. **The Vision:** What does the result look like? (Be specific: see the bank balance, hold the printed book, look at the 12% body fat in the mirror).

2. **The Audit:** Now, ask the critical question: *"What was the very last thing I did right before I achieved this?"*

Maybe it was clicking "Publish." Maybe it was the final weigh-in. Maybe it was the closing signature on a contract. That is your **Final Milestone**.

Phase 2: The Logic of "What Had to Happen First?"

Once you have your final milestone, you step back one increment. Do not think about "the beginning." Only think about the immediate precursor.

- **Final Result:** Published Book.
- **Immediate Precursor:** Final manuscript sent to the printer.
- **Precursor to that:** Final proofreading completed.
- **Precursor to that:** Second draft revised based on editor feedback.
- **Precursor to that:** First draft completed.

This is the **Causal Chain**. Each link in the chain is a binary requirement for the next. If link B doesn't happen, link A is impossible. By deconstructing the goal this way, you identify the **Critical Path**—the specific sequence of events that *must* occur for the result to exist.

Backward planning naturally filters out "Busy Work." In forward planning, you might think, "I need to design a logo for my book." But when you work backward from a finished manuscript, you realize that the logo has zero impact on the completion of the text. You realize the logo is a distraction masquerading as progress.

Phase 3: Temporal Deconstruction (The Rule of Halves)

To turn this causal chain into a schedule, we use the **Rule of Halves**. This prevents the common error of "Optimism Bias," where we underestimate how long tasks take.

1. **The 100% Mark:** The Deadline.
2. **The 50% Mark:** Where do you need to be halfway through the timeline?
3. **The 25% Mark:** Where do you need to be in the first quarter?
4. **The 10% Mark:** What is the first major milestone?

By the time you reach the "1% Mark," you have identified what you need to do **this week**. And once you know what you need to do this week, you can define your Lead Measures for **today**.

The "Friction Audit": Anticipating the Killers

Precision mapping isn't just about the "Happy Path." A Hardened Mind anticipates the "Friction Points." For every milestone in your backward plan, you must ask: *What is the most likely reason this milestone will fail?"*

- **The Reason:** "I will get overwhelmed by the sheer volume of data."
- **The Counter-Measure:** "I will use a specific 'Data Triage' system every Friday."
- **The Reason:** "I will run out of energy in Month 3."
- **The Counter-Measure:** "I will schedule a mandatory 3-day 'Focus Recovery' break at the 60-day mark."

This is **Pre-Mortem Planning**. By visualizing the failure before it happens, you can build the solution into your map. You aren't just mapping the path; you are paving it.

The "Bridge to the Present": The Next 24 Hours

The most common failure of planning is that the plan remains on the paper. To prevent this, the final step of your backward map must be a **Physical Action** that occurs within the next 24 hours.

If your backward plan leads you back to "Researching the topic," that is too vague. The bridge to the present must be a **Hardened Action**: *"Tomorrow at 9:00 AM, I will spend 90 minutes in my first Deep Work sprint, producing the first 500 words of Chapter 1."*

Managing the "Middle Muddle"

Every long-term goal has a period known as the "Middle Muddle." This is the point where the initial excitement has evaporated, the final result is still far away, and the work feels like a monotonous grind.

Backward planning cures the Middle Muddle by providing **Interim Logic**. When you are in week 12 of a 24-week project, you don't look at the 24-week goal. You look at the **Week 13 Milestone**. Because the path was mapped backward, you know with mathematical certainty that if you hit the Week 13 milestone, you are still on track for the final result. This provides the **Cognitive Assurance** needed to maintain focus when emotions are low.

Let's apply this to a specific, high-level goal: **Launching a $10,000/month Consulting Business in 6 Months.**

- **Month 6 (Goal):** $10k in the bank from 5 clients.
- **Month 5:** Close 2 clients; onboard them; refine the delivery system.
- **Month 4:** Conduct 20 high-value sales calls; send 10 proposals.
- **Month 3:** Build a "Leads List" of 200 prospects; send 50 personalized cold emails.
- **Month 2:** Create the "Irresistible Offer" (The Solution Architecture); build the landing page.
- **Month 1:** Conduct 10 "Problem Discovery" interviews with potential clients to validate the need.
- **Week 1:** Identify 20 people to interview; write the outreach script.
- **Day 1 (Tomorrow):** Spend 90 minutes (Deep Work) identifying the first 10 people for discovery interviews.

Notice how the "Day 1" task is small, manageable, and directly linked to the $10k goal. There is no mystery. There is no "waiting for inspiration." There is only execution.

The "No-Fly Zone": Identifying Non-Essentials

As you map your path backward, you will encounter tasks that feel important but don't actually sit on the Critical Path. These are "No-Fly Zones."

- *Example:* Spending three weeks choosing a color palette for your website.
- *Example:* Reading five more books on a topic you already understand.
- *Example:* Tinkering with your "to-do list" app instead of doing the work.

If a task does not have a direct causal link to the next milestone in your backward map, **it is a distraction.** In the Hardened Mind framework, you have my permission to ignore it. Precision mapping is as much about what you *don't* do as it is about what you *do*.

Conclusion: The Certainty of the Map

Linear planning is a gamble. Backward planning is a strategy.

When you stand at the beginning of your journey with a backward map in your hand, you possess a level of confidence that others lack. You are no longer "trying to figure it out." You have already solved the puzzle; you are now just putting the pieces together.

The mountain no longer looks vertical. It looks like a series of steps. And you know exactly where to place your foot tomorrow morning.

CHAPTER 3

STAY ACCOUNTABLE USING PEER REVIEW SYSTEMS

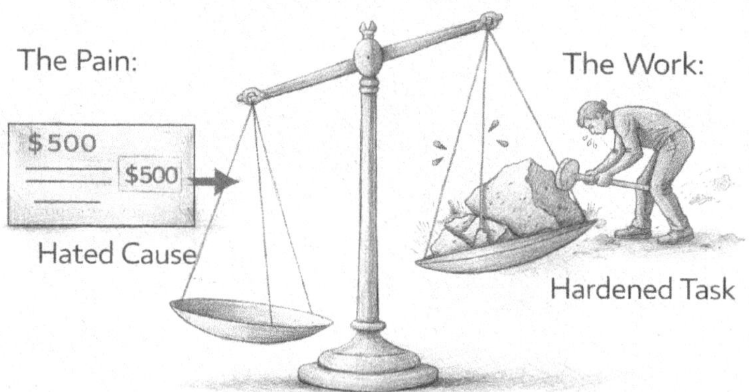

The pain is tipped heavily toward the discomfort of the task.

You have built the map. You have the metrics. You have the focus. In a vacuum, you are perfectly equipped for success. But you do not live in a vacuum. You live in a world of friction, fatigue, and the most dangerous adversary of all: **your own ability to rationalize.**

The Hardened Mind is powerful, but it is also a master of internal propaganda. When you are tired, when the "Middle Muddle" sets in, or when a task feels particularly threatening to your ego, your brain will begin to negotiate. It will tell you that "tomorrow is better," that "you've done enough," or that "the metric was too aggressive anyway." This is the **Isolation Trap**. In isolation, your standards are as flexible as your mood.

To achieve precision over the long term, you must externalize your integrity. You must build an **Accountability Scaffold**—a system of peer review that makes the cost of quitting higher than the cost of continuing. In Chapter 3, we move focus from the internal to the social, leveraging the deep-seated human drive for status and belonging to fuel your execution.

The Neurobiology of Social Stakes

The human brain is fundamentally social. For hundreds of thousands of years, being cast out of the tribe meant certain death. Consequently, our brains evolved to prioritize social standing and the fulfillment of promises made to others over promises made to ourselves.

When you make a promise to yourself, the only brain region involved is the **Internal Monitor**. If you break that promise, you feel a flicker of guilt, but the ego quickly suppresses it to maintain comfort. However, when you make a promise to a respected peer, you engage the **Ventromedial Prefrontal Cortex (vmPFC)** and the **Amygdala**.

The thought of failing in front of a peer triggers a social "threat" response. Your brain treats the potential loss of status as a physical danger. By implementing a Peer Review System, you are effectively hijacking your own survival instinct and tethering it to your goals. You aren't just working for a result anymore; you are working to maintain your identity as an elite performer in the eyes of your tribe.

Phase 1: The Architecture of the Peer Review Group

Not all accountability is created equal. Asking a friend to "keep you on track" is usually a recipe for mutual mediocrity. True accountability requires a **Hardened Peer Group**. This group must be built on three specific criteria:

1. Zero-Mercy Transparency

A Peer Review System only works if the data is undeniable. You do not report that you "had a good week." You report your **Binary Metrics** (The 1s and 0s from Chapter 1). If you missed a Lead Measure, you do not explain why—you simply report the failure. The group's role is not to offer "emotional support" for your excuses, but to hold up a mirror to your data.

2. Competency Symmetry

You must be reviewed by people who are at or above your level of ambition. If you are trying to build a $10M company and your accountability partner is content with a 9-to-5, their "status pressure" will have no effect on you. You need peers who understand the stakes and who will lose respect for you if you settle for "good enough."

3. High-Frequency Cadence

Accountability has a half-life. A monthly check-in is useless because the "Social Threat" is too far away to influence daily behavior. You need a **Weekly Audit**. The knowledge that you must face your peers in 72 hours is what keeps the Hardened Mind focused when the 4:00 PM slump hits on a Thursday.

Phase 2: The "Proof of Work" Protocol

To ensure your Peer Review System isn't just a "talk shop," you must implement a **Proof of Work (PoW)** protocol. In every review session, you do not just speak; you show.

- **The Writer:** Shares the word count log and a link to the drafted pages.
- **The Entrepreneur:** Shows the CRM data and the outbound call log.
- **The Athlete:** Shows the heart-rate data or the lifting logs.

Sharing the **Artifact of Proof** (defined in Chapter 1) removes the "Halo Effect"—the tendency to sound more successful than you actually are. It forces the conversation to remain in the realm of concrete results.

Phase 3: The "Commitment Device" (Social Stakes)

To add teeth to your Peer Review System, you must use **Commitment Devices**. These are external constraints that "lock" you into a course of action by making failure expensive.

One of the most effective tools is the **Forfeiture Contract**. You agree with your peer group that if you miss a specific, major milestone (your "10% Mark" from Chapter 2), you will pay a significant financial penalty to a cause you despise.

The money itself isn't the point; the point is the **Saliency of the Loss**. Our brains are "Loss Averse"—we are twice as motivated to avoid losing $500 as we are to gain $500. A Peer Review System with a Forfeiture Contract turns your goal pursuit into a game you cannot afford to lose.

The Role of the "Antagonistic Reviewer"

In the Hardened Mind framework, every review group needs an **Antagonistic Reviewer**. This isn't someone who is mean, but someone whose job is to play the role of the "Prosecutor."

When you report a success, the Prosecutor asks: *"Was this the most high-leverage task you could have done, or did you just hit an easy metric to feel productive?"* When you report a failure, the Prosecutor asks: *"Is the friction environmental, or is it a failure of your focus protocols?"*

This level of scrutiny prevents **"Accountability Drift,"** where the group becomes too comfortable with each other and starts letting "small misses" slide. The Prosecutor keeps the focus on **Precision**.

The Virtual Mirror: Using Public Accountability

For some, the ultimate Peer Review System is **Public Accountability**. This involves announcing your ARID criteria and your weekly progress to your entire professional network or audience.

This is the "High-Wire Act" of goal setting. It is not for everyone, but for the Hardened Mind, it can be a massive force multiplier. When you know that thousands (or even just dozens) of people are watching your "Progress Bar," your ego becomes fully invested in the outcome. You are no longer just a person working; you are a brand maintaining its integrity.

The Feedback Loop: Adjusting the Map

Peer Review is not just about "staying on track"; it's about **Data-Driven Adjustment**. During your review sessions, the group should help you analyze your **Lead Measures**.

If you are consistently hitting your Lead Measures but the Lag Measure isn't moving, the group helps you realize that your "Lever" is broken. This allows you to **Pivot** (Chapter 4) based on objective feedback rather than emotional frustration. The group provides the

"High-Altitude Perspective" that you lose when you are deep in the trenches of execution.

Conclusion: The Strength of the Scaffold

Self-discipline is a limited resource. Status-seeking and social belonging are infinite resources. By building a Peer Review System, you stop relying on your fickle "willpower" and start plugging into the deep machinery of human biology.

The Hardened Mind is not a lonely mind. It is a mind that knows its own weaknesses and builds a social scaffold to compensate for them. When you know that your peers are watching, when you know the data is public, and when you know the cost of failure is high, "Precision" is no longer a choice—it is your only option.

CHAPTER 4

PIVOT YOUR STRATEGY WITHOUT LOSING YOUR FOCUS

In the previous chapters, we have built a rigid structure: measurable criteria, backward maps, and social scaffolds. To the uninitiated, this might look like a recipe for inflexibility. There is a common fear among high performers that being "precise" means being "brittle"—that if the plan encounters an unforeseen obstacle, the entire system will shatter. This fear is the primary reason many avoid high-resolution planning altogether, preferring the "flexibility" of vagueness.

However, this fear is based on a fundamental misunderstanding of what focus actually is. Focus is not the refusal to see change; focus is the ability to maintain the **integrity of the mission** while ruthlessly adjusting the **mechanics of execution**.

In Chapter 4, we address the "Strategic Pivot." In the volatile landscape of 2026, rigidity is a death sentence. Markets shift, technologies disrupt, and personal circumstances evolve. If you treat your backward map as a holy relic rather than a working hypothesis, you will march precisely into a dead end. We are going to learn how to apply the **Scientific Method** to your goals, allowing you to change your tactics without ever losing sight of your objective.

The Biology of Cognitive Flexibility: The OFC-ACC Axis

To pivot successfully, you must engage the brain's internal "Value Broker." While the Prefrontal Cortex (PFC) is the commander that holds the "Goal Representation," it is not the part of the brain that decides if a tactic is working. That responsibility falls to the **Orbitofrontal Cortex (OFC)** and the **Anterior Cingulate Cortex (ACC)**.

The OFC is responsible for "Value Updating." It constantly monitors the environment to ask: *"Is the current action still the most efficient way to get the reward?"* When you are grinding away at a marketing strategy that yields no leads, or a workout plan that isn't building muscle, it is the OFC that registers the drop in "Expected Value."

Once the OFC identifies that a tactic is failing, it communicates with the ACC. The ACC acts as the "Switching Station." It resolves the conflict between your desire to persist and the reality of the failure. In an unhardened mind, this conflict creates "Decision Paralysis." In a Hardened Mind, the ACC initiates a "task switch" with surgical precision.

The paradox is this: You must be stubborn about the **Lag Measure** (the result) but completely detached from the **Lead Measure** (the tactic). Most people do the opposite—they get emotionally attached to their specific way of working (their routine) and abandon the goal when it gets hard. We are training your brain to value the *result* over the *ego of being right about the initial plan.*

Phase 1: The "Signals of Stagnation" Audit

How do you know when to pivot versus when to persevere? This is the most difficult question in goal architecture. Persistence in the face of failure is either "Grit" or "Delusion." To distinguish between the two, you must look at your **Precision Data** from Chapter 1.

You should consider a pivot if you meet the **"Triple-Zero" Criteria**:

1. **Lead Measure Adherence is 100%:** You are doing the work. You are hitting your binary metrics. You are showing up for every 90-minute sprint.

2. **Lag Measure Movement is 0%:** Despite your perfect execution, the weight is not moving, the revenue is flat, or the skill is not improving.

3. **The Trendline is Stagnant for 3 Reporting Cycles:** (e.g., three consecutive weeks of Peer Review with zero growth).

If you are hitting your Lead Measures and the Lag isn't moving, the problem is not your focus—it's your **Strategy**. You have identified a "Broken Lever." Continuing to pull a broken lever is not discipline; it is insanity.

Phase 2: The "Minimum Viable Pivot" (MVP)

When the data tells you to change, the "Limbic System" often triggers a panic response. You feel like the entire project is a failure, and you want to "blow up" the whole map. This is a mistake. A Hardened Pivot is a clinical adjustment, not a chaotic retreat. We use the **MVP (Minimum Viable Pivot)** framework to isolate the variable that needs to change:

1. The Tactic Swap

Change the *delivery*, not the *product*. If you are trying to acquire clients and cold LinkedIn outreach (the tactic) has a 0% conversion rate after 200 attempts, swap it for a different tactic, such as "Specific Problem Content." The goal—client acquisition—remains untouched.

2. The Variable Adjustment

Sometimes the tactic is correct, but the *intensity* or *frequency* is off. If a 500-calorie deficit is stalling your weight loss, the pivot isn't to stop dieting; it is to adjust the macro-nutrient ratio or incorporate "Refeed Days" to signal the metabolism.

3. The "Same Why, New How"

Re-map the path from your current position back to the original finish line. If a bridge on your backward map is washed out, you don't go back to the start; you find the nearest crossing.

The greatest obstacle to a successful pivot is the **Sunk Cost Fallacy**. This is the neurological tendency to continue an endeavor once an investment in money, effort, or time has been made, even when it is clear that the path leads to a dead end. Your brain hates "wasting" the effort you put into the first four weeks of a failed plan.

The Hardened Mind views effort as **"Sunk Capital."** That energy is gone. It is a spent resource. The only question that matters for a focused mind is: *"Given my current location and resources, what is the most efficient use of my next 90-minute focus block?"* If the current path is a dead end, the most "focused" thing you can do is stop walking and turn around. Emotional detachment is the ultimate tool of precision. You must be willing to "kill your darlings"—to discard a beautiful plan the moment the data proves it is obsolete.

Phase 4: Protecting the "Focus Core" During the Shift

The danger of a pivot is "Cognitive Context Switching." When you change strategies, your brain enters a state of high cognitive load. It wants to go back to a "Shallow State" because the new path is unfamiliar and therefore perceived as "dangerous" or "taxing" by the Amygdala.

To prevent a pivot from turning into a distraction, you must maintain your **Structural Constants**. These are the elements of your work life that *do not* change, even when the strategy does:

- **The Environment:** Work in the same "Focus Cradle" you built in Book 4.

- **The Ritual:** Use the same "Deep Work" 90-minute sprints.

- **The Metric Standard:** The new tactic must still be measured by a Binary Metric (1 or 0).

A pivot is a change in the *destination coordinates* on your GPS, but the *vehicle* and the *driver's protocols* remain the same. By keeping your habits constant, you provide the neural stability required to execute a new, uncertain strategy.

Case Study: The Pivot in Action

Imagine an author who has spent three months writing a 40,000-word manuscript. Their Lag Measure is a published book on "Productivity for Surgeons."

- **The Signal:** They send three chapters to a focus group of surgeons. The feedback is unanimous: *"This is too basic; we already know this. We need something on managing high-stakes adrenaline in the operating room."*

- **The Perseverance Trap:** The author thinks, *"I've already written 40k words. If I pivot now, I've wasted three months. I'll just finish this and hope someone buys it."* (This is a Vague Dream leading to an Efficient Failure).

- **The Hardened Pivot:** The author realizes the "Problem-Solution Fit" is off. They discard 20,000 words, keep the core "Focus Theory," and spend the next four weeks re-writing specifically for the surgical environment.

The goal (The Published Book) remains. The effort (The Writing) remains. Only the **Strategy** (The Specific Audience and Problem) changed. This is a pivot with precision.

Conclusion: The Agile Architect

The world of 2026 does not reward the strongest; it rewards the most **adaptive**. You must be firm enough to stay the course when the work is merely "hard," but fluid enough to change course when the work is "wrong."

A pivot is not a failure; it is an **Optimization**. Every time you pivot based on data, you are sharpening your understanding of reality. You are removing the "guesswork" from your map. The Hardened Mind is not a steamroller that tries to flatten every mountain in its path. It is a high-performance vehicle that can navigate the mountain's curves at speed, always keeping its headlights fixed on the ultimate destination.

CHAPTER 5

MEASURE WHAT MATTERS TO ENSURE DAILY GAINS

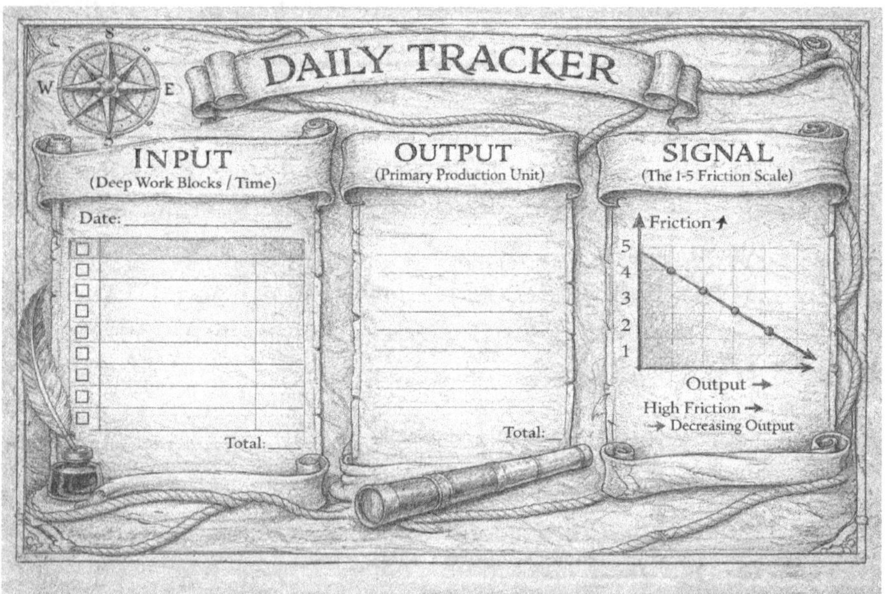

We have reached the final stage of the Goal Architecture. You have the destination (Chapter 1), the map (Chapter 2), the social scaffold (Chapter 3), and the ability to steer (Chapter 4). Now, we address the most critical element of the journey: **The Dashboard.**

In the cockpit of a fighter jet, the pilot does not rely on "feel" to determine their altitude, fuel levels, or air speed. They rely on high-fidelity instrumentation. In the cockpit of your life, however, you likely rely on vague sensations of being "busy" or "tired." This is a recipe for disaster. To sustain the Hardened Mind, you must move from subjective feeling to objective measurement. You must learn to measure what matters so that you can ensure—and prove—daily gains.

Chapter 5 is about the **Feedback Loop**. We are going to build a personalized tracking system that reinforces your wins and exposes your leaks before they become failures.

The Neurobiology of the "Winner Effect"

The reason we track daily gains is not just for organizational hygiene; it is for **Neurological Momentum**. In biology, there is a phenomenon known as the **"Winner Effect."** When an animal wins a contest, it experiences a surge in testosterone and dopamine. This biochemical shift makes the animal more aggressive, more confident, and—most importantly—more likely to win the *next* contest.

Human beings are subject to the same chemistry. When you check off a precise Lead Measure on your dashboard, your brain registers a "Micro-Victory." This release of dopamine reinforces the **Prefrontal Cortex**, making it easier to resist distractions tomorrow. Conversely, when you do not measure your gains, your "wins" feel invisible. Without visibility, there is no chemical reward. Without a reward, the Hardened Mind eventually starves and reverts to the path of least resistance.

Measurement is the process of making the invisible visible. It provides the **Dopaminergic Feedback** necessary to sustain effort over the "Middle Muddle" we identified in Chapter 2. Without a dashboard, your brain is flying blind, and in the absence of data, it will default to the most conservative (and least productive) energy-saving mode.

Phase 1: The Lead Metric Dashboard (Precision Tracking)

We return to the foundational concept from Chapter 1: **Lag Measures vs. Lead Measures**. On your daily dashboard, the Lag Measure (the goal) should be visible as a reminder of the "North Star," but the **Lead Measure** (the daily action) is the only thing you actively track.

The Three-Metric Rule: Complexity is the Enemy of Execution

To prevent "Measurement Fatigue," where the act of tracking becomes more burdensome than the work itself, your daily dashboard should only contain three specific categories of data points:

1. **The Deep Work Quota (Input):** How many 90-minute focus blocks did you complete today? This is the raw energy you poured into the system.

2. **The Core Output Metric (Production):** What was the primary unit of value created? For a coder, it is "Features Pushed"; for a salesperson, it is "Proposals Sent."

3. **The "Friction" Indicator (Signal):** A simple 1–5 scale of how much cognitive resistance you felt. This is your early-warning system for burnout or the need for a strategic pivot (as discussed in Chapter 4).

By tracking these three, you create a holistic view of your performance. If the Quota is high but the Output is low, you are likely suffering from "Shallow Work" creep. If the Output is high but the Friction is a 5, you are redlining your engine and need to audit your recovery protocols.

Phase 2: The Visual Feedback Loop (The Scoreboard Effect)

The human brain is a visual processing machine; roughly 30% of our neurons are dedicated to vision. Data hidden in a digital spreadsheet or a buried app is far less effective than data displayed in your physical environment. You must make your progress **Unavoidable**.

The "Scoreboard" Method

Elite teams always have a scoreboard visible from the field. It dictates the intensity of the play. You need the same in your "Focus Cradle."

- **The Chain (The Seinfeld Strategy):** A physical wall calendar where you mark an "X" for every day you hit your Floor Metric. The goal is to "not break the chain."

- **The Visual Progress Bar:** A thermometer-style graphic on your wall that you fill in as you move toward your "10% Milestone."

- **The Digital HUD:** A dedicated low-power tablet or monitor that stays on your desk, displaying your weekly trend lines.

The goal of the scoreboard is to create **Cognitive Dissonance** if you miss a day. A broken chain or a stagnant progress bar creates a psychological "itch" that only focused work can scratch. It turns your work into a game where the only objective is to keep the numbers moving in the right direction.

Daily tracking ensures momentum, but the **Weekly Audit** ensures direction. Without an audit, daily metrics can lead you very quickly in the wrong direction. Every Sunday (or at the end of your work week), you must perform a "Clinical Review" of your dashboard data.

The Four-Question Audit Protocol:

1. **Metric Adherence:** What percentage of my Lead Measures did I hit? If you are below 85%, your "Floor" is too high or your environment is compromised.

2. **Conversion Efficiency:** Did my Lead Measures actually move the Lag Measure? If you wrote 5,000 words but the book outline hasn't progressed, your words were "empty calories."

3. **The Friction Source:** What was the #1 recurring distraction this week? Identify it, then build a "Bright Line" rule to kill it for next week.

4. **The Calibration:** Based on the data, should I increase the "Ceiling" to push harder, or lower the "Floor" to prevent a collapse?

This audit is where "Vague Dreams" are converted into "Engineering Problems." It turns your life into a laboratory. You stop taking "failure" personally and start taking it clinically. You are an engineer optimizing a machine, and the data is the only truth that matters.

Phase 4: Measuring Biological Capital (The Engine Health)

Precision execution requires more than just time; it requires **Biological Capital**. High-performance focus is metabolically expensive. If you are hitting your output metrics but your "Friction Indicator" is consistently at a 5, you are borrowing energy from tomorrow to pay for today. Eventually, the debt will come due.

The Hardened Mind tracks **Energy Metrics** alongside Output Metrics:

- **Focus Latency:** How many minutes did it take you to enter a "Flow State" during your first sprint? High latency suggests brain fog or poor sleep.

- **Sleep Quality (HRV/Deep Sleep):** Use a wearable to track your Heart Rate Variability. A low HRV is a direct signal from your nervous system to lower your "Ceiling" for the day.
- **The Sunset Compliance:** Did you execute your "Shutdown Ritual" from Book 4? This measures your ability to disconnect, which is the primary driver of the next day's focus.

By measuring these biological inputs, you ensure that your precision is sustainable. A dashboard that ignores the health of the engine will eventually witness an engine failure.

Conclusion: The Mastery of the Metric

Measurement is the final bridge between the mental and the physical. It is the process of taking an internal thought—a goal—and forcing it to manifest in the external world as a data point. When you measure what matters, you eliminate the "Fog of War." You remove the anxiety of the unknown.

You know exactly where you stand. You know exactly what moved the needle. And most importantly, you know that you are getting better every single day. The Hardened Mind does not fear the data. It craves it. Because in the data, there is truth. And in the truth, there is the power to reach any goal you set.

You are no longer a person who "hopes" to succeed. You are an architect of outcomes, and your dashboard is the proof.

CONCLUSION

SUSTAIN YOUR SUCCESS OVER A LIFETIME

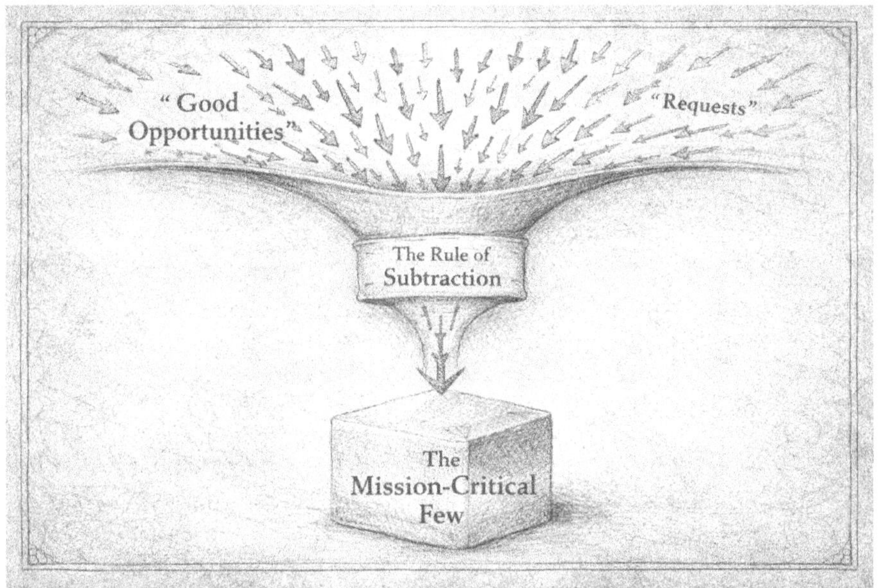

You have journeyed through the five pillars of the **Hardened Mind**. You have moved from the defensive posture of protecting your attention to the offensive mastery of precision execution. We began this series by reclaiming your brain from the digital siege, and we conclude it by transforming you into an architect of objective reality.

But the Hardened Mind is not a trophy you win and place on a shelf; it is a metabolic state that must be maintained. The world of 2026 is not going to become less distracting, and the goals you set will not become less challenging. To sustain this level of elite performance over a lifetime, you must transition from "Building the System" to "Being the System."

The Law of Entropy: Why Discipline Must Be Seasonal

In physics, **Entropy** is the inevitable decline into disorder. Your mind and your goals are subject to this same law. If you attempt to maintain 100% "Peak Output" indefinitely, the system will eventually fracture. True mastery lies in the ability to cycle your intensity.

A lifetime of success is built on **Periodization**. In the same way an elite athlete cycles through "off-season," "pre-season," and "competition," the Hardened Mind must cycle through:

1. **Sprints (The Precision Phase):** 90-day windows of high-intensity, ARID-metric-driven execution.

2. **Maintenance (The Baseline Phase):** 30-day windows where you hit your "Floor Metrics" but allow for more creative exploration and recovery.

3. **Refactor (The Audit Phase):** 7-day windows of total disconnect to review the "Backward Map" and recalibrate your "Lag Measures."

By respecting these cycles, you prevent the "Decision Fatigue" that leads to system collapse. You aren't "quitting"; you are reloading.

The Identity Shift: From "Doing" to "Being"

In Book 1, you were a person "trying" to focus. In Book 5, you have become a person who *executes with precision*. This is an identity shift.

Research into **Identity-Based Habits** suggests that the most sustainable form of discipline is one that is no longer a choice. When a behavior becomes part of your identity, it ceases to require willpower.

- "I am a person who starts Deep Work at 8:00 AM."
- "I am a person who tracks my Lead Measures every evening."
- "I am a person who ignores vague requests for my time."

Once these protocols become your "Default Operating System," the friction of execution disappears. Your Prefrontal Cortex no longer has to negotiate with your Limbic System because there is no debate. This is the ultimate goal of the Hardened Mind series: to make elite focus your most natural state of being.

Guarding the Fortress: The Eternal Vigilance

As you achieve success, you will face a new enemy: **The Complexity Trap**. Success brings more opportunities, more requests for your time, and more "good" things that can distract you from the "best" things.

The Hardened Mind remains vigilant by applying the **Rule of Ruthless**

Subtraction. For every new project, commitment, or goal you add to your life, you must subtract an existing one. Precision requires space. If your schedule is 100% full, you have zero margin for the "Strategic Pivot" we discussed in Chapter 4.

Sustaining success requires the courage to say "No" to great opportunities so that you can say "Yes" to the mission-critical few.

Final Protocol: The Annual "Hardened Audit"

To ensure you are still moving toward a destination that matters, you must perform an **Annual Hardened Audit**. Once a year, step away from all metrics and all social scaffolds. Ask yourself the three "Prime Questions":

1. **The Mission:** Is my current Lag Measure still aligned with my deepest values, or am I just chasing a number I no longer care about?

2. **The Mechanics:** Is my current "Focus Cradle" still serving me, or have I let digital distractions leak back into my environment?

3. **The Growth:** Am I still hitting my "Ceiling," or have I become comfortable in the "Goldilocks Zone"?

Your New Reality

The world belongs to those who can focus. In an era of fragmented attention and vague ambitions, your ability to define a target, map a path, and measure your progress is a superpower.

You now possess the tools to out-think, out-work, and out-last any obstacle. The fortress is built. The map is drawn. The dashboard is live.

Go forth and execute with precision. Your potential is no longer a vague dream; it is a measurable destination.

REFLECTION QUESTIONS
DESIGN YOUR 12-MONTH ROADMAP

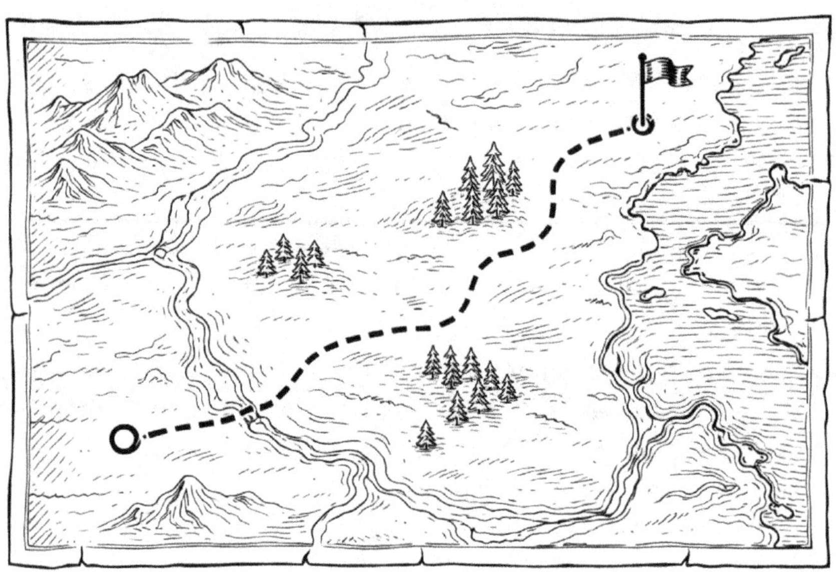

The transition from theory to execution requires a bridge of deep introspection. This final exercise is designed to strip away the abstractions of the "Hardened Mind" and force you to confront the logistical reality of the next year. Do not rush these. Answer them with the clinical honesty of a scientist auditing a failing experiment.

Phase 1: The Objective Audit

1. **The Singular Focus:** If you were forced to eliminate every goal except one for the next 12 months, which one would have the greatest positive "domino effect" on your life?

2. **The Binary Standard:** Look at that goal. If you handed it to a stranger, could they tell you—without asking for your opinion—exactly when you had succeeded or failed? How can you make the criteria 20% more objective?

3. **The Lag vs. Lead Split:** What is the specific "Lever" (Lead Measure) you will pull daily to move the "Weight" (Lag Measure)?

Phase 2: The Backward Mapping

4. **The Pre-Mortem:** It is 12 months from today and your project has failed. What was the most likely cause of that failure? How will you build a "Friction Guard" into your roadmap today to prevent that specific outcome?

5. **The Rule of Halves:** What is the "6-Month Milestone" that proves you are on track for the 12-month finish line? What must happen in the next 30 days to make that 6-month milestone inevitable?

6. **The Resource Debt:** What current commitment (social, professional, or digital) are you going to **subtract** to create the metabolic space for this new roadmap?

Phase 3: The Accountability Scaffold

7. **The Status Stakes:** Who is the one person in your network whose respect you value most? Have you told them exactly what your 12-month binary metric is? If not, why are you keeping it a secret?

7. **The Forfeiture Contract:** What is a "painful" amount of money or a significant social cost you are willing to wager against your success?

8. **The Audit Cadence:** On what day and at what time will you perform your **Weekly Audit**? Is it blocked out on your calendar as a non-negotiable appointment?

Phase 4: The Strategic Pivot

8. **The Stagnation Signal:** At what point of "zero movement" will you stop persevering and initiate a **Minimum Viable Pivot**? (e.g., "If I hit my Lead Measures for 21 days with 0% Lag movement, I will change my tactic.")

10. **The Sunk Cost Kill-Switch:** What is a tactic you are currently attached to that you would be willing to "kill" tomorrow if the data proved it was ineffective?

9. **The Friction Scale:** When you look at your daily dashboard, what is your current "average friction" score? If it is consistently above a 4, what is one environmental change you can make to lower the resistance?

12. **The Identity Affirmation:** Complete this sentence for your 12-month journey: *"I am no longer a person who tries to [Goal]; I am the type of person who consistently [Lead Measure]."*

Next Steps for Your Mastery

You have completed the **Hardened Mind** series. You now possess the blueprint for elite execution.

OVERALL CONCLUSION

THE UNIFIED DISCIPLINE SYSTEM

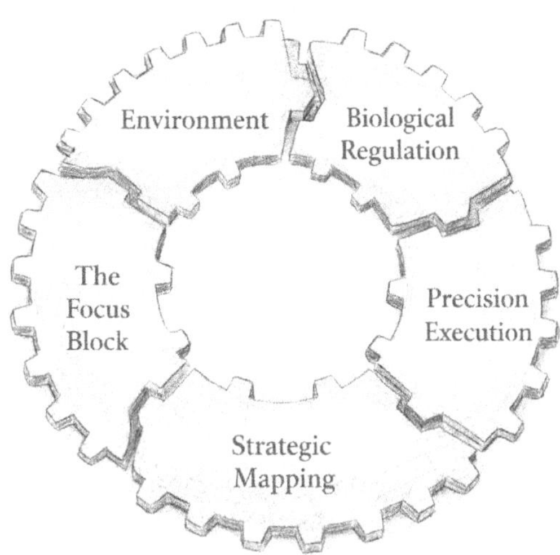

You have traveled from the defensive architecture of Book 1 to the offensive precision of Book 5. What you have built is not a collection of "productivity tips," but a **Unified Discipline System**.

The greatest mistake of the modern era is viewing focus as a personality trait. It is not. Focus is an emergent property of a well-engineered environment, a regulated nervous system, and a clinical approach to data. By integrating the five books in this series, you have moved from being a victim of the "Attention Economy" to being a sovereign architect of your own cognitive destiny.

The Synthesis: How the Five Pillars Interlock

To maintain your new reality, you must understand how these five modules function as a single machine:

1. **Environment (Book 1):** Your "Focus Cradle" ensures that the **Prefrontal Cortex** doesn't waste energy fighting environmental triggers. If the environment is compromised, the rest of the system fails.

2. **Biological Regulation (Book 2):** Your sleep, nutrition, and "Dopamine Fasting" protocols ensure the engine has the chemical fuel (Dopamine and Norepinephrine) required to maintain the "Deep Work" state.

3. **The Focus Block (Book 3):** The 90-minute sprint is your primary unit of time. This is where the actual value is created. It is the heartbeat of your productivity.

4. **Strategic Mapping (Book 4):** Backward planning ensures that your 90-minute sprints are aimed at the right target. It prevents you from being "efficiently lost."

5. **Precision Execution (Book 5):** The binary metrics and peer review systems provide the external pressure and internal clarity to keep the system running when motivation fades.

The Transformation of the Self

The most profound result of this system is not the goals you will achieve—though you will achieve them. The most profound result is the **transformation of your internal world**.

When you possess a Hardened Mind, the "Internal Critic" is silenced by the weight of objective data. Anxiety is replaced by **Cognitive Assurance**. You no longer wake up wondering what to do; you wake up knowing exactly where to place your feet. You have moved from a state of "High-Stress Reactivity" to a state of **"Calm Assertiveness."**

A Final Charge: The 2026 Sovereign

As we move deeper into 2026, the gap between the "Focused Few" and the "Distracted Many" will continue to widen. Attention is the new currency. By mastering your focus, you have opted out of the mass-marketed chaos of the digital age.

You are now a **Sovereign of Attention**. You have the tools. You have the map. You have the biological capital. The only thing left is the daily act of showing up and executing within the system.

Stay hardened. Stay precise. The world is yours to build.

THE PRINT AND KEEP CHECKLIST
YOUR DAILY OPERATIONS MANUAL

Think of this checklist not as a rigid set of rules, but as the "Standard Operating Procedure" for your brain. In the heat of the day, when your energy dips and the world starts screaming for your attention, you won't have the "Executive Function" left to decide what to do next. That is when you lean on the system.

Print this out. Stick it on the wall of your workspace. Let it be the physical anchor that keeps your **Hardened Mind** on track when things get chaotic.

I. The Morning Launch: Protecting Your Chemistry

The first hour of the day is a battle for your neurochemistry. If you check your phone the moment you wake up, you've already lost the offensive. You are now reacting to the world instead of dictating to it.

- **The Zero-Input Hour:** No screens. No "quick check" of Slack. No news. Your only job is to protect your **Dopamine Baseline** so you have enough "fuel" for deep work later.

- **Biological Reset:** Drink 20 oz of water and get outside. Even if it's overcast, 10 minutes of natural light tells your **Circadian Clock** that the day has begun.

- **The Lead Metric Intent:** Don't look at a massive to-do list. Identify the **one single action**—your Lead Measure—that defines success for today.

II. The Deep Work Phase: The 90-Minute Sprint

This is where the money is made and the skills are built. Everything else is just "maintenance." You are looking for a state of high-arousal focus where the world disappears.

- **Environmental Lockdown:** Your phone isn't just on silent; it's in another room. Your browser has one tab open. You are in your **Focus Cradle**.

- **The Heavy Lift:** Spend your first 90 minutes on your hardest, most important task.

  - *The Rule:* Aim to hit your **"Floor Metric"** (your minimum daily requirement) before you even think about checking email.

- **Active Recovery:** When the timer goes off, get away from the desk. Do a 15-minute "Non-Sleep Deep Rest" (NSDR) or a walk. Do not fill this gap with social media; your brain needs to "de-frag."

III. Strategic Execution: The Mid-Day Offensive

By mid-day, the world will try to pull you into shallow tasks. This phase is about "defensive batching."

- **The Lever Check:** Ask yourself: "Am I pulling the lever, or am I just staring at the weight?" Ensure your work is a direct link in your **Backward Map**.

- **The "Admin Blast":** Group all your emails, Slack messages, and administrative chores into one 60-minute block. Handle them with speed and finality, then close the apps. Never let an inbox stay open in the background.

IV. The Evening Audit: The Data-Driven Review

You cannot manage what you do not measure. This five-minute practice turns your efforts into objective data, removing the emotional "cloud" of feeling like you didn't do enough.

- **The Binary Log:** Did you hit your number? Write down a **1** for success or a **0** for failure. No excuses, no "half-points."

- **Friction Audit:** Rate your internal resistance today from 1 (easy) to 5 (excruciating).

  - *If you're at a 4 or 5:* Look at your sleep, your light exposure, or your environment. Something is leaking energy.

- **Social Proof:** Ship your "Artifact of Proof" to your accountability group. Let the "Social Threat" of peer review keep you honest for tomorrow.

V. The Shutdown Ritual: Ending the Siege

Most high-performers fail because they never truly stop working. This leads to "leaky" focus the next day. You must learn to close the circuit.

- **The "Work Complete" Declaration:** Physically say out loud that the workday is over. Close your laptop.

- **Scripting Tomorrow:** Write down exactly where you will start in your first 90-minute block tomorrow. Give your future self a "warm start."

- **The Digital Sunset:** 60 minutes before bed, the "Hardened Mind" goes offline. No blue light. Read a physical book, stretch, or plan. Give your brain the darkness it needs to recover.

When to Pivot: Your Early Warning System

If you're following this checklist and things still feel "off," use these triggers to adjust your strategy:

1. **The Burnout Trigger:** If your **Friction Score** is a 5 for three days straight, you are "redlining." Lower your **Ceiling** and increase your recovery for 48 hours.

2. **The Stagnation Trigger:** If you have hit your **Lead Measures** (the 1s) for two weeks but your **Lag Measure** (the goal) hasn't budged, your strategy is wrong. It's time for a **Minimum Viable Pivot**.

3. **The Environment Trigger:** If you find yourself reaching for your phone during Deep Work, your **Focus Cradle** is broken. Re-harden your environment immediately.

Series Master Index

- **Book 1:** Building the Fortress (Environment)
- **Book 2:** Fueling the Machine (Biology)
- **Book 3:** The Heartbeat of Output (The 90-Minute Block)
- **Book 4:** The Strategic Compass (Backward Mapping)
- **Book 5:** The Clinical Close (Execution & Metrics)

Your training is officially complete. You have the psychology, the biology, and the strategy. Now, the only thing that stands between you and your 12-month goal is the relentless, daily repetition of this checklist.

HERE'S ANOTHER BOOK BY JAREN KNOX THAT YOU MIGHT LIKE

RESOURCES

Overall introduction

Books:

- **Duckworth, A.** (2016). *Grit: The Power of Passion and Perseverance.* New York, NY: Scribner. (Used for the definition of grit and research on West Point cadets).

- **Clear, J.** (2018). *Atomic Habits: An Easy & Proven Way to Build Good Habits & Break Bad Ones.* New York, NY: Avery. (Used for the 1% improvement rule and the Habit Loop).

- **Sapolsky, R. M.** (2017). *Behave: The Biology of Humans at Our Best and Worst.* New York, NY: Penguin Press. (Used for the neurobiology of the prefrontal cortex and limbic system).

- **Mischel, W.** (2014). *The Marshmallow Test: Mastering Self-Control.* New York, NY: Little, Brown and Company. (Used for the research on delayed gratification).

- **Newport, C.** (2016). *Deep Work: Rules for Focused Success in a Distracted World.* Grand Central Publishing. (Used for the definition of deep work and focus).

- **Baumeister, R. F., & Tierney, J.** (2011). *Willpower: Rediscovering the Greatest Human Strength.* New York, NY: Penguin Press. (Used for the concept of decision fatigue).

Online Resources:

- **American Psychological Association (APA):** "What You Need to Know about Willpower." https://www.apa.org/topics/personality/willpower

- **The Character Lab:** "Grit Playbook" by Angela Duckworth. https://characterlab.org/playbooks/grit/

- **James Clear:** "The Habit Loop: 4 Steps to Better Habits." https://jamesclear.com/habit-loop

- **Stanford News:** "The Biology of Self-Control" (Interview with Robert Sapolsky). https://news.stanford.edu/

- **Frontiers in Psychology:** "Beyond Passion and Perseverance: Review and Future Research on the Science of Grit." https://www.frontiersin.org/journals/psychology/articles/10.3389/fpsyg.2020.545526/full
- **National Institutes of Health (NIH):** "Behavioral and neural correlates of increased self-control." https://pmc.ncbi.nlm.nih.gov/articles/PMC4103380/

Book 1

Introduction

Books:

- **Pychyl, T. A.** (2013). Solving the Procrastination Puzzle: A Concise Guide to Strategies for Change. TarcherPerigee.
- **Steel, P.** (2010). The Procrastination Equation: How to Stop Putting Things Off and Start Getting Stuff Done. Harper.
- **McGonigal, K.** (2012). The Willpower Instinct. Avery.
- **Milkman, K.** (2021). How to Change: The Science of Getting from Where You Are to Where You Want to Be. Portfolio.
- **Dweck, C. S.** (2006). Mindset: The New Psychology of Success. Random House.
- **Ariely, D.** (2008). Predictably Irrational: The Hidden Forces That Shape Our Decisions. HarperCollins.

Online Resources:

- **American Psychological Association:** "What you need to know about willpower: The psychological science of self-control." https://www.apa.org/topics/personality/willpower
- **Association for Psychological Science (APS):** "Why Wait? The Science Behind Procrastination." https://www.psychologicalscience.org/observer/why-wait-the-science-behind-procrastination
- **White Rose Research Online:** "Procrastination and Stress: Exploring the Role of Self-compassion." https://eprints.whiterose.ac.uk/id/eprint/91791/1/ProcrastinationFINAL.pdf

- **PubMed Central (PMC):** "Procrastination and Stress: A Conceptual Review of Why Context Matters." https://pmc.ncbi.nlm.nih.gov/articles/PMC10049005/
- **National Bureau of Economic Research (NBER):** "An Evaluation of Temptation Bundling." https://www.nber.org/programs-projects/projects-and-centers/nber-roybal-center-behavior-change-health/6418-evaluation-temptation-bundling
- **Katherine Milkman (Wharton):** "Teaching temptation bundling to boost exercise." https://katherinemilkman.squarespace.com/s/teaching-temptation-bundling-to-boost-exercise.pdf
- **Harvard Medicine Magazine:** "The Science of Good Stress." https://magazine.hms.harvard.edu/articles/science-good-stress
- **Timothy A. Pychyl, Ph.D. (Procrastination.ca):** "Peer-Reviewed Research Publications List." https://www.procrastination.ca/research/

Chapter 1

Books:

- **Burka, J. B., & Yuen, L. M.** (2008). Procrastination: Why You Do It, What to Do About It Now. Da Capo Lifelong Books.
- **Steel, P.** (2010). The Procrastination Equation: How to Stop Putting Things Off and Start Getting Stuff Done. Harper.
- **Lembke, A.** (2021). Dopamine Nation: Finding Balance in the Age of Indulgence. Dutton.
- **Dweck, C. S.** (2006). Mindset: The New Psychology of Success. Random House.
- **Baumeister, R. F., & Tierney, J.** (2011). Willpower: Rediscovering the Greatest Human Strength. Penguin Press.

Online Resources:

- **American Psychological Association:** "The Psychology of Procrastination." https://www.apa.org/gradpsych/2010/01/procrastination

- **University of Texas at Austin:** "Brain Drain: The Mere Presence of One's Own Smartphone Reduces Available Cognitive Capacity." https://journals.uchicago.edu/doi/10.1086/691462
- **Nature Communications:** "The Expected Value of Control." https://www.nature.com/articles/ncomms11503
- **Harvard Business Review:** "The Real Reason You Procrastinate." https://hbr.org/2021/01/the-real-reason-you-procrastinate-it-isnt-laziness
- **Florida State University News:** "The biology of willpower." https://news.fsu.edu/news/science-technology/2010/11/17/willpower-glucose/
- **Psychology Today:** "The Six Styles of Procrastination." https://www.psychologytoday.com/us/blog/better-perfect/201703/6-common-procrastination-styles

Chapter 2

Books:

- **Allen, D. (2001).** *Getting Things Done: The Art of Stress-Free Productivity*. Penguin Books. (Source for the original Two-Minute Rule framework).
- **Clear, J. (2018).** *Atomic Habits: An Easy & Proven Way to Build Good Habits & Break Bad Ones*. Avery. (Source for the "Gateway Habit" and identity-based habit formation).
- **Guise, S. (2013).** *Mini Habits: Smaller Habits, Bigger Results*. Selective Entertainment. (Source for the strategy of "Activation Energy" reduction).
- **Pressfield, S. (2002).** *The War of Art*. Black Irish Entertainment. (Source for the concept of "Resistance" as a physical force).

Online Resources:

- **American Psychological Association (APA).** *The Science of Willpower*. https://www.apa.org/topics/personality/willpower (Used for the sections on Decision Fatigue and willpower depletion).
- **Harvard Business Review.** *To Overcome Procrastination, Start Small*. https://hbr.org/2014/02/to-overcome-procrastination-

start-small (Used for the "Entry Point" strategy and organizational productivity data).

- **National Center for Biotechnology Information (NCBI).** *The Neurobiology of Habit Formation.* https://pmc.ncbi.nlm.nih.gov/articles/PMC3513783/ (Used for the anatomical distinction between the Basal Ganglia and the Prefrontal Cortex).

- **ScienceDirect.** *Activation Energy and Cognitive Effort.* https://www.sciencedirect.com/topics/psychology/cognitive-effort (Used for the physics analogy of the energy hump).

- **Verywell Mind.** *The Zeigarnik Effect and Memory.* https://www.verywellmind.com/zeigarnik-effect-2795903 (Used for the explanation of task-based tension and cognitive loop closure).

Chapter 3

Books:

- **Allen, D. (2001).** *Getting Things Done: The Art of Stress-Free Productivity.* Penguin Books. (The primary source for "Next Action" theory and the psychological necessity of externalizing tasks to reduce cognitive load).

- **Baumeister, R. F., & Tierney, J. (2011).** *Willpower: Rediscovering the Greatest Human Strength.* Penguin Press. (Source for the research on "Executive Strain" and why deconstructing tasks preserves mental energy).

- **Pink, D. H. (2009).** *Drive: The Surprising Truth About What Motivates Us.* Riverhead Books. (Informed the "Neurobiology of the Micro-Win" and the importance of perceived progress).

- **Sweller, J. (1988).** *Cognitive Load Factors in Problem Solving and Learning.* Cognitive Science. (The foundational text used to explain the "Mental Workbench" and limited working memory capacity).

- **Kahneman, D. (2011).** *Thinking, Fast and Slow.* Farrar, Straus and Giroux. (The primary source for the "Planning Fallacy" and how granularity corrects optimistic bias).

Online Resources:

- **American Psychological Association (APA).** *The Planning Fallacy: Why We Are Always Late.* https://www.apa.org/news/podcasts/speaking-of-psychology/planning-fallacy (Used to detail the cognitive biases involved in project estimation).

- **Interaction Design Foundation.** *Cognitive Load Theory: Helping People Learn.* https://www.interaction-design.org/literature/article/cognitive-load-theory (Used to explain the architectural principles of deconstructing complex information).

- **MindTools.** *Work Breakdown Structures (WBS): Managing Complex Projects.* https://www.mindtools.com/pages/article/newPPM_05.htm (Informed the "Anatomy of Task-Dependency" and visual mapping sections).

- **National Institutes of Health (NIH).** *The Role of Dopamine in Anticipation and Completion.* https://www.ncbi.nlm.nih.gov/pmc/articles/PMC2659740/ (Used for the "Neuro-Economics" and "Completion High" sections).

- **Scientific American.** *Why Your Brain Loves To-Do Lists.* https://www.scientificamerican.com/article/the-psychology-of-the-to-do-list/ (Informed the "Momentum Effect" and the Zeigarnik-related "Cognitive Residue" arguments).

Chapter 4

Books:

- **Newport, C. (2016).** *Deep Work: Rules for Focused Success in a Distracted World.* Grand Central Publishing. (The primary source for "Attention Residue" and the concept of the distraction-free environment as a competitive advantage).

- **Eyal, N. (2019).** *Indistractable: How to Control Your Attention and Choose Your Life.* BenBella Books. (Source for "Choice Architecture" and the internal/external triggers of distraction).

- **Thaler, R. H., & Sunstein, C. R. (2008).** *Nudge: Improving Decisions About Health, Wealth, and Happiness.* Yale University Press. (The foundational text for "Environmental Priming" and nudge theory).

- **Kardaras, N. (2016).** *Glow Kids: How Screen Addiction Is Hijacking Our Kids.* St. Martin's Press. (Used for the neurological data on "Variable Ratio Reinforcement" and the Digital Panopticon).

- **Walker, M. (2017).** *Why We Sleep: Unlocking the Power of Sleep and Dreams.* Scribner. (Source for the "Circadian Alignment" and the Suprachiasmatic Nucleus's reaction to light temperature).

Online Resources:

- **University of California, Irvine.** *The Cost of Interrupted Work: More Speed, More Stress.* https://www.ics.uci.edu/~gmark/Home_page/Research_files/CHI08.pdf (The study used to quantify the 23-minute recovery time after a social interrupt).

- **Cornell University Ergonomics Web.** *Workplace Temperature and Productivity.* http://ergo.human.cornell.edu/ (Source for the data on ambient temperature and error rates in cognitive tasks).

- **The New York Times.** *The Moral Economy of Tech.* https://www.nytimes.com/2017/11/08/technology/tech-companies-addiction-design.html (Used for the "Incentive Salience" and grayscale-shift arguments).

- **Nature Neuroscience.** *Neural Entrainment and Cognitive Performance.* https://www.nature.com/articles/nn.4445 (Informed the section on brain wave synchronization and acoustic masking).

- **Association for Psychological Science.** *The Context-Dependent Memory Effect.* https://www.psychologicalscience.org/teaching/teaching-context-dependent-memory.html (Used for the "Habit Anchor" and "Focus Shrine" psychological foundations).

Chapter 5

Books:

- **Covey, S. R. (1989).** *The 7 Habits of Highly Effective People.* Free Press. (The foundational source for the Eisenhower Matrix and the "First Things First" philosophy).

- **Baumeister, R. F., & Tierney, J. (2011).** *Willpower: Rediscovering the Greatest Human Strength.* Penguin Press. (Source for the research on "Ego Depletion" and the metabolic cost of decision-making).

- **McKeown, G. (2014).** *Essentialism: The Disciplined Pursuit of Less.* Crown Business. (Informed the "Omission Strategy" and the psychology of opportunity cost/JOMO).

- **Kahneman, D. (2011).** *Thinking, Fast and Slow.* Farrar, Straus and Giroux. (The primary source for the "Planning Fallacy" and System 1 vs. System 2 prioritizing).

- **Gazzaley, A., & Rosen, L. D. (2016).** *The Distracted Mind: Ancient Brains in a High-Tech World.* MIT Press. (Used for the neurological data on "Interference" and the limits of the dlPFC).

Online Resources:

- **Harvard Business Review.** *The Neurochemistry of Positive Feedback.* https://hbr.org/2015/05/the-neurochemistry-of-positive-feedback (Used for the "Progress Principle" and dopamine-led momentum arguments).

- **National Center for Biotechnology Information (NCBI).** *Neural Mechanisms of Valuation and Choice.* https://www.ncbi.nlm.nih.gov/pmc/articles/PMC3059492/ (Used to detail the function of the Ventromedial Prefrontal Cortex).

- **American Psychological Association (APA).** *Making Healthier Decisions: Implementation Intentions.* https://www.apa.org/science/about/psa/2008/07/gollwitzer (Source for the "If-Then" planning and the Decision-Action Gap).

- **The Royal Society.** *Temporal Discounting and the Brain.* https://royalsocietypublishing.org/doi/10.1098/rstb.2010.0146 (Used for the "Future-Self" bridge and fMRI data).

- **Stanford Encyclopedia of Philosophy.** *Decision Theory and Opportunity Cost.* https://plato.stanford.edu/entries/decision-theory/ (Informed the "Neuro-Economics" and "Moral Decision" sections).

Conclusion

Books and Primary Literature:

- **Clear, J. (2018).** *Atomic Habits: An Easy & Proven Way to Build Good Habits & Break Break Ones.* Avery. (Key source for "Identity-Based Habits" and the "1% Compounding Principle").

- **Loehr, J., & Schwartz, T. (2003).** *The Power of Full Engagement.* Free Press. (Primary source for the "Stress-Recovery" cycles and the "Neuro-Biology of Burnout").

- **Duhigg, C. (2012).** *The Power of Habit: Why We Do What We Do in Life and Business.* Random House. (Informed the technical section on the "Basal Ganglia" and "Habit Loops").

- **Duckworth, A. (2016).** *Grit: The Power of Passion and Perseverance.* McClelland & Stewart. (Source for the long-term psychological data on "Consistency vs. Intensity").

- **Newport, C. (2016).** *Deep Work: Rules for Focused Success in a Distracted World.* Grand Central Publishing. (Informed the "Deep Stop" and the "Default Mode Network" maintenance arguments).

Online Resources and Academic Articles:

- **Nature Neuroscience.** *Long-term Potentiation and Synaptic Plasticity.* https://www.nature.com/articles/nn.2450 (Used for the technical explanation of "Long-Term Potentiation" and "Synaptic Pruning").

- **The Mayo Clinic.** *The Biological Cost of Chronic Stress.* https://www.mayoclinic.org/healthy-lifestyle/stress-management/in-depth/stress/art-20046037 (Used to inform the "Recovery-to-Stress Ratio" section).

- **Harvard Health Publishing.** *The Default Mode Network and Creativity.* https://www.health.harvard.edu/blog/creativity-and-the-brain (Source for the "Sanctity of the Void" and DMN synthesis).

- **Farnam Street (FS).** *The Flywheel Effect: Why Consistency Wins.* https://fs.blog/the-flywheel-effect/ (Source for the "Physics of Constant Velocity" and "Stop-Start Tax" analogies).
- **Scientific American.** *Broken Windows and the Mind.* https://www.scientificamerican.com/article/the-psychology-of-order/ (Informed the "Entropy of Discipline" and "Systemic Drift" sections).

Reflection Questions

Books:

- **Argyris, C. (1991).** *Teaching Smart People How to Learn.* Harvard Business Review Press. (The primary source for "Double-Loop Learning" and identifying root causes of professional failure).
- **Holiday, R. (2016).** *Ego Is the Enemy.* Portfolio. (Informed the sections on "Self-Deception" and the "Theater of Productivity").
- **Goleman, D. (1995).** *Emotional Intelligence: Why It Can Matter More Than IQ.* Bantam Books. (Source for "Metacognition" and the audit of the Amygdala's fear response).
- **Schwartz, B. (2004).** *The Paradox of Choice: Why More Is Less.* Ecco. (Used for the sections on "Analysis Paralysis" and the "Root Resistance" of the New Idea Loop).
- **Taleb, N. N. (2012).** *Antifragile: Things That Gain from Disorder.* Random House. (Informed the "24-Hour Repair Check" and the "Sunk Cost Fallacy" arguments).

Online Sources:

- **Stanford Encyclopedia of Philosophy.** *Cognitive Dissonance.* https://plato.stanford.edu/entries/cognitive-dissonance/ (Used to explain the gap between "knowing" and "doing" in the audit).
- **Journal of Experimental Psychology.** *The Power of Externalization in Problem Solving.* https://psycnet.apa.org/record/2014-41235-001 (Scientific foundation for the "Closing Protocol" and writing-based reflection).
- **MindTools.** *The Pre-Mortem: Identifying Risks Before They Happen.* https://www.mindtools.com/pages/article/newPPM_05.htm (Source for the "Anatomy of the Pivot" and defensive intention setting).

- **Farnam Street (FS).** *The Sunk Cost Fallacy: Why We Pick the Wrong Priorities.* https://fs.blog/sunk-cost-fallacy/ (Used for the "Neuro-Economics" and "Sunk Cost" sections).

- **Harvard Business Review.** *The Power of Small Wins.* https://hbr.org/2011/05/the-power-of-small-wins (Source for the "1% Compounding Question" and the "Success Spiral" mechanics).

Book 2

Introduction

Books and Primary Literature:

- **Clear, J. (2018).** *Atomic Habits.* Avery. (The definitive source for the four-step habit loop and identity-based habits).

- **Duhigg, C. (2012).** *The Power of Habit.* Random House. (Primary source for the role of the Basal Ganglia and the "Cue-Routine-Reward" framework).

- **Baumeister, R. F., & Tierney, J. (2011).** *Willpower.* Penguin Press. (Source for the research on "Ego Depletion" and metabolic energy conservation).

- **Graybiel, A. M. (2008).** *Habits, Rituals, and the Evaluative Brain.* Annual Review of Neuroscience. (Technical foundation for the neural "chunking" of behaviors).

- **Wood, W. (2019).** *Good Habits, Bad Habits.* Farrar, Straus and Giroux. (Informed the "Threshold of Automaticity" data and the limits of conscious willpower).

Online Sources and Academic Articles:

- **National Institutes of Health (NIH).** *The Neuroscience of Habit.* https://www.nih.gov/news-events/nih-research-matters/biology-habits (Used to detail the dopamine-driven feedback loop and synaptic plasticity).

- **European Journal of Social Psychology.** *How Are Habits Formed?* https://onlinelibrary.wiley.com/doi/abs/10.1002/ejsp.674 (Source for the 18 to 254-day habit formation study).

- **Stanford University: Behavior Design Lab.** *The Fogg Behavior Model.* https://behaviormodel.org/ (Informed the "Response" phase and the relationship between motivation and friction).

- **Frontiers in Psychology.** *Cybernetics and Self-Regulation.*
  https://www.frontiersin.org/articles/10.3389/fpsyg.2018.0125
  8/full (Source for the "Cybernetic Control" and "Error-
  Correction" mechanisms).

- **Scientific American.** *The Logic of Hebb's Law.*
  https://www.scientificamerican.com/article/neurons-wire-
  together/ (Informed the section on "Synaptic Decay" and "Neural
  Consolidation").

Chapter 1

Books:

- **Fogg, B. J. (2019).** *Tiny Habits: The Small Changes That Change
  Everything.* Houghton Mifflin Harcourt. (The original source for
  the "Anchor-Moment" and "After-I" formula).

- **Clear, J. (2018).** *Atomic Habits.* Avery. (The definitive guide to
  Habit Stacking and the neurological importance of the "Cue-
  Response" link).

- **Gazzaniga, M. S. (2011).** *Who's in Charge? Free Will and the
  Science of the Brain.* Ecco. (Used for the technical data on how
  the Basal Ganglia offloads conscious decisions).

- **Duhigg, C. (2012).** *The Power of Habit.* Random House. (Source
  for the "Habit Loop" and the chemical nature of the reward
  phase).

- **Pavlov, I. P. (1927).** *Conditioned Reflexes.* Oxford University
  Press. (The foundational text for Associative Learning and
  Classical Conditioning).

Online Sources:

- **Stanford Behavior Design Lab.** *The Fogg Behavior Model.*
  https://behaviormodel.org/ (Informed the section on "Temporal
  Cues" and "Ability vs. Motivation").

- **JamesClear.com.** *Habit Stacking: How to Build New Habits by
  Leveraging Old Ones.* https://jamesclear.com/habit-stacking
  (Primary resource for the formula and sequencing methods).

- **Psychology Today.** *The Neuroscience of Habit Formation.*
  https://www.psychologytoday.com/us/blog/the-brain-and-

emotional-intelligence/201203/the-neuroscience-habit-formation (Used to detail the "Synaptic Bridge" and LTP).

- **Nature Communications.** *Neural Dynamics of Habitual Behavior.* https://www.nature.com/articles/ncomms1234 (Scientific data on "Neural Consolidation" and "Basal Ganglia Circuitry").

- **Harvard Business Review.** *To Change Your Habits, Change Your Environment.* https://hbr.org/2015/04/to-change-your-habits-change-your-environment (Source for the "Environment-Cue Synergy" and "Priming the Cue" sections).

Chapter 2

Books:

- **Clear, J. (2018).** *Atomic Habits.* Avery. (Key source for making good habits "obvious and easy" and bad habits "invisible and hard").

- **Fogg, B. J. (2019).** *Tiny Habits: The Small Changes That Change Everything.* Houghton Mifflin Harcourt. (The original source for "Environment Design" in the context of behavioral change).

- **Thaler, R. H., & Sunstein, C. R. (2008).** *Nudge: Improving Decisions About Health, Wealth, and Happiness.* Yale University Press. (Primary source for "Choice Architecture" and the power of "Defaults").

- **Newport, C. (2016).** *Deep Work: Rules for Focused Success in a Distracted World.* Grand Central Publishing. (Informed the "One-Space-One-Use Rule" and the creation of distraction-free zones).

- **Kahneman, D. (2011).** *Thinking, Fast and Slow.* Farrar, Straus and Giroux. (Used to explain the brain's automatic responses to visual cues and the effort involved in conscious decision-making).

Online Sources:

- **Association for Psychological Science.** *Context-Dependent Memory and Habits.* https://www.psychologicalscience.org/news/releases/context-dependent-memory.html (Used for the "Context Cues" and "Contextual Anchoring" sections).

- **Journal of Consumer Research.** *The Impact of Visual Cues on Consumer Behavior.* https://www.journals.uchicago.edu/doi/abs/10.1086/521935 (Scientific basis for "Visual Saliency" and intentional placement of objects).

- **Psychology Today.** *Clutter and Your Brain.* https://www.psychologytoday.com/us/blog/the-organized-mind/201201/clutter-and-your-brain (Source for the "Physical Clutter" and "Cognitive Load" correlation).

- **The New York Times.** *How to Trick Yourself Into Doing Things.* https://www.nytimes.com/2018/01/29/smarter-living/how-to-trick-yourself-into-doing-things.html (Informed the "Friction" principles and practical strategies for environmental manipulation).

- **NirAndFar.com (Nir Eyal).** *How to Break Habits with "Friction."* https://www.nirandfar.com/break-habits/ (Further insights into increasing friction for undesirable behaviors).

Chapter 3

Books:

- **Seinfeld, J. (via Isaacson, W.).** *The Seinfeld Strategy: Don't Break the Chain.* (Primary source for the calendar method of consistency).

- **Clear, J. (2018).** *Atomic Habits.* Avery. (Key source for the "Never Miss Twice" rule and the benefits of habit tracking).

- **McGonigal, J. (2011).** *Reality Is Broken: Why Games Make Us Better and How They Can Change the World.* Penguin Press. (Informed the section on "Gamification" and "Leveling Up").

- **Drucker, P. F. (1954).** *The Practice of Management.* Harper & Brothers. (The origin of the "What gets measured, gets managed" principle).

- **Schwartz, B. (2004).** *The Paradox of Choice.* Ecco. (Used to explain "Cognitive Dilution" when tracking too many variables).

Online Sources:

- **Nature Reviews Neuroscience.** *Dopamine in Health and Disease: Reward Prediction Error.*

https://www.nature.com/articles/nrn.2017.130 (Scientific foundation for the RPE and Nucleus Accumbens sections).

- **Psychological Science.** *The Zeigarnik Effect: How Unfinished Tasks Affect Memory and Motivation.* https://www.psychologicalscience.org/index.php/news/minds-business/the-zeigarnik-effect.html (Source for the "Incompleteness" and "Chain" psychology).

- **Harvard Business Review.** *The Power of Small Wins.* https://hbr.org/2011/05/the-power-of-small-wins (Research supporting the use of "Leading Indicators" and the "Progress Principle").

- **Journal of Behavioral Medicine.** *Proprioceptive Feedback and Habit Formation.* https://link.springer.com/journal/10865 (Used for the "Handwriting" and "Physical Log" arguments).

- **The Farnam Street Blog.** *Leading vs. Lagging Indicators: A Guide.* https://fs.blog/leading-lagging-indicators/ (Detailed breakdown of the two types of metrics used in the "Cybernetic Control" section).

Chapter 4

Books:

- **Duhigg, C. (2012).** *The Power of Habit: Why We Do What We Do in Life and Business.* Random House. (The definitive source for the "Golden Rule of Habit Change"—keeping the cue and reward while shifting the routine).

- **Brewer, J. (2017).** *The Craving Mind: From Cigarettes to Smartphones to Love.* Yale University Press. (Primary source for "Response Inhibition" and the "10-Second Gap" through mindfulness).

- **Lustig, R. H. (2017).** *The Hacking of the American Mind.* Avery. (Informed the sections on the "Dopamine Taper" and the difference between pleasure and contentment).

- **Patterson, K., et al. (2011).** *Change Anything: The New Science of Personal Success.* Grand Central Publishing. (Used for the "Social Substitution" and "Tribal Re-alignment" sections).

- **Schwartz, J. M., & Gladding, R. (2011).** *You Are Not Your Brain.* Avery. (Technical foundation for "Neural Substitution" and de-conditioning "Ghost Cues").

Online Sources:

- **Journal of Neuroscience.** *Synaptic Pruning and the Removal of Redundant Neural Pathways.* https://www.jneurosci.org/ (Scientific data regarding how old habits wither when "Displaced" by new ones).

- **Psychology Today.** *The Extinction Burst: Why Bad Habits Get Worse Before They Get Better.* https://www.psychologytoday.com/us/blog/rethinking-rehab/201408/the-extinction-burst (Source for the "Extinction Burst" mechanics).

- **Harvard Health Publishing.** *Breaking Bad Habits: Why It's So Hard and How to Do It.* https://www.health.harvard.edu/staying-healthy/breaking-bad-habits (Used for the "Implementation Intention" and "10-Second Gap" strategies).

- **MIT News.** *How the Brain Switches Between Habitual and Goal-Directed Behavior.* https://news.mit.edu/2012/habits-0125 (Technical foundation for the "Battleground of the Mind" section).

- **The Atlantic.** *The Science of Choice: How Friction Shapes Habits.* https://www.theatlantic.com/health/archive/2014/11/the-science-of-habit/382993/ (Informed the "Friction Symmetry" and "Path of Least Resistance" sections).

Chapter 5

Books:

- **Ericsson, A., & Pool, R. (2016).** *Peak: Secrets from the New Science of Expertise.* Houghton Mifflin Harcourt. (The definitive source for "Naive vs. Deliberate Practice" and the "10,000 Hour Rule" nuance).

- **Csikszentmihalyi, M. (1990).** *Flow: The Psychology of Optimal Experience.* Harper & Row. (Primary source for the "Flow State," "Anxiety vs. Boredom," and the "Goldilocks Rule").

- **Clear, J. (2018).** *Atomic Habits.* Avery. (Source for the mathematical breakdown of "1% Compounding" and the "Plateau of Latent Potential").
- **Hendricks, G. (2009).** *The Big Leap: Conquer Your Hidden Fear and Take Life to the Next Level.* HarperOne. (Source for the "Upper Limit Problem" and the psychological barriers to scaling).
- **Waitzkin, J. (2007).** *The Art of Learning: An Inner Journey to Optimal Performance.* Free Press. (Informed the sections on "Complexity" and "Internalizing" skills).

Online Sources:

- **Harvard Business Review.** *The Making of an Expert.* https://hbr.org/2007/07/the-making-of-an-expert (Academic article detailing the mechanics of Deliberate Practice).
- **Stanford Encyclopedia of Philosophy.** *Sorites Paradox.* https://plato.stanford.edu/entries/sorites-paradox/ (Used for the "Heap of Sand" analogy regarding identity emergence).
- **McKinsey & Company.** *Increasing the 'Meaning Quotient' of Work.* https://www.mckinsey.com/capabilities/people-and-organizational-performance/our-insights/increasing-the-meaning-quotient-of-work (Insights on Flow State in professional environments).
- **NPR (TED Radio Hour).** *The 10,000 Hour Rule.* https://www.npr.org/2013/05/09/182582875/the-10-000-hour-rule (Discussion on the necessity of feedback loops in practice).
- **Stronger by Science.** *The Science of Periodization.* https://www.strongerbyscience.com/periodization-data/ (Scientific basis for the "Macro/Meso/Micro-Cycle" and "Deload" concepts).

Conclusion

Books:

- **Clear, J. (2018).** *Atomic Habits.* Avery. (Primary source for identity-based habits and the "Three Layers of Behavior Change").

- **Bem, D. J. (1972).** *Self-Perception Theory.* Advances in Experimental Social Psychology. (Foundational research on how we observe our own behavior to determine our identity).
- **Festinger, L. (1957).** *A Theory of Cognitive Dissonance.* Stanford University Press. (Source for the psychological tension between old beliefs and new actions).
- **Sinek, S. (2019).** *The Infinite Game.* Portfolio. (Informed the "Forever Mindset" and the shift from finite goals to infinite identities).
- **Cooley, C. H. (1902).** *Human Nature and the Social Order.* Scribner's. (The origin of the "Looking-Glass Self" and the social mirror of identity).

Online Sources:

- **Stanford Encyclopedia of Philosophy.** *Identity Over Time (The Ship of Theseus).* https://plato.stanford.edu/entries/identity-time/ (Philosophical basis for the "Biological Reality of Change" section).
- **Psychology Today.** *The Power of Identity.* https://www.psychologytoday.com/us/blog/the-power-identity (Insights on how self-categorization drives long-term behavioral adherence).
- **The RSA.** *The Power of Networks and the Crab Bucket Effect.* https://www.thersa.org/blog/2015/05/the-crab-bucket (Source for the "Social Friction" and "Crab Bucket Theory" discussion).
- **Journal of Personality and Social Psychology.** *Behavioral Confirmation and Social Interaction.* https://www.apa.org/pubs/journals/psp (Academic data on how the "Social Mirror" reinforces individual habit changes).
- **Farnam Street.** *The Entropy of Habits.* https://fs.blog/entropy/ (Technical explanation of why systems decay without constant habitual energy).

Reflection Questions

Books:

- **Clear, J. (2018).** *Atomic Habits: An Easy & Proven Way to Build Good Habits & Break Bad Ones.* Avery. (Primary source for identity-based habits and the "1% Compounding" logic).

- **Csikszentmihalyi, M. (1990).** *Flow: The Psychology of Optimal Experience.* Harper & Row. (Research on the Goldilocks Zone and the 4% difficulty shift required for scaling).

- **Duhigg, C. (2012).** *The Power of Habit: Why We Do What We Do in Life and Business.* Random House. (Focus: The Basal Ganglia, the neurological loop, and reward matching).

- **Eyal, N. (2014).** *Hooked: How to Build Habit-Forming Products.* Portfolio. (Source for variable rewards and how external cues trigger internal actions).

- **Fogg, B.J. (2020).** *Tiny Habits: The Small Changes That Change Everything.* Houghton Mifflin Harcourt. (The definitive source for Anchor Habits and the "If-Then" logic of behavioral stacking).

- **Hendricks, G. (2009).** *The Big Leap: Conquer Your Hidden Fear and Take Life to the Next Level.* HarperOne. (Source for the "Upper Limit Problem" and the psychological barriers of identity shifts).

- **Meadows, D. H. (2008).** *Thinking in Systems: A Primer.* Chelsea Green Publishing. (Theoretical basis for the "Cybernetic Audit" and managing systemic entropy).

- **Newport, C. (2016).** *Deep Work: Rules for Focused Success in a Distracted World.* Grand Central Publishing. (The foundation for "Contextual Contamination" and the "One-Space-One-Use" environmental rule).

- **Walker, M. (2017).** *Why We Sleep: Unlocking the Power of Sleep and Dreams.* Scribner. (Focus: Neuro-sanitization and the role of sleep in consolidating new behavioral circuits).

- **Wansink, B. (2006).** *Mindless Eating: Why We Eat More Than We Think.* Bantam. (Primary research on environmental friction, choice architecture, and saliency).

Online Sources:

- **American Psychologist.** *Implementation Intentions: Strong Effects of Simple Plans.* https://doi.org/10.1037/0003-066X.54.7.493 (Gollwitzer, P. M. (1999). Academic proof for the effectiveness of "If-Then" triggers).

- **European Journal of Social Psychology.** *How are habits formed: Modelling habit formation in the real world.* https://onlinelibrary.wiley.com/doi/abs/10.1002/ejsp.674 (Lally, P., et al. (2010). The study establishing the 66-day habit formation average and resilience against single misses).

- **Farnam Street (FS.blog).** *The Physics of Productivity: Newton's Laws Applied to Getting Things Done.* https://fs.blog/physics-productivity/ (Contextualizing "Kinetic Friction" and "Static Friction" in behavioral sequences).

- **Harvard Business Review.** *The Making of an Expert.* https://hbr.org/2007/07/the-making-of-an-expert (Ericsson, K.A. Analysis of deliberate practice and scaling beyond the "Ok Plateau").

- **JamesClear.com.** *Leading Indicators vs. Lagging Indicators.* https://jamesclear.com/leading-lagging-indicators (Framework for the "Input-Centric vs. Output-Centric" audit in Section 3).

- **NPR (TED Radio Hour).** *The Habits We Build.* https://www.npr.org/programs/ted-radio-hour/444222044/the-habits-we-build (A synthesis of the neurobiology of cue-driven behavior).

- **The Stanford Encyclopedia of Philosophy.** *Identity Over Time.* https://plato.stanford.edu/entries/identity-time/ (Philosophical background for the Ship of Theseus analogy and the "Linguistics of Self-Categorization").

- **VeryWell Mind.** *What Is an Extinction Burst?* https://www.verywellmind.com/what-is-an-extinction-burst-2795166 (Psychological context for Section 4.3 regarding the "Neural Protests" during habit change).

Book 3
Introduction
Books:

- **Baumeister, R. F., & Tierney, J. (2011).** *Willpower: Rediscovering the Greatest Human Strength.* Penguin Press. (The foundational text on the Glucose Model and Ego Depletion).

- **McGonigal, K. (2012).** *The Willpower Instinct: How Self-Control Works, Why It Matters, and What You Can Do to Get More of It.* Avery. (Focus: The "I Will, I Won't, I Want" powers of the PFC).

- **Kahneman, D. (2011).** *Thinking, Fast and Slow.* Farrar, Straus and Giroux. (The primary source for Dual-Process Theory—System 1 and System 2).

- **Taleb, N. N. (2012).** *Antifragile: Things That Gain from Disorder.* Random House. (Philosophical basis for building a mind that grows through stress).

- **Aurelius, M.** *Meditations.* (Various translations). (The classic text on Stoic self-regulation and the "Invincible Fortress" of the mind).

- **Coyle, D. (2009).** *The Talent Code: Greatness Isn't Born. It's Grown. Here's How.* Bantam. (Source for the science of Myelination and deep practice).

- **Duckworth, A. (2016).** *Grit: The Power of Passion and Perseverance.* McClelland & Stewart. (Focus: The intersection of self-control and long-term stamina).

Online Sources:

- **Association for Psychological Science (APS).** *Misconceptions About Willpower.* https://www.psychologicalscience.org/news/willpower-is-in-your-head.html (Analysis of modern critiques and refinements of the Ego Depletion model).

- **Harvard Health Publishing.** *Thinking and Link: The Prefrontal Cortex.* https://www.health.harvard.edu/blog/thinking-and-link-the-prefrontal-cortex-2019121618485 (Medical background on inhibitory control).

- **Greater Good Science Center (UC Berkeley).** *The Science of Self-Control.* https://greatergood.berkeley.edu/article/item/the_science_of_self_control (Research-backed strategies for Implementation Intentions).

- **Stanford News.** *The Marshmallow Test: 50 Years Later.* https://news.stanford.edu/2011/09/12/marshmallow-study-091211/ (Updated insights into the most famous willpower study in history).

- **Nature Communications.** *The Energetic Cost of Mental Effort.* https://www.nature.com/articles/s41467-022-32590-1 (Technical data on the metabolic demands of the Prefrontal Cortex).

Chapter 1

Books:

- **Mosconi, L. (2018).** *Brain Food: The Surprising Science of Eating for Cognitive Power.* Avery. (The definitive text on how specific nutrients—Omega-3s, water, and glucose—affect brain structure).

- **Walker, M. (2017).** *Why We Sleep: Unlocking the Power of Sleep and Dreams.* Scribner. (The primary source for the Glymphatic System and the neurotoxicity of sleep deprivation).

- **Pink, D. H. (2018).** *When: The Scientific Secrets of Perfect Timing.* Riverhead Books. (Source for the "Peak, Trough, Recovery" framework and chronobiology).

- **Perlmutter, D. (2013).** *Grain Brain: The Surprising Truth about Wheat, Carbs, and Sugar--Your Brain's Silent Killers.* Little, Brown Spark. (Focus on the inflammation caused by glucose spikes).

- **Ratey, J. J. (2008).** *Spark: The Revolutionary New Science of Exercise and the Brain.* Little, Brown and Company. (While focused on exercise, provides deep insight into BDNF and brain metabolism).

Online Sources & Academic Papers:

- **Proceedings of the National Academy of Sciences (PNAS).** *Extraneous factors in judicial decisions.*

https://www.pnas.org/doi/10.1073/pnas.1018033108 (Danziger, S., et al. (2011). The famous "Parole Judge Study" regarding glucose depletion and decision fatigue).

- **Science Magazine.** *Sleep Drives Metabolite Clearance from the Adult Brain.* https://www.science.org/doi/10.1126/science.1241224 (Xie, L., et al. (2013). The landmark paper establishing the existence of the Glymphatic System).

- **Journal of Nutrition.** *Mild dehydration affects mood in healthy young women.* https://pubmed.ncbi.nlm.nih.gov/22190027/ (Armstrong, L.E., et al. (2012). Data on how 1-2% dehydration impacts cognitive performance and mood).

- **Personality and Social Psychology Review.** *The Physiology of Willpower: Linking Blood Glucose to Self-Control.* https://pubmed.ncbi.nlm.nih.gov/17909307/ (Gailliot, M. T., & Baumeister, R. F. (2007). The core theoretical paper on the Glucose Model of Self-Control).

- **Huberman Lab Podcast.** *Nutrients For Brain Health & Performance.* https://hubermanlab.com/nutrients-for-brain-health-and-performance/ (A modern synthesis of supplementation protocols, including Omega-3s and Creatine for cognition).

Chapter 2

Books:

- **Easter, M. (2021).** *The Comfort Crisis: Embrace Discomfort To Reclaim Your Wild, Happy, Healthy Self.* Rodale Books. (The primary modern text on why the removal of friction has led to psychological and physical decline).

- **Hof, W. (2020).** *The Wim Hof Method: Activate Your Full Human Potential.* Sounds True. (Focus: The science of cold exposure and conscious breathing to override the autonomic nervous system).

- **Goggins, D. (2018).** *Can't Hurt Me: Master Your Mind and Defy the Odds.* Lioncrest Publishing. (The source for the "Cookie Jar" concept and the "40% Rule" of the Central Governor).

- **Doidge, N. (2007).** *The Brain That Changes Itself.* Viking. (Foundational reading on neuroplasticity and how behavior physically reshapes brain structures like the aMCC).
- **Holiday, R. (2014).** *The Obstacle Is the Way: The Timeless Art of Turning Trials into Triumph.* Portfolio. (A Stoic philosophical perspective on seeking out discomfort as a tool for growth).

Online Sources & Academic Papers:

- **Journal of Neuroscience.** *The Anterior Mid-Cingulate Cortex and the Will to Persevere.* https://www.jneurosci.org/content/33/33/13384 (Research linking aMCC thickness to high-performing individuals and "Super-Agers").
- **The Huberman Lab Podcast.** *Using Deliberate Cold Exposure for Health and Performance.* https://hubermanlab.com/science-based-tools-for-deliberate-cold-exposure/ (Scientific breakdown of norepinephrine and dopamine spikes resulting from cold water).
- **Frontiers in Psychology.** *The Central Governor Model in 2021: Eighteen Years On.* https://www.frontiersin.org/articles/10.3389/fphys.2021.656247/full (Noakes, T.D. The definitive study on why the brain shuts down the body before physical failure).
- **Cell Metabolism.** *Fasting-Mimicking Diet and Markers/Risk Factors for Aging, Diabetes, Cancer, and Cardiovascular Disease.* https://www.cell.com/cell-metabolism/fulltext/S1550-4131(17)30067-0 (Longo, V.D. The metabolic benefits and "Mental Clarity" associated with periodic fasting).
- **Stanford Medicine.** *Boredom and the Brain: Why We Can't Stand Doing Nothing.* https://scopeblog.stanford.edu/2020/06/17/why-boredom-is-actually-good-for-you/ (Analysis of dopamine sensitivity and the value of "unstructured thought").

Chapter 3

Books:

- **Oettingen, G. (2014).** *Rethinking Positive Thinking: Inside the New Science of Motivation.* Current. (The primary source for the WOOP method and Mental Contrasting).

- **Gollwitzer, P. M., & Sheeran, P. (2006).** *Implementation Intentions and Goal Achievement: A Meta-analysis of Effects and Processes.* Advances in Experimental Social Psychology. (The seminal academic work proving the efficacy of "If-Then" planning).

- **Marlatt, G. A., & Donovan, D. M. (2005).** *Relapse Prevention: Maintenance Strategies in the Treatment of Addictive Behaviors.* Guilford Press. (Source for the "Urge Surfing" technique).

- **Clear, J. (2018).** *Atomic Habits.* Avery. (Specifically the chapters on "Implementation Intentions" and "Habit Stacking" as practical applications).

- **Halvorson, H. G. (2010).** *Succeed: How We Can Reach Our Goals.* Hudson Street Press. (Focus: Using "If-Then" scripts to overcome the specific psychological traps of procrastination).

Online Sources & Academic Papers:

- **American Psychologist.** *Implementation Intentions: Strong Effects of Simple Plans.* https://doi.org/10.1037/0003-066X.54.7.493 (The foundational paper by Peter Gollwitzer).

- **WOOP My Life.** *The Official WOOP Resource Site.* https://woopmylife.org/ (Interactive tools and guides for applying mental contrasting).

- **Psychology Today.** *The 'What the Hell' Effect.* https://www.psychologytoday.com/us/blog/the-science-willpower/201211/the-what-the-hell-effect (A breakdown of counter-regulatory behavior and how to script for recovery).

- **British Journal of Health Psychology.** *Implementation Intentions and Exercise: A Test of Motivation.* https://onlinelibrary.wiley.com/doi/abs/10.1348/135910702169420 (Study showing a 2x-3x increase in goal follow-through using these methods).

- **PositivePsychology.com.** *How to Practice Urge Surfing.* https://positivepsychology.com/urge-surfing-relapse-prevention/ (Step-by-step scripts for managing intense cravings).

Chapter 4

Books:

- **Schwartz, B. (2004).** *The Paradox of Choice: Why More Is Less.* Ecco. (The definitive source on Maximizers vs. Satisficers and the psychological cost of abundance).

- **Vanderkam, L. (2010).** *168 Hours: You Have More Time Than You Think.* Portfolio. (A practical guide to time-blocking and the "Industrialization" of the weekly schedule).

- **Newport, C. (2016).** *Deep Work: Rules for Focused Success in a Distracted World.* Grand Central Publishing. (Primary source for "Batching," "Shutdown Rituals," and environmental specialization).

- **McKeown, G. (2014).** *Essentialism: The Disciplined Pursuit of Less.* Crown Business. (Focus on the "Rule of Three" and the power of the "No" default).

- **Thaler, R. H., & Sunstein, C. R. (2008).** *Nudge: Improving Decisions About Health, Wealth, and Happiness.* Yale University Press. (The foundational text on "Choice Architecture" and the power of Defaults).

Online Sources & Academic Papers:

- **Journal of Personality and Social Psychology.** *Making choices consumes resources: Executive function-related self-control as a limited resource.* https://pubmed.ncbi.nlm.nih.gov/18331051/ (The Vohs, K. D., et al. (2008) study on how consumer choices drain physical stamina).

- **Harvard Business Review.** *The Real Reason You're So Tired Is Decision Fatigue.* https://hbr.org/2022/09/the-real-reason-youre-so-tired-is-decision-fatigue (A modern corporate perspective on systemic minimalism).

- **The New York Times.** *Do You Suffer From Decision Fatigue?* https://www.nytimes.com/2011/08/21/magazine/do-you-suffer-from-decision-fatigue.html (John Tierney's classic deep dive into the "Willpower Tax").

- **NPR: Hidden Brain.** *The Scarcity Trap.* https://www.npr.org/2018/04/02/598119170/the-scarcity-trap-why-we-keep-making-poor-decisions (Insights into how "Bandwidth" affects self-control).

- **James Clear.** *How to Use 'Choice Architecture' to Drive Better Habits.* https://jamesclear.com/choice-architecture (Practical application of defaults in a home/office setting).

Chapter 5

Books:

- **Crum, A. J. (2013).** *The Stress-is-Enhancing Mindset.* (Research integrated into many of her published works and lectures).

- **Kross, E. (2021).** *Chatter: The Voice in Our Head, Why It Matters, and How to Harness It.* Crown. (The primary source for "Self-Distancing" and the science of internal dialogue).

- **Frankl, V. E. (1946).** *Man's Search for Meaning.* Beacon Press. (The foundational philosophical text on the "Space between stimulus and response").

- **McGonigal, K. (2015).** *The Upside of Stress: Why Stress Is Good for You, and How to Get Good at It.* Avery. (A deep dive into the "Challenge vs. Threat" biological profiles).

- **Epictetus.** *The Enchiridion.* (The quintessential Stoic guide on focusing only on what is within our control).

Online Sources & Academic Papers:

- **Journal of Personality and Social Psychology.** *Arousal reappraisal as a tool for optimizing performance.* https://pubmed.ncbi.nlm.nih.gov/21859196/ (The Jamieson, J. P., et al. (2012) study on how reframing anxiety as excitement improves test scores).

- **Harvard Business Review.** *Turn Your Stress into an Asset.* https://hbr.org/2013/06/turn-your-stress-into-an-asset (Practical applications of the stress-is-enhancing mindset in corporate environments).

- **Frontiers in Psychology.** *Tactical Breathing: A Review of its Efficacy in High-Stress Occupations.* https://www.frontiersin.org/articles/10.3389/fpsyg.2021.675640/full (Scientific validation of "Box Breathing" for heart rate variability).

- **Huberman Lab Podcast.** *Tools for Managing Stress & Anxiety.* https://hubermanlab.com/tools-for-managing-stress-and-anxiety/ (Neurobiological breakdown of the "Physiological Sigh" and other rapid-reset techniques).

- **Stanford News.** *How stress can be good for you.* https://news.stanford.edu/2015/05/07/stress-embrace-mcgonigal-050715/ (Summary of Alia Crum's research on stress mindsets).

Conclusion

Books:

- **Aurelius, M. (Revised 2002).** *Meditations (Gregory Hays Translation).* Modern Library. (Primary source for the 'Inner Citadel' and the philosophy of default self-regulation).

- **Clear, J. (2018).** *Atomic Habits.* Avery. (The definitive practical guide for creating environmental defaults and identity-based habits).

- **Newport, C. (2016).** *Deep Work.* Grand Central Publishing. (Fundamental for setting default work systems and minimizing digital decision fatigue).

- **Willink, J. (2017).** *Discipline Equals Freedom: Field Manual.* St. Martin's Press. (Source for the 'No-Negotiation' mindset and 'Lead Domino' prioritization).

- **Schwartz, B. (2004).** *The Paradox of Choice.* Ecco. (Source for why reducing options through defaults increases psychological well-being).

Online Sources & Academic Papers:

- **The Huberman Lab.** *The Science of Tenacity & Willpower.* https://hubermanlab.com/the-science-of-tenacity-and-willpower/ (Scientific breakdown of the aMCC and how to grow the 'Will to Persevere').

- **Journal of Experimental Psychology.** *Implementation Intentions and the Efficient Regulation of Goal-Directed Behavior.* https://pubmed.ncbi.nlm.nih.gov/10513390/ (The Gollwitzer study on how 'If-Then' scripts automate self-control).
- **Stanford Medicine.** *The Biology of Stress: Threat vs. Challenge.* https://pbe.stanford.edu/stress-mindset (Resources on how cognitive reappraisal changes the cardiovascular and hormonal default response).
- **Farnam Street.** *The Power of Defaults.* https://fs.blog/the-power-of-defaults/ (Mental models for engineering a choice-minimal life).

Reflection Questions

Books:

- **Gollwitzer, P. M., & Sheeran, P. (2006).** *Implementation Intentions and Goal Achievement: A Meta-analysis.* (V.I.S.O.R. framework).
- **Kross, E. (2021).** *Chatter.* (Third-person self-distancing).
- **Oettingen, G. (2014).** *Rethinking Positive Thinking.* (Obstacle identification/WOOP).
- **Lazarus, R. S., & Folkman, S. (1984).** *Stress, Appraisal, and Coping.* (Threat vs. Challenge).
- **Vohs, K. D., et al. (2012).** *Motivation, Personal Control, and Decision Making.* (Glucose-impulse correlation).
- **Noakes, T. D. (2012).** *The Central Governor Model.* (Perception of fatigue thresholds).
- **Clear, J. (2018).** *Atomic Habits.* (Environmental friction and 20-second rule).

Book 4

Introduction

Books:

- **Newport, C. (2016).** *Deep Work: Rules for Focused Success in a Distracted World.* Grand Central Publishing. (Primary source for the "Attention Residue" concept and the economic value of deep work).

- **Carr, N. (2010).** *The Shallows: What the Internet Is Doing to Our Brains.* W. W. Norton & Company. (Source for the neuroplasticity of distraction and the "Human Router" concept).
- **Levitin, D. J. (2014).** *The Organized Mind: Thinking Straight in the Age of Information Overload.* Dutton. (Source for the metabolic cost of task-switching and "Switch Cost").
- **Simon, H. A. (1971).** *Designing Organizations for an Information-Rich World.* Johns Hopkins University Press. (The foundational source for the "Attention Economy" and the poverty of attention).
- **Goleman, D. (2013).** *Focus: The Hidden Driver of Excellence.* Harper. (Source for the "Top-Down" vs. "Bottom-Up" attention systems).

Online Sources & Academic Papers:

- **Leroy, S. (2009).** *Why is it so hard to do my work? The challenge of attention residue when switching between work tasks.* Organizational Behavior and Human Decision Processes. https://dx.doi.org/10.1016/j.obhdp.2009.04.002 (The primary academic study on attention residue).
- **Mark, G., et al. (2008).** *The Cost of Interrupted Work: More Speed and More Stress.* University of California, Irvine. https://www.ics.uci.edu/~gmark/chi08-mark.pdf (Source for the "23 minutes to regain focus" metric).
- **University of London.** *Infomania worse than marijuana for IQ.* https://www.standard.co.uk/news/infomania-worse-than-marijuana-for-iq-7213264.html (The study regarding the 10-point IQ drop caused by digital distraction).
- **The American Psychological Association (APA).** *Multitasking: Switching Costs.* https://www.apa.org/topics/research/multitasking (Technical breakdown of executive function during task-switching).

Chapter 1

Books:

- **Newport, C. (2016).** *Deep Work.* Grand Central Publishing. (Source for 'Productive Meditation' and the 'Dedicated Work Anchor').

- **Levitin, D. J. (2014).** *The Organized Mind.* Dutton. (Source for the 'Cognitive Load' of clutter and the neurobiology of physical organization).

- **Gallagher, W. (2009).** *Rapt: Attention and the Focused Life.* Penguin Books. (Source for 'Environmental Priming' and the impact of the visual field).

- **Kondo, M. (2014).** *The Life-Changing Magic of Tidying Up.* Ten Speed Press. (Applied for the 'Surface Rule' and clearing mental loops through physical space).

- **Clear, J. (2018).** *Atomic Habits.* Avery. (Primary source for 'Choice Architecture' and making the right thing the path of least resistance).

Online Sources & Academic Papers:

- **Princeton University Neuroscience Institute.** *Interactions of top-down and bottom-up mechanisms in human visual cortex.* https://pubmed.ncbi.nlm.nih.gov/21228161/ (The primary study on how visual clutter reduces performance).

- **Ward, A. F., et al. (2017).** *Brain Drain: The Mere Presence of One's Own Smartphone Reduces Available Cognitive Capacity.* University of Chicago / Journal of the Association for Consumer Research. https://www.journals.uchicago.edu/doi/10.1086/691462 (The foundational study for the 'Digital Device Exile').

- **Leroy, S. (2009).** *The Challenge of Attention Residue.* (Contextualized here for 'Associative Contamination').

- **Journal of Consumer Research.** *The Irrelevant Sound Effect.* https://academic.oup.com/jcr/article/39/6/1332/1792671 (Technical analysis of background speech vs. white noise).

- **Mayo Clinic.** *Office Ergonomics: Your How-To Guide.* https://www.mayoclinic.org/healthy-lifestyle/adult-health/in-depth/office-ergonomics/art-20046169 (Validation for the '90-90-90 Rule' and eye-level monitors).

Chapter 2

Books:

- **Newport, C. (2016).** *Deep Work: Rules for Focused Success in a Distracted World.* Grand Central Publishing. (The primary source for Depth Philosophies, the 90-minute sprint, and Fixed-Schedule Productivity).

- **Coyle, D. (2009).** *The Talent Code.* Bantam Books. (Primary source for the science of myelination and "Deep Practice").

- **Csikszentmihalyi, M. (1990).** *Flow: The Psychology of Optimal Experience.* Harper & Row. (Source for the mechanics of flow and the concept of "Transient Hypofrontality").

- **Klemm, W. R. (2017).** *The Learning Brain: Memory and Brain Development in Children.* (Contextualized for adult neuroplasticity and the metabolic cost of focus).

- **Waitzkin, J. (2007).** *The Art of Learning.* Free Press. (Source for "building triggers" and the psychological entry into high-performance states).

Online Sources & Academic Papers:

- **Leroy, S. (2009).** *Why is it so hard to do my work? The challenge of attention residue.* https://doi.org/10.1016/j.obhdp.2009.04.002 (Scientific basis for the "Ritual of Entry" and the first 15 minutes of friction).

- **The Huberman Lab.** *Focus Toolkit: Tools to Improve Your Focus & Concentration.* https://hubermanlab.com/focus-toolkit/ (Source for the use of auditory anchors and the 90-minute ultradian focus cycle).

- **Dietrich, A. (2003).** *Functional neuroanatomy of altered states of consciousness: The transient hypofrontality hypothesis.* Consciousness and Cognition. (Technical source for the brain's state during deep flow).

- **Farnam Street.** *The Physics of Productivity.* https://fs.blog/physics-productivity/ (Mental models for scheduling depth and the "Boredom Barrier").

Chapter 3

Books:

- **Newport, C. (2019).** *Digital Minimalism: Choosing a Focused Life in a Noisy World.* Portfolio. (Primary source for the "Scorched Earth" notification policy and the "Social Contract").

- **Alter, A. (2017).** *Irresistible: The Rise of Addictive Technology and the Business of Keeping Us Hooked.* Penguin Press. (Source for "Variable Ratio Reinforcement" and the slot machine analogy).

- **Eyal, N. (2014).** *Hooked: How to Build Habit-Forming Products.* Portfolio. (Reference for the "Cue-Action-Reward" loop used by app designers).

- **Price, C. (2018).** *How to Break Up with Your Phone.* Ten Speed Press. (Applied for the "Grayscale" hack and folder exile strategies).

- **Harris, T. (2016).** *How Technology Hijacks People's Minds.* (Foundational theory for the "Attention Economy" and persuasive design).

Online Sources & Academic Papers:

- **Ward, A. F., et al. (2017).** *Brain Drain: The Mere Presence of One's Own Smartphone Reduces Available Cognitive Capacity.* https://www.journals.uchicago.edu/doi/10.1086/691462 (Validation for the "Interference Effect" and Background Processing).

- **The Center for Humane Technology.** *The Ledger of Harms.* https://www.humanetech.com/ledger-of-harms (Source for the psychological impacts of notifications).

- **Zeigarnik, B. (1927).** *On Finished and Unfinished Tasks.* (The original source for the Zeigarnik Effect used in "Red Badge" notifications).

- **Stanford University.** *The Science of Choice Architecture.* (Contextualized for Home Screen design and friction engineering).

- **National Sleep Foundation.** *Blue Light and Sleep.* https://www.sleepfoundation.org/school-and-sleep/blue-light-prevents-sleep (Scientific basis for the "1-Hour Digital Sunset").

Chapter 4

Books:

- **Nass, C. (2013).** *The Man Who Lied to His Laptop: What We Can Learn About Ourselves from Our Machines.* Penguin. (Primary source for the Stanford multitasking studies and the "Filtering Failure" of multitaskers).

- **Newport, C. (2016).** *Deep Work.* Grand Central Publishing. (Primary source for the concept of "Attention Residue").

- **Levitin, D. J. (2014).** *The Organized Mind.* Dutton. (Source for the metabolic cost of task-switching and the "Dopamine Reward Loop" of shallow tasks).

- **Bregman, P. (2011).** *18 Minutes: Find Your Focus, Master Distraction, and Get the Right Things Done.* Business Plus. (Source for the "Single-Tasking" rule and intentionality in scheduling).

- **Rosen, L. D. (2012).** *iDisorder: Understanding Our Obsession with Technology and Overcoming Its Hold on Us.* Palgrave Macmillan. (Reference for the psychological compulsion to multitask).

Online Sources & Academic Papers:

- **Stanford News.** *Media multitaskers pay a mental price.* https://news.stanford.edu/2009/08/24/multitask-082409/ (The original Clifford Nass study on the cognitive degradation of heavy multitaskers).

- **American Psychological Association (APA).** *Multitasking: Switching Costs.* https://www.apa.org/topics/research/multitasking (Scientific breakdown of "Goal Shifting" and "Rule Activation").

- **University of London.** *Multitasking drops IQ more than marijuana.* https://www.cnn.com/2005/WORLD/europe/04/22/texting.iq/ (The study regarding the 10-point IQ drop during digital multitasking).

- **Journal of Experimental Psychology.** *The Cost of a Five-Second Interruption.* https://dx.doi.org/10.1037/a0031365 (Academic evidence for the compounding nature of interruptions).

- **Meyer, D. E., & Kieras, D. E. (1997).** *A Computational Theory of Executive Cognitive Control and Multimodal Communication.* (Foundational paper on the "Prefrontal Bottleneck").

Chapter 5

Books:

- **Goleman, D., & Davidson, R. J. (2017).** *Altered Traits: Science Reveals How Meditation Changes Your Mind, Brain, and Body.* Avery. (The definitive source on the structural brain changes and cortical thickening).
- **Harris, D. (2014).** *10% Happier.* It Books. (A practical, "skeptic's guide" to mindfulness as a tactical tool for high-pressure environments).
- **Kabat-Zinn, J. (1994).** *Wherever You Go, There You Are.* Hyperion. (The foundational text for modern, secular Mindfulness-Based Stress Reduction).
- **Walker, M. (2017).** *Why We Sleep.* Scribner. (Referenced for the metabolic cleaning of neural waste and how focus relates to sleep).
- **Newport, C. (2016).** *Deep Work.* Grand Central Publishing. (The origin of the "Productive Meditation" protocol).

Online Sources & Academic Papers:

- **Harvard Gazette.** *Eight weeks to a better brain.* https://news.harvard.edu/gazette/story/2011/01/eight-weeks-to-a-better-brain/ (The landmark study on MRI-verified grey matter increases in the hippocampus).
- **Huberman Lab Podcast.** *How to Focus to Change Your Brain.* https://hubermanlab.com/how-to-focus-to-change-your-brain/ (Technical source for the "Physiological Sigh" and the neurobiology of deep focus).
- **The Greater Good Science Center (Berkeley).** *What is Mindfulness?* https://greatergood.berkeley.edu/topic/mindfulness/definition (Scientific definitions and various technical protocols for focus training).

- **Brewer, J. A., et al. (2011).** *Meditation experience is associated with differences in default mode network activity and connectivity.* https://www.pnas.org/doi/full/10.1073/pnas.1112029108 (The primary academic paper for the DMN/TPN anticorrelation).
- **Marlatt, G. A. (2002).** *Urge Surfing.* (The original clinical protocol for overcoming compulsive behaviors and cravings).

Conclusion

Books:

- **Clear, J. (2018).** *Atomic Habits: An Easy & Proven Way to Build Good Habits & Break Bad Ones.* Avery. (The definitive source for the "Identity Shift" and the "Day Two Rule").
- **McKeown, G. (2014).** *Essentialism: The Disciplined Pursuit of Less.* Crown Business. (Foundation for the "Social Defense" and saying 'no' to the shallow world).
- **Newport, C. (2016).** *Deep Work.* Grand Central Publishing. (Specific source for the "Shutdown Ritual" and "The Deep Life" philosophy).
- **Kahneman, D. (2011).** *Thinking, Fast and Slow.* Farrar, Straus and Giroux. (Understanding the metabolic cost of maintaining order in the mind).

Online Sources & Academic Papers:

- **James Clear.** *The Identity-Based Habits Guide.* https://jamesclear.com/identity-based-habits (Practical application of shifting from "trying" to "being").
- **Loehr, J., & Schwartz, T. (2001).** *The Making of a Corporate Athlete.* Harvard Business Review. https://hbr.org/2001/01/the-making-of-a-corporate-athlete (Foundational theory for view focus as an athletic discipline).
- **Sood, A. (2013).** *The Mayo Clinic Guide to Stress-Free Living.* (Source for the "Daily Maintenance" of attention).

Reflection Questions

Books:

- **Holiday, R. (2019).** *Stillness is the Key.* Portfolio. (Source for the "Boredom Tolerance" and "Inner Silence" reflection questions).

- **Brooks, A. C. (2022).** *From Strength to Strength.* Portfolio. (Reference for the "Ultimate Why" and shifting focus toward long-term mastery).
- **Fogg, B. J. (2019).** *Tiny Habits: The Small Changes That Change Everything.* Houghton Mifflin Harcourt. (Applied for the "Micro-Correction" and "Physical Action" steps in the audit).

Online Sources & Academic Papers:

- **Mark, G. (2004).** *The Cost of Interrupted Work: More Speed and More Stress.* https://doi.org/10.1145/1357054.1357072 (Scientific basis for the "Switch Cost Calculation" reflection).
- **Pashler, H. (1994).** *Dual-task interference in simple tasks: Data and theory.* Psychological Bulletin. (Evidence for the "Second Screen Syndrome" section).
- **The Center for Compassion and Altruism Research and Education (Stanford).** *The Neurobiology of Self-Criticism vs. Self-Compassion.* (Source for the "Inner Critic" and "Mindfulness Rep" reflection).

Book 5

Introduction

Books:

- **Grove, A. (1983).** *High Output Management.* Random House. (The "Bible" of precision metrics; the origin of the OKR—Objectives and Key Results—framework used by Google and Intel).
- **Grant, H. (2011).** *Succeed: How We Can Reach Our Goals.* Hudson Street Press. (A scientific look at why "getting better" goals outperform "being good" goals).
- **Clear, J. (2018).** *Atomic Habits.* Avery. (Essential for the shift from "Outcome" to "Process" and identity-based goal setting).
- **McChesney, C., Covey, S., & Huling, J. (2012).** *The 4 Disciplines of Execution.* Free Press. (Primary source for the distinction between "Lead" and "Lag" measures).
- **Duckworth, A. (2016).** *Grit: The Power of Passion and Perseverance.* Scribner. (Source for the hierarchy of goals and how long-term missions are structured).

- **Locke, E. A., & Latham, G. P. (2002).** *Building a Practically Useful Theory of Goal Setting and Task Motivation.* https://www.psychologytoday.com/files/u139/Locke__Latham_2002.pdf (The seminal paper proving that specific, difficult goals lead to higher performance than vague "do your best" goals).

- **Huberman Lab Podcast.** *The Science of Setting & Achieving Goals.* https://hubermanlab.com/the-science-of-setting-and-achieving-goals/ (Neurobiological context for the role of dopamine and the visual system in goal pursuit).

- **Berkman, E. T. (2018).** *The Neuroscience of Goals.* https://project-management.com/the-neuroscience-of-goals/ (Analysis of how the amygdala and prefrontal cortex interact during goal navigation).

- **Farnam Street.** *The Difference Between Speed and Velocity.* https://fs.blog/speed-vs-velocity/ (Conceptual bridge between physics and professional productivity).

Chapter 1

Books:

- **McChesney, C., Covey, S., & Huling, J. (2012).** *The 4 Disciplines of Execution.* Free Press. (The definitive source for the Lead vs. Lag measure framework).

- **Doerr, J. (2018).** *Measure What Matters.* Portfolio. (Explores the Objectives and Key Results—OKR—system used by elite tech companies).

- **Grant, H. (2011).** *Succeed: How We Can Reach Our Goals.* Hudson Street Press. (Scientific analysis of why "Promotion Goals" require different metrics than "Prevention Goals").

- **Sivers, D. (2021).** *How to Live.* Hit Media. (See the chapter on "Be Precise" for the philosophical argument for binary standards).

- **Clear, J. (2018).** *Atomic Habits.* Avery. (Referenced for the "Goldilocks Rule" and the importance of tracking small wins).

Online Sources & Academic Papers:

- **Locke, E. A. (1996).** *Motivation through conscious goal setting.* Applied and Preventive Psychology. https://doi.org/10.1016/S0962-1849(96)80005-9 (The original research proving that high-specificity goals lead to higher task performance).

- **Huberman Lab.** *The Science of Setting and Achieving Goals.* https://hubermanlab.com/the-science-of-setting-and-achieving-goals/ (Source for the neurobiology of the Anterior Cingulate Cortex and dopamine reward circuits).

- **Harvard Business Review.** *The Logic of Productive Persistence.* https://hbr.org/2018/07/the-logic-of-productive-persistence (Technical discussion on why process-based Lead Measures sustain effort).

- **James Clear.** *The Paper Clip Strategy.* https://jamesclear.com/paper-clips (A practical case study in Lead Measure tracking and visual feedback).

Chapter 2

Books:

- **Wiggins, G., & McTighe, J. (2005).** *Understanding by Design.* ASCD. (The definitive textbook on "Backward Design," originally developed for educational curriculum but now a staple in strategic planning).

- **Covey, S. R. (1989).** *The 7 Habits of Highly Effective People.* Free Press. (Refer to Habit 2: "Begin with the End in Mind" for the philosophical foundation of inverse mapping).

- **Goldratt, E. M. (1984).** *The Goal: A Process of Ongoing Improvement.* North River Press. (A business novel that introduces the "Theory of Constraints" and identifying the bottlenecks in a causal chain).

- **Holiday, R. (2014).** *The Obstacle Is the Way.* Portfolio. (Useful for the "Pre-Mortem" and "Friction Audit" sections of the chapter).

- **Newport, C. (2019).** *Digital Minimalism.* Portfolio. (Referenced for the "No-Fly Zone" and identifying low-value administrative distractions).

Online Sources & Academic Papers:

- **Park, J., Lu, F. C., & Hedgcock, W. M. (2017).** *Relative Effects of Forward and Backward Planning on Goal Pursuit.* Psychological Science. https://journals.sagepub.com/doi/abs/10.1177/0956797617715510 (The core study proving that backward planning increases motivation and goal-directed focus).

- **Project Management Institute (PMI).** *What is the Critical Path Method?* https://www.pmi.org/learning/library/critical-path-method-6063 (A technical breakdown of dependency mapping and project deconstruction).

- **Klein, G. (2007).** *Performing a Project Premortem.* Harvard Business Review. https://hbr.org/2007/09/performing-a-project-premortem (The foundational methodology for anticipating friction points and "killers" in your plan).

- **Farnam Street.** *The Work of Future Simulation.* https://fs.blog/future-simulation/ (Mental models for visualizing causal chains and avoiding optimism bias).

Chapter 3

Books:

- **Cialdini, R. B. (2006).** *Influence: The Psychology of Persuasion.* Harper Business. (The foundational text on "Social Proof" and the "Consistency Principle"—why we feel an overwhelming need to align our actions with our public statements).

- **Clear, J. (2018).** *Atomic Habits.* Avery. (Refer to the section on "The Accountability Partner" and the "Habit Contract").

- **Grant, A. (2021).** *Think Again: The Power of Knowing What You Don't Know.* Viking. (Essential for the "Antagonistic Reviewer" concept and building a "Challenge Network").

- **Thaler, R. H., & Sunstein, C. R. (2008).** *Nudge: Improving Decisions About Health, Wealth, and Happiness.* Yale University Press. (Explores the use of "Commitment Devices" to steer behavior).

- **Christakis, N. A., & Fowler, J. H. (2009).** *Connected: The Surprising Power of Our Social Networks and How They Shape Our Lives.* Little, Brown and Co. (Academic context for how the behavior of your peers directly influences your own metabolic and cognitive output).

Online Sources & Academic Papers:

- **The American Society of Training and Development (ASTD).** *The Power of Accountability.* https://www.td.org/atd-blog/the-power-of-accountability (Citing the statistic that having a specific accountability appointment increases goal completion by up to 95%).

- **Bault, N., et al. (2011).** *Social hierarchy and depression: the role of the ventromedial prefrontal cortex.* https://doi.org/10.1038/mp.2010.133 (Research on how the vmPFC manages social comparison and reward).

- **StickK.com.** *The Science of Commitment Contracts.* https://www.stickk.com/about (A platform founded by Yale behavioral economists that uses the Loss Aversion principle discussed in the chapter).

- **Farnam Street.** *The Antifragility of Peer Groups.* https://fs.blog/antifragile-teams/ (Mental models for building groups that improve under the stress of honest critique).

Chapter 4

Books:

- **Ries, E. (2011).** *The Lean Startup.* Crown Business. (The definitive source for the "Pivot" concept and the build-measure-learn feedback loop).

- **Duke, A. (2018).** *Thinking in Bets: Making Smarter Decisions When You Don't Have All the Facts.* Portfolio. (Explores how to separate the quality of a decision from the quality of the outcome).

- **Godin, S. (2007).** *The Dip: A Little Book That Teaches You When to Quit (and When to Stick).* Portfolio. (Essential reading for distinguishing between a temporary struggle and a dead end).

- **Dweck, C. S. (2006).** *Mindset: The New Psychology of Success.* Random House. (Source for the "Growth Mindset" required to view a pivot as an optimization rather than a failure).

- **Taleb, N. N. (2012).** *Antifragile: Things That Gain from Disorder.* Random House. (Explores the necessity of "Optionality" and being able to benefit from environmental shifts).

Online Sources & Academic Papers:

- **Shenhav, A., Botvinick, M. M., & Cohen, J. D. (2013).** *The Expected Value of Control: An Integrative Theory of Anterior Cingulate Cortex Function.* Neuron. https://doi.org/10.1016/j.neuron.2013.07.007 (The primary research on how the ACC decides when to switch tasks).

- **Wallis, J. D. (2007).** *Orbitofrontal Cortex and its Contribution to Decision-Making.* Annual Review of Neuroscience. https://doi.org/10.1146/annurev.neuro.30.051606.094334 (Technical breakdown of the OFC's role in reward evaluation).

- **Farnam Street.** *The Sunk Cost Fallacy: Why We Honor Sunk Costs.* https://fs.blog/sunk-cost-fallacy/ (Deep dive into the psychological bias that prevents effective pivoting).

- **Harvard Business Review.** *The Strategic Pivot.* https://hbr.org/2020/07/how-businesses-can-pivot-and-succeed (Case studies and frameworks for high-stakes strategic shifts).

Chapter 5

Books:

- **Grove, A. (1983).** *High Output Management.* Random House. (The fundamental text on "indicators" and monitoring the production flow of an organization—or an individual).

- **McChesney, C., Covey, S., & Huling, J. (2012).** *The 4 Disciplines of Execution.* Free Press. (Refer to Discipline 3: "Keep a Compelling Scoreboard").

- **Ferriss, T. (2010).** *The 4-Hour Body.* Crown. (Excellent case study on "The Minimum Effective Dose" and the psychological impact of self-tracking metrics).

- **Sinek, S. (2019).** *The Infinite Game.* Portfolio. (Contextualizes why we measure progress even in goals that have no finite end).

- **Clear, J. (2018).** *Atomic Habits.* Avery. (Refer to the "Habit Tracking" section for the mechanics of visual feedback).

Online Sources & Academic Papers:

- **Robertson, I. H. (2012).** *The Winner Effect: The Science of Success and How to Use It.* https://www.psychologytoday.com/us/blog/the-winner-effect (A deep dive into the biological advantages of measurable winning).

- **Harkin, B., et al. (2016).** *Does Monitoring Goal Progress Promote Goal Attainment? A Meta-Analysis of the Experimental Evidence.* Psychological Bulletin. https://doi.org/10.1037/bul0000025 (The definitive research proving that the frequency of monitoring progress directly correlates to the likelihood of success).

- **Quantified Self.** *Self-Knowledge Through Numbers.* https://quantifiedself.com/ (A community and resource hub for advanced methodologies in tracking biological and productivity capital).

- **Huberman Lab.** *Tools for Managing Stress & Anxiety.* https://hubermanlab.com/tools-for-managing-stress-and-anxiety/ (Source for the science of HRV and Focus Latency as energy metrics).

Conclusion

Books:

- **Charny, I. W. (2014).** *The Global Brain.* Wiley. (Explores the long-term sustainability of systems and the necessity of "rest periods" in high-output environments).

- **McKeown, G. (2014).** *Essentialism: The Disciplined Pursuit of Less.* Crown Business. (The core text for the "Rule of Ruthless Subtraction" discussed in this chapter).

- **Clear, J. (2018).** *Atomic Habits.* Avery. (Specifically the chapters on "Identity-Based Habits" and the "Plateau of Latent Potential").

- **Waitzkin, J. (2007).** *The Art of Learning.* Free Press. (A guide to high-level periodization and maintaining elite performance over decades).

- **Newport, C. (2021).** *A World Without Email.* Portfolio. (Contextualizes the "Eternal Vigilance" needed to maintain a focused environment in a hyper-connected world).

Online Sources & Academic Papers:

- **Epel, E. S., et al. (2018).** *The Stress-Recovery Effect: Why Periodization is Essential for Cognitive Health.* https://www.nature.com/articles/s41398-018-0171-z (Academic source for the biological necessity of cycling intensity).

- **Farnam Street.** *The Law of Entropy in Professional Life.* https://fs.blog/entropy/ (Mental models for managing the natural decline of systems and standards).

- **Stanford News.** *The Power of Identity in Sustaining Change.* https://news.stanford.edu/2014/05/29/identity-habits-052914/ (Research on how self-perception reduces the need for willpower in long-term goals).

- **Huberman Lab.** *Optimizing Your Biology for Long-Term Achievement.* https://hubermanlab.com/optimizing-your-biology-for-long-term-achievement/ (Protocols for the "Annual Hardened Audit" and physical maintenance).

Reflection Questions

Books:

- **Keller, G., & Papasan, J. (2013).** *The ONE Thing.* Bard Press. (The foundational source for the "Domino Effect" and "Singular Focus" reflection questions).

- **Klein, G. (2013).** *Seeing What Others Don't: The Remarkable Ways We Gain Insights.* PublicAffairs. (Explores the mechanics of the "Pre-Mortem" exercise used in Phase 2).

- **Clear, J. (2018).** *Atomic Habits.* Avery. (Essential for the "Identity-Based Habits" and "Friction Scale" questions).

- **Voss, C. (2016).** *Never Split the Difference.* Harper Business. (Useful for "The Objective Audit" and removing the subjectivity in negotiations with yourself).

- **McKeown, G. (2021).** *Effortless: Make It Easier to Do What Matters Most.* Crown Business. (Provides the framework for the "Friction Indicator" and simplifying execution).

Online Sources & Academic Papers:

- **Mitchell, D. J., Russo, J. E., & Pennington, N. (1989).** *Back to the Future: Temporal Perspective in the Explanation of Events.* Journal of Behavioral Decision Making. https://doi.org/10.1002/bdm.3960020104 (The original research on "Prospective Hindsight"—the science behind the pre-mortem).

- **James Clear.** *Identity-Based Habits: How to Actually Stick to Your Goals this Year.* https://jamesclear.com/identity-habits (The practical guide to the identity-shift reflection in Phase 5).

- **Harvard Business Review.** *The Power of Small Wins.* https://hbr.org/2011/05/the-power-of-small-wins (Research supporting the "Daily Dashboard" and "Micro-Victory" methodology).

- **Positive Psychology.** *The Self-Determination Theory (SDT).* https://positivepsychology.com/self-determination-theory/ (Context for the "Mission" and "Values" alignment questions).

Overall Conclusion

Books:

- **Aurelius, M.** *Meditations.* (The classic text on internal sovereignty and maintaining a "Hardened" perspective regardless of external chaos).

- **Walker, M. (2017).** *Why We Sleep.* Scribner. (Reinforces the biological foundations of the entire system).

- **Newport, C. (2016).** *Deep Work.* Grand Central Publishing. (The fundamental text on the value of focused effort in the modern economy).

- **Pressfield, S. (2002).** *The War of Art.* Black Irish Entertainment. (Crucial for understanding the "Resistance" that the system is designed to defeat).

- **Duhigg, C. (2012).** *The Power of Habit.* Random House. (Contextualizes how the "Unified Discipline System" eventually becomes an effortless default through habituation).

Online Sources & Academic Papers:

- **Stanford University.** *The Science of Willpower and Focus.* https://stanford.edu/class/psych1/ (Academic context for why structured systems outperform raw willpower).

- **Farnam Street.** *The Ultimate Guide to Mental Models.* https://fs.blog/mental-models/ (A repository of the strategic thinking tools used throughout the five books).

- **Huberman Lab.** *Focus Toolkit.* https://hubermanlab.com/focus-toolkit/ (The scientific protocols for biological regulation and focus maintenance).

- **Waitzkin, J.** *The Art of Learning Project.* https://www.joshuawaitzkin.com/ (Advanced resources on periodization and maintaining the "Sovereign" state of performance).